Features of person and society in Swat
Collected essays on Pathans

International Library of Anthropology

Editor: Adam Kuper, University of Leiden

Arbor Scientiae
Arbor Vitae

A catalogue of other Social Science books published by Routledge &
Kegan Paul will be found at the end of this volume.

Features of person and society in Swat
Collected essays on Pathans

Selected essays of Fredrik Barth
Volume II

Routledge & Kegan Paul
London, Boston and Henley

First published in 1981
by Routledge & Kegan Paul Ltd
39 Store Street
London WC1E 7DD,
9 Park Street,
Boston, Mass. 02108, USA, and
Broadway House,
Newtown Road,
Henley-on-Thames,
Oxon RG9 1EN
Set in Press Roman 10 on 12 point
and printed in Great Britain by
Billing & Sons Limited
Guildford, London, Oxford and Worcester

British Library Cataloguing in Publication Data

Barth, Fredrik
Selected essays of Fredrik Barth. (International
library of anthology).
Vol. 2: Features of person and society in Swat
1. Ethnology
I. Series
301.2'08   GN325   80-41524

ISBN 0-7100-0620-9

Contents

Introduction

Swat Pathans have figured prominently in my writing, and perhaps at times overmuch in my thinking in anthropology. Swat was my second proper fieldwork, better prepared and more confidently pursued than my first one among the Kurds, yet subjectively still novel and momentous, and therefore more formative than subsequent field experiences elsewhere. Perhaps for this reason, Swat Pathans impressed themselves very forcefully on my awareness. I have been variously criticized for casting my analysis of Swat in theoretical moulds adopted from other sources, such as Norwegian entrepreneurs (Ahmed, 1976:9 ff., though my brief study of Norwegian entrepreneurship was made subsequently to my main publications on Swat), or from Hobbes (Asad, 1972:8 ff., though Hobbes had been one of many lacunae in my reading). My own judgment would be to the contrary, that perhaps the experience of Swat Pathans has at times unduly dominated my general understanding of Man, and thus my theoretically intended formulations. Their remarkable vitality and individualism proved both easy to recognize and subjectively compelling. The relatively undisguised harshness of their lives and their explicitly strategic reasoning in their dealings with and understanding of others, seemed to lay bare basic and elementary forces in society. Their yearning for social independence, for honour and security through self-sufficiency, were easy to identify and admire, and seemed to provide a key to what propelled them and guided them in many of their activities even when the collective result sometimes spelled dependence and defeat. Their cultural focus on 'real' things — land, gold, and women in their own terms — rather than on more obviously symbolically transformed idioms and prizes, seemed elemental and fathomable. Yet these were all features that appeared to fit uneasily into the prevailing structural-functional paradigm which dominated the anthropology of the 1950s. To me all these features seemed to provide elements for a more realistic and truer paradigm of the (inter-)relation of the individual and society for which I was searching — one which would allow us to identify the goals and rationality of many patterns of individual behaviour without prejudging the rationality, or functionalism, of many of the collective consequences of such behaviour.

Each of the essays reprinted below was a step in the effort to analyse major substantive features of the social organization of Swat while at the same time uncovering the elements for such a general paradigm. With the hindsight of subsequent fieldwork in other cultures, I would judge the former purpose to have been more fully achieved than the latter, and that it may not have been till the 1970s that my generally intended statements were given a form where the stamp of Swat had been reduced to appropriate dimensions.

The essays also address other, more specific, theoretical challenges that I felt arose from the nature of the material. These include an early venture in ecologic analysis, the application of the Theory of Games to the main lineaments of a political system, an analysis of social stratification and caste, and the processes at work in ethnic differentiation and identity in a situation of social inequality and wide dispersal. A persistent challenge also arises from the large scale and complexity of the social system in Swat, posing problems that are still troublesome in anthropology today. The last chapter is new to this volume, and readdresses several of these issues, as well as some that have been raised by others in critiques and commentaries to my analysis of Swat. It is based in part on additional data from brief visits to Swat in 1960, 1974, 1978 and 1979.

Fredrik Barth
Oslo

1 Ecologic relationships of ethnic groups in Swat, North Pakistan

The importance of ecologic factors for the form and distribution of cultures has usually been analysed by means of a culture area concept. This concept has been developed with reference to the aboriginal cultures of North America (Kroeber, 1939). Attempts at delimiting culture areas in Asia by similar procedures have proved extremely difficult (Bacon, 1946; Kroeber 1947; Miller, 1953), since the distribution of cultural types, ethnic groups, and natural areas rarely coincide. Coon (1951) speaks of Middle Eastern society as being built on a mosaic principle – many ethnic groups with radically different cultures co-reside in an area in symbiotic relations of variable intimacy. Referring to a similar structure, Furnivall (1944) describes the Netherlands Indies as a plural society. The common characteristic in these two cases is the combination of ethnic segmentation and economic interdependence. Thus the 'environment' of any one ethnic group is not only defined by natural conditions, but also by the presence and activities of the other ethnic groups on which it depends. Each group exploits only a section of the total environment, and leaves large parts of it open for other groups to exploit.

This interdependence is analogous to that of the different animal species in a habitat. As Kroeber (1947:330) emphasizes, culture area classifications are essentially ecologic; thus detailed ecologic considerations, rather than geographical areas of subcontinental size, should offer the point of departure. The present paper attempts to apply a more specific ecologic approach to a case study of distribution by utilizing some of the concepts of animal ecology, particularly the concept of a *niche* – the place of a group in the total environment, its relations to resources and competitors (cf. Allee, 1949:516).

* First published in *American Anthropologist* (1956), Vol. 58, no. 6, 1079-89.

Groups

The present example is simple, relatively speaking, and is concerned with the three major ethnic groups in Swat state, North-West Frontier Province, Pakistan.[1] These are: (1) *Pathans* — Pashto-speaking (Iranian language family) sedentary agriculturalists; (2) *Kohistanis* — speakers of Dardic languages, practising agriculture and transhumant herding; and (3) *Gujars* — Gujri-speaking (a lowland Indian dialect) nomadic herders. Kohistanis are probably the ancient inhabitants of most of Swat; Pathans entered as conquerors in successive waves between A.D. 1000-1600, and Gujars probably first appeared in the area some 400 years ago. Pathans of Swat State number about 450,000, Kohistanis perhaps 30,000. The number of Gujars in the area is difficult to estimate.

The centralized state organization in Swat was first established in 1917, and the most recent accretion was annexed in 1947, so the central organization has no relevance for the distributional problems discussed here.

Area

Swat state contains sections of two main valleys, those of the Swat and the Indus rivers. The Swat river rises in the high mountains to the North, among 18,000-foot peaks. As it descends and grows in volume, it enters a deep gorge. This upper section of the valley is thus very narrow and steep. From approximately 5,000 feet, the Swat valley becomes increasingly wider as one proceeds southward, and is flanked by ranges descending from 12,000 to 6,000 feet in altitude. The river here has a more meandering course, and the valley bottom is a flat, extensive alluvial deposit.

The east border of Swat state follows the Indus river; only its west bank and tributaries are included in the area under discussion. The Indus enters the area as a very large river; it flows in a spectacular gorge, 15,000 feet deep and from 12 to 16 miles wide. Even in the north, the valley bottom is less than 3,000 feet above sea level, while the surrounding mountains reach 18,000 feet. The tributary valleys are consequently short and deeply cut, with an extremely steep profile. Further to the south, the surrounding mountain ranges recede from the river banks and lose height, the Indus deposits some sediment, and the tributary streams form wider valleys.

Climatic variations in the area are a function of altitude. Precipitation is low throughout. The southern low-altitude areas have long, hot summers and largely steppe vegetation. The Indus gorge has been described as 'a desert embedded between icy gravels' (Spate, 1954:381). The high mountains are partly covered by permanent ice and snow, and at lower levels by natural mountain meadows in the brief summer season. Between these extremes is a broad belt (from 6,000 to 11,000 feet) of forest, mainly of pine and deodar.

Pathan-Kohistani distribution

Traditional history, in part relating to place-names of villages and uninhabited ruins, indicates that Kohistani inhabitants were driven progressively northward by Pathan invaders (cf. Stein, 1929:33, 83). This northward spread has now been checked, and the border between Kohistani and Pathan territories has been stable for some time. The last Pathan expansion northward in the Swat valley took place under the leadership of the Saint Akhund Sadiq Baba, eight generations ago. To understand the factors responsible for the stability of the present ethnic border, it is necessary to examine the specific ecologic requirements of the present Pathan economy and organization.

Pathans of Swat live in a complex, multi-caste society. The landholding Pakhtun caste is organized in localized, segmentary, unilineal descent groups; other castes and occupational groups are tied to them as political clients and economic serfs. Subsistence is based on diversified and well-developed plough agriculture. The main crops are wheat, maize, and rice; much of the ploughed land is watered by artificial irrigation. Manuring is practised, and several systems of crop rotation and regular fallow-field rhythms are followed, according to the nature of the soil and water supply. All rice is irrigated, with nursery beds and transplantation.

Only part of the Pathan population is actively engaged in agriculture. Various other occupational groups perform specialized services in return for payment in kind, and thus require that the agriculturalists produce a considerable surplus. Further, and perhaps more importantly, the political system depends on a strong hierarchical organization of landowners and much political activity, centering around the men's houses (*hujra*). This activity diverts much manpower from productive pursuits. The large and well-organized Pathan tribes are found in the lower parts of the Swat valley and along the more southerly tributaries of the Indus, occupying broad and fertile alluvial plains. A simpler form of political organization is found along the northern fringes of Pathan territory. It is based on families of saintly descent, and is characterized by the lack of men's houses. This simplification renders the economy of the community more efficient (a) by eliminating the wasteful potlatch-type feasts of the men's houses, and (b) by vesting political office in saintly persons of inviolate status, thus eliminating the numerous retainers that protect political leaders in other Pathan areas.

Pathan territory extends to a critical ecologic threshold: the limits within which two crops can be raised each year. This is largely a function of altitude. Two small outliers of Pashto-speaking people (Jag, in Duber valley, and a section of Kalam) are found north of this limit. They are unlike other Pathans, and similar to their Kohistani neighbours in economy and political organization.

The conclusion that the limits of double cropping constitute the effective check on further Pathan expansion seems unavoidable. Pathan economy and political organization requires that agricultural labour produce considerable surplus. Thus in the marginal, high-altitude areas, the political organization is modified and 'economized' (as also in the neighboring Dir area), while beyond these limits of double cropping the economic and social system cannot survive at all.

Kohistanis are not restricted by this barrier. The Kohistani ethnic group apparently once straddled it; and, as they were driven north by invading Pathans, they freely crossed what to Pathans was a restricting barrier. This must be related to differences between Kohistani and Pathan political and economic organization, and consequent differences in their ecologic requirements.

Kohistanis, like Pathans, practise a developed plough agriculture. Due to the terrain they occupy, their fields are located on narrow artificial terraces, which require considerable engineering skill for their construction. Parts of Kohistan receive no summer rains; the streams, fed from the large snow reserves in the mountains, supply water to the fields through complex and extensive systems of irrigation. Some manuring is practised. Climatic conditions modify the types of food crops. Maize and millet are most important; wheat and rice can only be raised in a few of the low-lying areas. The summer season is short, and fields produce only one crop a year.

Agricultural methods are thus not very different from those of Pathans, but the net production of fields is much less. Kohistanis, however, have a two-fold economy, for transhumant herding is as important as agriculture. Sheep, goats, cattle and water buffalo are kept for wool, meat, and milk. The herds depend in summer on mountain pastures, where most of the Kohistanis spend between four and eight months each year, depending on local conditions. In some areas the whole population migrates through as many as five seasonal camps, from winter dwellings in the valley bottom to summer campsites at a 14,000 foot altitude, leaving the fields around the abandoned low-altitude dwellings to remain practically untended. In the upper Swat valley, where the valley floor is covered with snow some months of the year, winter fodder is collected and stored for the animals.

By having two strings to their bow, so to speak, the Kohistanis are able to wrest a living from inhospitable mountain areas which fall short of the minimal requirements for Pathan occupation. In these areas, Kohistanis long retained their autonomy, the main territories being conquered by Swat state in 1926, 1939, and 1947. They were, and still are, organized in politically separate village districts of from 400 to 2000 inhabitants. Each community is subdivided into a number of loosely connected patrilineal lineages. The central political institution is the village council, in which all landholding minimal lineages have their representatives. Each community also includes a family of blacksmith-cum-carpenter specialists, and a few households of tenants or farm laborers.

Neighboring communities speaking the same dialect or language[2] could apparently fuse politically when under external pressure, in which case they were directed by a common council of prominent leaders from all constituent lineages. But even these larger units were unable to withstand the large forces of skilled fighters which Pathans of the Swat area could mobilize. These forces were esimated at 15,000 by the British during the Ambeyla campaign in 1862 (cf. Roberts, 1898, Vol. 2:7).

'Natural' subareas

The present Swat state appears to the Kohistanis as a single natural area, since, as an ethnic group, they once occupied all of it, and since their economy can function anywhere within it. With the advent of invading Pathan tribes, the Kohistanis found themselves unable to defend the land. But the land which constitutes one natural area to Kohistanis is divided by a line which Pathans were unable to cross.

From the Pathan point of view, it consists of two natural areas, one containing the ecologic requisites for Pathan occupation, the other uninhabitable.[3] Thus the Kohistanis were permitted to retain a part of their old territory in spite of their military inferiority, while in the remainder they were either assimilated as serfs in the conquering Pathan society or were expelled.

From the purely synchronic point of view, the present Pathan-Kohistani distribution presents a simple and static picture of two ethnic groups representing two discrete culture areas, and with a clear correspondence between these culture areas and natural areas: Pathans in broad valleys with a hot climate and scrub vegetation as against Kohistanis in high mountains with a severe climate and coniferous forest cover. Through the addition of time depth, the possibility arises of breaking down the concept of a 'natural area' into specific ecologic components in relation to the requirements of specific economies.

Analysis of the distribution of Gujars in relation to the other ethnic groups requires such a procedure. Gujars are found in both Pathan and Kohistani areas, following two different economic patterns in both areas: transhumant herding, and true nomadism. But while they are distributed throughout all of the Pathan territory, they are found only in the western half of Kohistan, and neither reside nor visit in the eastern half. The division into mountain and valley seems irrelevant to the Gujars, while the mountain area – inhospitable to Pathans and usable to Kohistanis – is divided by a barrier which Gujars do not cross. The economy and other features of Gujar life must be described before this distribution and its underlying factors can be analysed.

Gujars constitute a floating population of herders, somewhat ill-defined due to a variable degree of assimilation into the host populations. In physical type, as well as in dress and language, the majority of them are easily distinguishable. Their music, dancing, and manner of celebrating rites of passage differ from those of their hosts. Their political status is one of dependence on the host population.

The Gujar population is subdivided into a number of named patrilineal tribes or clans – units claiming descent from a common known or unknown ancestor, but without supporting genealogies. There are sometimes myths relating to the clan origin, and these frequently serve as etymologies for the clan name. The clans vary greatly in size and only the smallest are localized. The effective descent units are patrilineal lineages of limited depth, though there is greater identification between unrelated Gujars bearing the same clan name than between strangers of different clans. These clans are irrelevant to marriage regulations. There is little intermarriage between Gujars and the host group.

The economy of the Gujars depends mainly on the herding of sheep, goats, cattle, and water buffalo. In addition to animal products, Gujars require some grain (maize, wheat, or millet) which they get by their own agriculture in marginal, high-altitude fields or by trade in return for clarified butter, meat, or wool. Their essential requirements may be satisfied by two rather different patterns of life – transhumance and true nomadism. Pathans differentiate persons pursuing these two patterns by the terms Gujar and Ajer, respectively, and consider them to be ethnic subdivisions. In fact, Gujars may change their pattern of life from one to the other.

Transhumance is practised mainly by Gujars in the Pathan area, but also occasionally in Kohistan (see map 1). Symbiotic relationships between Gujars and Pathans take various forms, some quite intimate. Pathans form a multicaste society, into which Gujars are assimilated as a specialized occupational caste of herders. Thus most Pathan villages contain a small number of Gujars – these may speak Gujri as their home language and retain their separate culture, or may be assimilated to the extent of speaking only Pashto. Politically they are integrated into the community in a client or serf status. Their role is to care for the animals (mainly water buffalo and draft oxen) either as servants of a landowner or as independent buffalo owners. They contribute to the village economy with milk products (especially clarified butter), meat, and manure, which is important and carefully utilized in the fields.

In addition to their agricultural land, most Pathan villages control neighboring hills or mountainsides, which are used by Pathans only as a source of firewood. The transhumant Gujars, however, shift their flocks to these higher areas for summer pasture, for which they pay a fixed rate, in kind, per animal. This rent supplies the landholders with clarified butter for their own consumption. Gujars also serve as agricultural laborers in the seasons of peak activity, most importantly during the few hectic days of rice transplantation. They also seed fields of their own around their summer camps for harvest the following summer.

In Kohistan there is less symbiosis between Gujars and their hosts but the pattern is similar, except that the few fields are located by the winter settlements.

The transhumant cycle may be very local. Some Gujars merely move

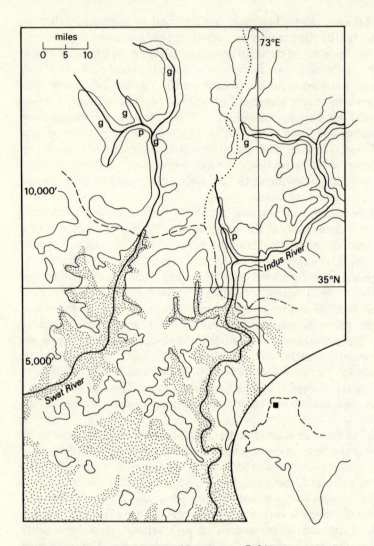

MAP 1 *Sketch map of area of Swat state, Pakistan*
Stippled area: *under cultivation by Pathans.* Broken line: *border
between Pathan and Kohistani areas.* Dotted line: *border of area
utilized by Gujars (the two borders coincide towards the south east).*
p: *outlying Pathan communities.* g: *outlying communities of transhumant Gujars. Gujar nomads spend the summer in the mountains
central and north on the map, and winter in the southernmost area of
the map. Inset: location of sketch map.*

from Pathan villages in the valley bottom to hillside summer settlements 1,000 or 1,500 feet above, visible from the village. Others travel 20 or 30 miles to summer grazing grounds in the territory of a different Pathan tribe from that of their winter hosts.

Nomads travel much farther, perhaps 100 miles, utilizing the high mountain pastures in the summer and wintering in the low plains. While the transhumant Gujars place their main emphasis on the water buffalo, the nomads specialize in the more mobile sheep and goats. None the less, the two patterns are not truly distinct, for some groups combine features of both. They spend the spring in the marginal hills of Pathan territory, where they seed a crop. In summer the men take the herds of sheep and goats to the high mountains while the women remain behind to care for the buffalo and the fields. In autumn the men return with the herds, reap the crops, and utilize the pastures. Finally, they store the grain and farm out their buffalo with Pathan villagers, and retire to the low plains with their sheep and goats for the winter.

The true nomads never engage in agricultural pursuits; they may keep cattle, but are not encumbered with water buffalo. The degree of autonomous political organization is proportional to the length of the yearly migration. Households of locally transhumant Gujars are tied individually to Pathan leaders. Those crossing Pathan tribal borders are organized in small lineages, the better to bargain for low grazing tax. The true nomads co-ordinate the herding of flocks and migrations of people from as many as fifty households, who may also camp together for brief periods. Such groups generally consist of several small lineages, frequently of different clans, related by affinal or cognatic ties and under the direction of a single leader. Thus, though migrating through areas controlled by other political organizations, they retain a moderately well-defined organization of their own.

Gujar distribution

The co-existence of Gujars and Pathans in one area poses no problem, in view of the symbiotic relations sketched above. Pathans have the military strength to control the mountainous flanks of the valleys they occupy, but have no effective means of utilizing these areas. This leaves an unoccupied ecologic niche which the Gujar ethnic group has entered and to which it has accommodated itself in a politically dependent position through a pattern of transhumance. Symbiotic advantages make the relationship satisfactory and enduring. It is tempting to see the expansion of Gujars into the area as resulting from the Pathan expulsion of Kohistanis from the valley. The Kohistanis, through their own pattern of transhumance, formerly filled the niche and it became vacant only when the specialized agricultural Pathans conquered the valley bottom and replaced the Kohistanis.

But the co-existence of Gujars and Kohistanis poses a problem, since the two groups appear to utilize the same natural resources and therefore to occupy the same ecologic niche. One would expect competition, leading to the expulsion of one or the other ethnic group from the area. However, armed conflict between the two groups is rare, and there is no indication that one is increasing at the expense of the other. On the other hand, if a stable symbiotic or non-competitive relationship may be established between the two groups, why should Gujars be concentrated in West Kohistan, and not inhabit the essentially similar East Kohistan area? The answer must be sought not only in the natural environment and in features of the Gujar economy, but also in the relevant social environment – in features of Kohistani economy and organization which affect the niche suited to utilization by Gujars.

East vs. West Kohistan

As indicated, Kohistanis have a two-fold economy combining agriculture and transhumant herding, and live in moderately large village communities. Although most Gujars also practise some agriculture, it remains a subsidiary activity. It is almost invariably of a simple type dependent on water from the melting snow in spring and monsoon rains in summer, rather than on irrigation, and on shifting fields rather than manuring. The Kohistanis have a more equal balance between agriculture and herding. The steep slopes require complex terracing and irrigation, which preclude shifting agriculture and encourage more intensive techniques. The size of herds is limited by the size of fields, which supply most of the winter fodder, since natural fields and mountain meadows are too distant from the winter dwellings to permit haying. Ecologic factors relevant to this balance between the two dominant economic activities become of prime importance for Kohistani distribution and settlement density.

There are significant differences in this respect between East and West Kohistan, i.e. between the areas drained by the Indus and the Swat rivers respectively. While the Indus and the lowest sections of its tributaries flow at no more than 3,000 feet, the Swat river descends from 8,000 to 5,000 feet in the section of its valley occupied by Kohistanis. The higher altitude in the west has several effects on the economic bases for settlement: (a) Agricultural production is reduced by the shorter season and lower temperatures in the higher western valley. (b) The altitude difference combined with slightly higher precipitation in the west results in a greater accumulation of snow. The Indus bank is rarely covered with snow, but in the upper Swat valley snow tends to accumulate through the winter and remains in the valley bottom until April or May. Thus the sedentary stock-owner in West Kohistan must provide stored fodder for his animals throughout the four months of winter. (c) The shorter season of West Kohistan eliminates rice (most productive per land unit) as a food crop and reduces maize (most advantageous in return per weight of seed) in favor of the hardier millet.

These features serve to restrict the agricultural production of West Kohistan, and therefore the number of animals that can be kept during the winter season. No parallel restrictions limit the possibility for summer grazing. Both East and West Kohistan are noteworthy for their large, lush mountain meadows and other good summer grazing, and are thus rich in the natural resources which animal herders are able to exploit. However, these mountain pastures are only seasonal; no population can rely on them for year-round sustenance. Consequently, patterns of transhumance or nomadism are developed to utilize the mountain areas in its productive season, while relying on other areas or techniques the rest of the year. True nomads move to a similar ecologic niche in another area. People practising transhumance generally utilize a different niche by reliance on alternative techniques, here agriculture and the utilization of stored animal fodder. There appears to be a balance in the productivity of these two niches, as exploited by local transhumance in East Kohistan. Thus, in the Indus drainage, Kohistanis are able to support a human and animal population of sufficient size through the winter by means of agriculture and stored food, so as to utilize fully the summer pastures of the surrounding mountains. In an ecologic sense, the local population fills both niches. There is no such balance in the Swat valley. Restrictions on agricultural production limit the animal and human population, and prevent full exploitation of the mountain pastures. This niche is thus left partly vacant and available to the nomadic Gujars, who winter in the low plains outside the area. Moreover, scattered communities of transhumant Gujars may be found in the western areas, mainly at the very tops of the valleys. With techniques and patterns of consumption different from those of Kohistanis, they are able to survive locally in areas which fall short of the minimal requirements for permanent Kohistani occupation. The present distribution of Gujars in Kohistan, limiting them to the western half of the area, would seem to be a result of these factors.

A simple but rather crucial final point should be made in this analysis: why do Kohistanis have first choice, so to speak, and Gujars only enter niches left vacant by them? Since they are able to exploit the area more fully, one might expect Gujars eventually to replace Kohistanis. Organizational factors enter here. Kohistanis form compact, politically organized villages of considerable size. The Gujar seasonal cycle prevents a similar development among them. In winter they descend into Pathan areas, or even out of tribal territory and into the administered areas of Pakistan. They are thus seasonally subject to organizations more powerful than their own, and are forced to filter through territories controlled by such organizations on their seasonal migrations. They must accommodate themselves to this situation by travelling in small, unobtrusive groups, and wintering in dispersed settlements. Though it is conceivable that Gujars might be able to develop the degree of political organization required to replace Kohistanis in a purely Kohistani environment, their dependence on more highly organized neighboring areas still makes this impossible.

The transhumant Gujar settlements in Kohistan represent groups of former nomads who were given permission by the neighboring Kohistanis to settle, and they are kept politically subservient. The organizational superiority of the already established Kohistanis prevents them, as well as the nomads, from appropriating any rights over productive means or areas. What changes will occur under the present control by the state of Swat is a different matter.

This example may serve to illustrate certain viewpoints applicable to a discussion of the ecologic factors in the distribution of ethnic groups, cultures, or economies, and the problem of 'mosaic' co-residence in parts of Asia.

1 The distribution of ethnic groups is controlled not by objective and fixed 'natural areas' but by the distribution of the specific ecologic niches which the group, with its particular economic and political organization, is able to exploit. In the present example, what appears as a single natural area to Kohistanis is subdivided as far as Pathans are concerned, and this division is cross-cut with respect to the specific

requirements of Gujars.

2 Different ethnic groups will establish themselves in stable co-residence in an area if they exploit different ecologic niches, and especially if they can thus establish symbiotic economic relations, as those between Pathans and Gujars in Swat.

3 If different ethnic groups are able to exploit the same niches fully, the militarily more powerful will normally replace the weaker, as Pathans have replaced Kohistanis.

4 If different ethnic groups exploit the same ecologic niches but the weaker of them is better able to utilize marginal environments, the groups may co-reside in one area, as Gujars and Kohistanis in West Kohistan.

Where such principles are operative to the extent they are in much of West and South Asia, the concept of 'culture areas', as developed for native North America, becomes inapplicable. Different ethnic groups and culture types will have overlapping distributions and disconforming borders, and will be socially related to a variable degree, from the 'watchful co-residence' of Kohistanis and Gujars to the intimate economic, political, and ritual symbiosis of the Indian caste system. The type of correspondence between gross ecologic classification and ethnic distribution documented for North America by Kroeber (1939) will rarely if ever be found. Other conceptual tools are needed to the study of culture distribution in Asia. Their development would seem to depend on analysis of specific detailed distributions in an ecologic framework, rather than by speculation on a larger geographical scale.

Notes

1   Based on fieldwork February to November 1954, aided by a grant from the Royal Norwegian Research Council.
2   There are four main Dardic languages spoken in Swat state: Torwali, Gawri, and Eastern and Western dialect of Kohistái or Mayán (Barth and Morgenstierne, 1957).
3   The Pathan attitude toward the Kohistan area might best be illustrated by the warnings I was given when I was planning to visit the area: 'Full of terrible mountains covered by many-colored snow and emitting poisonous gases causing head and stomach pains when you cross the high passes; inhabited by robbers, and snakes that coil up and leap ten feet into the air; with no villages, only scattered houses on the mountain tops!'

2 The system of social stratification in Swat, North Pakistan

Introduction

The present paper describes the system of social stratification in the Swat area of North Pakistan. It is a hierarchical system of stable social groups, differing greatly in wealth, privilege, power, and the respect accorded to them by others. The local term for such groups is *qoum*. In any such system the organization of one stratum can only meaningfully be described with reference to its relations to the other strata, and in the pages which follow the various *qoum* are analysed as parts of a single, larger system embracing the whole community, and not as autonomous social units. My concern is with social structure, not with ritual or religion, and, for my purpose, although the people of Swat, as Sunni Muslims, fall far outside the Hindu fold, their system of social stratification may meaningfully be compared to that of Hindu caste systems.

Caste, as a pattern of social stratification, is characterized by the simpliciy of its basic schema, and its comprehensiveness. In contrast, class systems (in the sense used by Warner and Lunt, 1942) give simultaneous recognition to a multiplicity of conflicting hierarchical criteria, while systems of rank, though single in the scale which each defines, are generally restricted in their fields of relevance.

The simultaneous comprehensiveness and clear definition of units which characterizes caste systems results from the summation of many part-statuses into standardized clusters, or social persons, each identified with a specific caste position. Thus, in a Hindu caste system, there is a diversity of economic statuses and ritual statuses, but these are interconnected so that all Priests are sacred and all Leatherworkers are untouchable.

* First published in E.R. Leach (ed.) (1960) *Aspects of Caste in South India, Ceylon and North-West Pakistan*, Cambridge Papers in Social Anthropology, No. 2, Cambridge University Press.

A sociological analysis of such a system naturally concentrates on the principles governing the summation of statuses, and the consequent structural features of the clusters of connected statuses or caste positions. Every individual has statuses in the occupational framework of the community, in the framework of kinship relations, etc. The caste system defines clusters of such statuses, and one particular cluster is imposed on all individual members of each particular caste.

The coherence of the system depends upon the compatibility of such associated statuses. The members of the society itself justify the clusters by asserting an inherent compatibility in a moral or ultimate sense. Thus, among Hindus, the concept of pollution serves to define which statuses should be combined, and which are incompatible. In Swat, other concepts, such as privilege and shame, serve similarly as explicit justifications. But sociological principles are also involved in the question of compatibility. Each caste position must be such that the requirements implied by its component statuses may be simultaneously satisfied; and the alignment of each individual in terms of his different statuses should also be consistent and not fraught with interminable dilemmas. The former aspect of compatibility relates to roles, the latter to the degree of congruence between different organizational frameworks. In the essay which follows both aspects will be explored.

The area under discussion constitutes the main section of a large, fertile valley, roughly seventy by thirty miles, in tribal territory in the northern part of West Pakistan.[1] A major part of the valley lies within the borders of Swat state, a small part in Dir state, and the remaining, lower part, in Malakand agency – all recent political subdivisions of minor significance to the present problem.[2] The climate is fairly dry, but water for irrigation is plentiful. In the valley bottom, the population depends on cereal agriculture, particularly of rice, for its subsistence. This valley area has a population density of roughly 1,000 per square mile, and is extensively irrigated by the Swat river and its main tributaries. Settlement is in compact villages numbering from 100 to 5,000 houses (each occupied by an elementary family). The mountainous areas bordering on the valley have a much sparser population, scattered in hamlets of five to twenty houses. In these hill settlements, maize is the main cereal, but pastoral pursuits are important as well.

The total population of the whole Swat region is about half a million, dependent throughout on a complex subsistence economy. Agricultural techniques are sophisticated, and include crop rotation, the use of decomposed natural fertilizer, etc. Craft specialization is also highly developed. In contrast, communications are poor. Each community is largely self-sufficient and all are of similar type, though varying in size. Politically, the area is anarchic. The self-sufficient communities do not depend on wider co-ordinating agencies of any kind, and internally there is much conflict and factionalism. Swat communities have never been subject to external government. Such centralized institutions as exist are weak and are a recent internal development. All major political decisions, the conduct of law, and the protection of life and property are the responsibility of members of the local community, whose actions are governed mainly by internal considerations.

Each Swat community contains a number of unequal groups, known as *qoum* (sing.) in the Pokhto (Pashtu) dialect of Swat. The general meaning of this term is 'tribe, sect, people, nation, family' (Raverty, 1867), but in Swat it is used predominantly as a term for these hierarchically-ordered social groups, though occasionally also for religion or sect. A full list of such groups will be given below; in a general way they fall into the following categories, in descending rank order: (1) persons of holy descent; (2) landowners and administrators; (3) priests; (4) craftsmen; (5) agricultural tenants and labourers; (6) herders; and (7) despised groups. All these groups are represented in nearly every village; in varying degrees each is dependent on the skills and services of all the others, and together they form the community.

The various *qoum* are not strictly homologous − the kinds of criteria which define membership, and the internal organization of each group, differ quite profoundly. Furthermore, there is no ritual system in terms of which the groups are compared and ordered with respect to each other. In contrast to a Hindu caste system there is no symbolic framework within which the homology of the groups may be expressed. Social stratification is expressed in everyday profane situations in a vast number of different ways, but never as a single, comprehensive system. Moreover, the Muslim religion, to which the whole population subscribes, explicitly repudiates the very social differences which the existence of *qoum* implies. Sacred activities continually assert the basic unity and equality of all Muslims.

Swat *qoum* are thus not castes in the Hindu sense of the word; yet they are too diverse and rigidly separate to be described simply as social classes. Furthermore, Swat lies on the edge of the Indian world and partakes to a certain extent in Indian traditions. Thus the different *qoum* within a single community participate in non-monetary reciprocal services on the model of the Hindu *jajmani* system, and the relative ranking of many occupations, and even their names, correspond to those of the villages in the Indian plains, and so on. For the rest of this paper I shall in fact refer to the Swat *qoum* as castes. It must be remembered that they are castes only in a very general sense. Taking Hindu caste as the ideal type, the Swat variety is a limiting case.

Historical summary

Something needs to be said here concerning the historical background of contemporary Swat society. History explains the presence of Indian cultural influences and illustrates the ethnic multiplicity of the 'castes' which make up the communities of modern Swat. In addition, history is used by the people of Swat themselves to explain the relative social standing of different castes.

Though Swat lies in the middle of a turbulent cultural shatter zone, it is geographically isolated in that no major routes of communication pass through the valley. Within the last century neighbours within a radius of 100 miles have variously paid taxes to Peking, Bokhara, Kabul, and Delhi, but Swat has probably never paid tax to any external government. Yet it has had contact with all the major political currents in the area, and the first historical mention of the valley goes back to a hymn of the Rigveda (Stein, 1929: viii). Very dense populations were established at an early date, as is shown by Greek (327 B.C.) and Chinese (A.D. 519) records. After a Buddhist phase Hindu religion reasserted itself, so that, at the time of the Muslim invasions (A.D. 1000) the population was solidly Hindu (*ibid.*, ix). These invasions caused no break in local traditions: in the place-names given in the early Greek sources may be recognized the names of the major villages of modern Swat (*ibid.*, 47, 60). Conversion to Islam was thus something imposed by a small group of warrior lords, with the bulk of the population maintaining its secular Indian traditions. The main body of the modern agricultural tenants in Swat, who are without known ancestry, probably descend from this formerly Hindu population. Some basic modern village institutions may reasonably be assumed to represent continuations of ancient Indian originals.

The first Muslim masters of Swat were non-Pathan Dilazak tribes from south-east Afghanistan. These were later ousted by Swati Pathans, who were in turn succeeded in the sixteenth century by Yusufzai Pathans. Both groups of Pathans came from the Kabul valley. The Yusufzai form the present caste of landowners. Some groups of agricultural tenants trace Dilazak and Swati descent, while a group of Swatis whose ancestors were displaced by the Yusufzai invasion form the landowners along the east bank of the Indus. The present political and economic dominance of the Yusufzai landowners is justified by the people themselves by reference to this history of conquest.

The diversity of castes in Swat has also been augmented by infiltration. Since the time of the conversion to Islam, a number of local lineages claiming descent from the Prophet Mohammed, or from prominent Saints, have swelled the ranks of the Saintly caste. These migrant 'Saints' came mostly from Turkistan. Rival 'Saint' groups from Persia, representing the Shiah schism, have been unsuccessful in the exclusively Sunni Swat. From lowland India, Gujar pastoralists speaking the Gujri language have moved up into the area and appropriated the occupation of herders. These same people have also established themselves as a dependent tribe of nomads and hill cultivators. Other small tribelets of unknown origin are today assimilated to the Gujar caste by virtue of their pastoralist way of life. Certain occupational castes are alleged to be recent immigrants from the lowlands, a view supported by their physical characteristics. Thus the caste of Muleteers which monopolizes trade and transport is supposed to be of Bengali origin; these people are said to have arrived in Swat about 200 years ago. Similarly the Leatherworkers are thought to be recent immigrants from Panjab. Barbers regard themselves as the local representatives of a homogeneous barber caste found throughout Pakistan and northern India. Finally, with the growing sophistication of Pathan chiefs, a need has arisen for the services of sweepers. During the past thirty years about a dozen families of sweeper caste have been brought into the valley from the Pakistan plains.

This historical sketch highlights the capacity of the Swat *qoum* system to accommodate diverse ethnic groups within a framework of discrete categories, and the intimate connection of this system with the traditions of India. But unlike the Hindu caste system, the basic organizational framework is defined, not by ritual, but by occupation and division of labour. I shall therefore first describe the positions of the castes of Swat with regard to occupation and then proceed to discuss other types of relationships.

Occupational framework

A complete list of all the caste groups to be found in the Swat area would have to be based on very extensive census surveys, for many groups are small and found in a few localities only. The following list, based on censuses of six villages in different parts of the area, includes all groups of any numerical importance. They are:

Occupational category	Pashtu name
1. Descendant of the Prophet	Sayyid
	Sahibzada
2. Saints of various degrees, all land-owners and mediators in conflict	Mian
	Akhundzada
	Pirzada
3. Landowners and warriors	Pakhtun
4. Priest	Mullah
5. Shopkeeper	Dukandar
6. Muleteer	Paracha
7. Farmer, tenant	Zamidar
8. Goldsmith	Zərger
9. Tailor	Sarkhamar
10. Carpenter	Tarkarn
11. Blacksmith	Inger
12. Potter	Kulal
13. Oil-presser	Tili
14. Cotton-carder	Landap
15. Weaver	Jola
16. Leatherworker	Mochi
17. Agricultural labourer	Dehqan
18. Herdsman	Gujar
19. Ferryman	Jalawan
20. Musician and dancer	Dəm
21. Washerman	Dobi
22. Barber	Nai
23. Thong- and sieve-maker, dancer	Kashkol

These are the alternative names by which persons will identify themselves when asked what is their *qoum* (caste).

Let us first regard this simply as a system of occupational statuses, a scheme for the division of labour. These occupational statuses are rigidly segregated and cannot be combined, except in the following cases: a priest, as well as being in charge of a mosque, is expected to support himself by agriculture (as proprietor of dedicated lands or as a tenant) and by trade; carpentry may be combined with blacksmithing, as a basis for specializing in the construction of watermills; and herdsmen may engage in agriculture, as tenants or labourers. But it is impossible to work simultaneously as an oil-presser and as a tenant, as a tailor and as a shopkeeper, as a leatherworker and as a thong- and sieve-maker. Even personal versatility is unusual; it is regarded as quite inappropriate for a tenant to mend his own plough. On the other hand the products or services of specialists in each of these twenty-two occupations are all equally essential. All the occupations must therefore be represented in each self-sufficient community.

Pathans, however, distinguish quite clearly between caste status (*qoum*) and occupational status (*kasb, kar*); it is quite possible for a man to say: 'I am a Carpenter, but I am working as a muleteer.' This does not mean that he is at one and the same time both carpenter and muleteer; it means that his caste status is 'Carpenter', but his occupational status is 'muleteer'. Despite this the occupational system provides the basic conceptual framework for the interrelations of castes. Caste status is ascribed to individuals by virtue of their paternity, while occupations are the subject of individual choice. But 'being of Carpenter caste' means, in Swat, that you are *expected* to work as a carpenter; any other occupation, though formally open, is regarded as anomalous. Caste status and occupational status are not identical, but each caste position is identified with an occupational position. As well as being the ideal, this identification corresponds very closely to empirical facts: of the 476 heads of households registered in the complete censuses of four small villages, only 16 per cent were engaged in occupations inappropriate to their caste. The correlation of caste status and occupational status in one of these villages is shown diagramatically in Figure 2.1.

The significance of this discrepancy between caste and occupation will be discussed in the second part of this essay but, for the moment, I shall ignore it. First, I shall describe the productive system of Swat, and show how this is relevant to (a) the rigid segregation of statuses in the occupational system, (b) the effects which each occupational position has on the position and organization of the caste occupying it, and (c) the composition of local communities which results from these factors.

The distinguishing feature of the productive system of Swat is that, although it depends on a high degree of individual specialization and division of labour, it functions with a very small volume of exchange medium in an essentially non-monetary economy. The rigid segregation of occupational statuses follows directly from these facts. Because the volume of money is small it is difficult to provide for the extensive exchange of services and goods. What is exchanged is *services*, rather than either money or goods. There is a complex pattern of reciprocal services within groups of persons who have direct social relations with one another. To make such a system of exchange function, the respective services due from each participating member must be clearly defined, and kept rigidly separate. The Swat 'caste' system may thus be seen as a device whereby a high degree of occupational specialization may be achieved in a non-monetary economy.

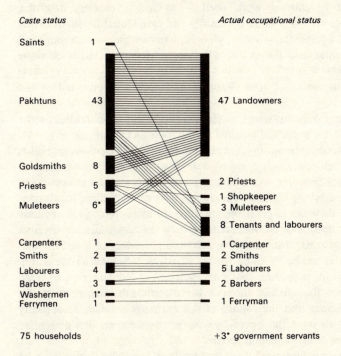

FIGURE 2.1   *Castes and occupation in Worejo*

*   Two men of Muleteer caste and one of Washerman caste worked as government servants and were outside the occupational hierarchy.

The main products of the Swat valley are agricultural and a predominant fraction of the population is engaged, directly or indirectly, in agricultural activity. Agricultural production is maintained by pooling the resources and labour of a number of specialists, including as a minimum: landowner, tenant and/or labourer, carpenter, smith, muleteer, and rope- and thong-maker. Each of these contributes to the total production in the following manner:

1 By and large only members of the Pakhtun or Saintly castes own land and among these most land is concentrated in the hands of a small number of prominent chiefs and landlords who do not themselves engage in manual labour. Their contribution to the productive team is to provide the land. Sometimes they also supply seed and equipment.

2 The agricultural work itself − ploughing, seeding, irrigating, harvesting, etc. − is done by tenants and agricultural labourers. Their tools and equipment − yokes, ploughs, harrows, etc. − are wrought by the carpenter and the smith, who also perform all repairs on these implements.

3 Transport − of seed, fertilizer and crop − is provided by the muleteer.

4 Ropes, brooms, sieves, pitchforks tied with thongs, bridles for the mules, etc. are made and repaired by the rope- and thong-maker.

In a monetary economy, the co-ordination of such various specialists could be achieved through a system of wages or cash payments between dyads, such as employer/employee, buyer/seller, etc. But the people of Swat, though long familiar with money, have no centralized institutions to which they would grant the authority to mint coins, and they have not developed any convenient alternative exchange media. Grain is extensively used in payment for contractual services of long duration, but grain is too bulky to be readily transferred. Substantial quantities of money (now predominantly in the form of Pakistan rupees) reach Swat from the outside through government subsidies, exports and migrant labour. But the volume of this exchange medium is not nearly sufficient to serve the internal exchange requirements of a diversified population of half a million people.

The co-ordination of these occupational specialists must thus be achieved in an essentially non-monetary economy. This is done through the formation of productive teams, in many ways analogous to the European medieval manor. Within such teams each specialist contributes with the skills and equipment or resources appropriate to his status, and receives in return a fraction of the resultant product. The members of each team are in constant communication with one another, and co-ordinate their activities in a manner analogous to what industrial

that is a man who has contributed labour only, not, as the tenant, with seed and bullocks as well), one in every twenty to the muleteer, one in every forty to the carpenter, one in every forty to the smith, and occasional piles as alms to the poor. The rope- and thong-maker usually receives a set amount yearly. In this way, every member of the team receives his fraction of the gross product, while the remainder — in fact a lion's share — goes to the landowner.

Variations from this most common procedure all follow the same general pattern. Sometimes one productive team works the land of several landowners; but in such cases, although the work in the different fields is co-ordinated, the landlords themselves do not pool their resources. The product of each field is divided separately.

The historical connexion of this pattern of organization with the Hindu *jajmani* system is obvious. More important in the present context is its effect on the occupational status system. The organization of work depends on a clear delimitation and allotment of duties to each member of the group, while the pattern of remuneration similarly requires adherence to a traditional schema for the allocation of duties and rights. The system breaks down if any individual assumes duties which are proper to status positions other than his own. The smith who services an estate will claim his contractual share of the produce even if a tenant has done some of the smith's work; and there is no way to adjust the division of the produce so that both parties will accept the adjustment as a fair settlement.

If the occupational contracts are to retain their functional simplicity, they must cover the complete roles of the traditional statuses. The remuneration goes to the holder of a role; it is not a reward for 'piece-work'. And these roles are furthermore so balanced in relation to the yearly cycle of labour requirements that it is very difficult for an individual to combine two roles at once. For example, in the peak season of agricultural activity, at the times of harvests and rice transplantation, there are brief periods when, under the traditional system, all the available labour both agricultural and non-agricultural is in full employment at the same time. A man who was at once both a tenant and a smith would be unable to carry out his seasonal smith duties because he would already be fully committed to agricultural duties in his capacity as tenant. The system thus requires a strict segregation of the different occupational roles. This segregation is achieved, in Swat, by the close identification of occupational status with caste status.

The other specialists in the community are mostly the parties to similar contracts. Priests serve local sections of communities which have the form of territorially delimited wards or parts of wards. In return the priest obtains the use of dedicated land and certain kinds of yearly tax, in kind. Most landowners have a potter, a tailor, a herder, and a washerman attached to their households on a yearly contract, whereby each is expected to perform all services appropriate to his caste in return for a stipulated weight of grain per year. Apart from such dyadic contractual relations the services of such professional craftsmen are also available to others on a piecework basis. This is true too of the other, rarer, specialists not discussed so far. These sporadic and limited 'piecework' exchanges require money payment and haggling over prices. The only case where goods are paid for in kind as opposed to money is in exchanges between agriculturalists and herders, where the traditional equation of equal volumes of milk for maize holds good.

There is one further field of non-monetary exchange which should be mentioned. This concerns the status position of barbers and the exchange of the goods and services required for the *rites de passage* of every individual. Villagers in Swat mark the birth, circumcision (for boys), betrothal, marriage and death of individuals by fairly large-scale public celebrations. For the purpose of mutual assistance in performing these celebrations they form neighbourhood associations, *təltole*. Each such association is administered by a barber; he holds service contracts with each individual household in the association, whereby he agrees to perform the service appropriate to his caste in return for a stipulated yearly payment and traditional gifts. These services include haircutting (of men by the barber, of women by his wife) and shaving, but they also include the organization of celebrations, the announcement of the event to appropriate outsiders, and the mobilization of the assistance from fellow association members to which each family is entitled. This assistance includes contributions of foodstuffs and cooked foods, firewood and crockery, and help in cooking and serving. The 'low', 'taboo' status of the barber stems from this special role. Because it involves intimate contact with the domestic life of each family, in breach of the usual barriers of prudery and seclusion, the barber's status needs to be clearly segregated from that of other persons in the community.

Corporate organization and spatial distribution of castes

While caste is closely identified with occupation, the relation between caste and political organization is more remote. The political organization of the villages of Swat depends on a system of balanced opposition between landowners competing within a feudal framework. Politically, the whole region is insecure and anarchic, and individuals seek security by attaching themselves to powerful chiefs. Such attachments are contractual, and are immediately linked with the individual's house tenancy. A landowner automatically gains administrative authority over the individuals residing on his property; in return, he is responsible for protecting their lives and interests.

The administration of each community is in the hands of public assemblies of landowners. A landowner will act as advocate for all his non-landowning tenants. After a legal decision has been reached in this forum, it is left to the aggrieved party to compensate himself at the expense of his opponents. It is therefore important for every non-landowner to have a powerful landowner as political patron. A good patron is one whose word carries weight in the assembly, and who will thereafter be able to extract restitution on behalf of his political clients.

But the landowner in turn depends for his position on the fact that he controls many followers. Every landlord therefore endeavours to reinforce his authority by binding his followers with additional economic obligations. By making gifts to the occupants of his 'men's house' he seeks to obtain their exclusive allegiance. In awarding house tenancy contracts he tries to restrict the allocation to those who are willing to make other kinds of dependency contract with him at the same time. In the simplest case, the productive teams described above emerge as corporate political groups under the leadership of the landlord. In all cases, the economic bonds of dependence between persons of differentiated status are utilized to increase the authority of the political lord. Through this organization, the community is split up into homologous sections under rival leaders on the basis mainly of house tenancy contracts. Each such section forms a political group which contains within it a number of different mutually dependent statuses having the landowner as common political patron of all.

Such an organization is entirely independent of caste; it further prevents the castes themselves from developing corporate administrative functions in any system like that of the local and regional caste pan-

chayats of India. In Swat, no form of organization which cuts across
the attachment of the clients to their patrons would be tolerated. Thus,
with some minor exceptions, which we shall discuss below, the castes
of Swat do not form corporate groups. Indeed, it is hardly possible
that they should. The productive system which I have described has the
necessary implication that the membership of each of the inferior
dependent castes is widely dispersed and consists of small pockets of
population located in the feudal domains of a large number of different
land-owning chieftains. The membership of such a dispersed group has
no common interest or estate in terms of which it might be 'corporate'.

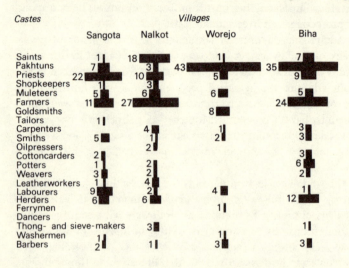

FIGURE 2.3   *The caste composition of four Swat villages*

In different local communities the proportions of each caste vary.
Figure 2.3 shows the caste composition of four particular small villages.
The main differences are of two kinds: (a) There is variation in the
ratio of Saints to Pakhtuns – some communities are dominated by the
former, but most by the latter. (b) There is an inverse variation in the
ratio of landowners to tenants. The ratio of total agriculturalists (owners
plus labourers): to total craftsmen: to total service castes is roughly
constant, though adjusted to the differing labour requirements of
different areas. The constancy of these ratios seems to be maintained
by migration in response to a free labour market – for it must be
remembered that all economic relations are based on voluntary individual

contracts; there is no serfdom. Some specialized castes are found in a few communities only. Ferrymen are distributed only among the communities on the banks of the Swat river, butchers are found only in major towns. Where they occur such specialists constitute only a small minority of the population.

To this pattern of distribution there are certain exceptions. In the hilly and mountainous areas of Swat are many small hamlets which do not participate fully in Pathan economic and social life. They are inhabited in part by Gujar pastoralists and farmers ethnically distinct from Pathans, and in part by remnant lineage segments of former landowning groups who were driven off their estates in the main valley during past conflicts. In the feudal framework of Swat, these hamlets correspond to the *coloni* settlements of the Roman marches — they are nominally owned by landowners who reside in the valley bottom and who exact irregular corvée labour and military service; but the land is too poor and the area too difficult to control for the landlord to extract regular tax. These hamlets maintain their own political authorities and organization, based on caste and descent, and fall in most respects outside the system discussed here.

The villages of the valley are nearly all multi-caste in composition, and in these the feudal organization is combined with the caste system in a different way. The necessary degree of congruence between the two structures is secured by ascribing feudal ascendancy in any one community to a single high-ranking caste. True corporate structure is then given to this one caste only. This is done by making one caste the sovereign landowners. Thus, in each community, the members of the one dominant caste serve as political patrons to all the members of all other castes. In these circumstances the feudal rights of the landlord may be interpreted, within the caste framework, as merely one further set of rights pertaining to high-caste position. We find that, depending on their relative positions of dominance as landowners, either Pakhtuns or Saints may assume these feudal privileges. In any one community all the individual feudal patrons, being of a single caste, are equal in rank but are ranged in opposition against the feudal patrons of rival neighbouring communities, especially if these are of another caste. In this case the political boundary between territorial ('feudal') domains coincides with the caste boundary between Saint and Pakhtun, so that the political ideology and the caste ideology serve to reinforce each other.

The members of a dominant caste must sometimes join in corporate action for purposes of government and the defence of their privileges. The land tenure system involves the periodic re-allotment of fields to title-holders over a considerable area, and this presupposes a corporate organization of landowners (Barth, 1957). Although they differ in power according to the number of their clients, all landowners are equal in rank, and the institution which provides a corporate expression of the local dominant caste is simply a plenary assembly of all its members; this assembly simultaneously constitutes the governing body of the whole local community.

The caste unity of the landlord group is not easily maintained. Land is held as individual, private property and can be bought and sold. Since feudal powers go with land, the structure calls for some legal device which will (a) prevent lower-caste individuals acquiring both land and feudal powers, and (b) eliminate those members of the dominant caste who have lost their land and feudal powers.

The former requirement is satisfied by restrictions on the individual's right to alienate land, and by distinguishing between different kinds of title to land. First, close agnates, neighbours and the headman of the ward (administrative division of the village) have first option, in that order, to buy any land offered for sale. Secondly, the transfer of complete title is not permitted across caste boundaries. The vast majority of land is owned by Pakhtuns, who trace descent from patrilineal ancestors who are supposed to have acquired holdings by conquest during the sixteenth century. Such land is classified as *daftar* and the title-holder has full rights of sovereignty. *Daftar* title gives the holder the right to speak in the assembly. *Daftar* land sold to another Pakhtun remains *daftar*, and the new owner succeeds to the complete rights. If however it is alienated to an individual of another caste, whether Saint or lower caste, it is classified as *siri* land. The buyer of such land obtains full rights to the land as private, disposable property; but its conversion to *siri* has divorced it from the administrative framework of the feudal system and removed the right of its owner to speak in the assembly. The exclusive right of members of the Pakhtun caste to serve as patrons is thus maintained in spite of the alienation of full economic rights over part of the original Pakhtun land. A tenant resident on *siri* lands cannot be the political client of his landlord; he must find some other patron, either through land tenancy contracts with a *daftar*-owning Pakhtun or by establishing other ties of obligation and service.

Conversely, the Pakhtun who loses all his land loses his caste status.

Since his claim to Pakhtun status can no longer be validated by the possession of *daftar*, his right to speak in the assembly of landowners is lost, and he must become the client of another man. In spite of his descent, he is then sloughed off from the higher caste and assimilated into the caste of farmer-tenants.

An essentially similar system is enforced in the villages ruled by Saints — the right to speak in the assembly, and thus to serve as political patron to others, depends on the ownership of land plus membership in the Saint caste.

It should be noted that, while the caste unity of local landowners is essential in both cases, unity of descent is not required. Patrons of different grades of Sainthood, with different ancestors, sometimes rule together within a single village, while, occasionally, villages dominated by Pakhtuns contain non-Yusufzai as well as Yusufzai lineage segments.[3]

The development of trade and the increase in money circulation have lately introduced special factors which are influencing the pattern of caste distribution, and hence the degree to which particular castes are 'corporate'. Most money income in Swat comes from the sources I have mentioned. This money is used to buy a great variety of foreign trade goods. These include foodstuffs such as refined sugar and tea, and industrial products such as crockery, factory-made rifles, cloth, and medicines.

Under the more anarchic political conditions which formerly prevailed, trade caravans required military protection. Each chief provided the defence equipment for the caravans run by his own dependent muleteers. In this way trade remained under the control of the feudal leaders. However, with the improved communications and greater security which developed about the turn of the century, trade became more regular, and trading bazaars grew up in the main communication centres. This bazaar trade has remained predominantly in the hands of former muleteers, now liberated from their dependence on military protectors. Such groups of muleteer traders now tend to congregate in the trading centres.

Within the limits imposed by the shortage of exchange media this same type of trade is also used for internal exchanges between the different local communities. This makes it possible for fellow specialists who are not directly involved in agricultural labour to congregate in a village by themselves where they can maintain themselves by exporting their specialized products to neighbouring villages and buying the necessities of life from outside. This arrangement is particularly feasible for weavers. Throughout the Swat valley there are to be found occasional villages inhabited almost exclusively by weavers; these form centres for the production of cloth.

Here, then, two kinds of localized caste groups have developed: (a) groups of traders located in communication centres who are independent of agriculture but possess money resources, and (b) small villages of uniform caste serving as centres of specialized production for a monetary market. Both types of localized caste group tend to develop a corporate structure. This takes the form of a ritual association (*təltole*), the general nature of which has already been explained above (p. 28) in connection with the role of barber. In both cases independent action by the localized castes is opposed by the landowners, but the castes are able to maintain the autonomy because of their freedom from dependence on feudal patronage. As individuals the traders are mostly house-tenants of various landowners, but they are able to repudiate their individual obligations of clientage in favour of the organized support of their own local caste group. Traders organized in local groups can be useful to the feudal leaders as providers of capital. Also, the possession of money allows such people to protect their interests with occasional bribes. Weavers, on the other hand, generally congregate on the land of a single, non-resident owner; and being economically independent they can combine to keep the landlord's influence at a minimum, in much the same way as do the Gujar hamlets mentioned above (p. 31).

The communities of traders and weavers both tend to recognize, informally, as local leader and spokesman, a *masher* ('elder' or senior man), but in both cases the web of community relations evoked through joint participation in the feasts of *təltole rites de passage* provides the main mechanism for co-ordinating common caste action. New arrivals, such as traders transferring their business from another village, or weavers settling in a new community, are not expected or compelled to join their fellow caste members in any formal organization. There is no 'guild' and no coercion to accept the authority of a *masher*. Only when the newcomer has established a set of informal or formal social ties with his fellow caste members, and started to participate in their association for *rites de passage*, is he expected to show solidarity with the group and to participate in their efforts at corporate action.

The Pathan combination of feudal and caste organization thus depends on the maintenance, in the ruling groups only, of an approximate identity between feudal and caste lines of cleavage. Where economic statuses based on trade and a monetary economy are established outside the feudal framework, other inferior castes also tend to develop corporate organizations. It is remarkable that, in this strongly Muslim area, these latter incipient corporate organizations do not take the form of guilds; instead they appear as ceremonial commensal units concerned with the celebration of the *rites de passage* of caste members.

Kinship and caste

Caste, in this essay, is analysed not as a set of ritual groups, but as a pattern of social stratification — that is, a conceptual scheme for ordering the individuals of a community, each occupying multiple statuses, in terms of a limited set of hierarchical categories. Caste systems are considered to be characterized by the relatively high degree of congruence that obtains between (a) the various status frameworks found in the community, with their internal hierarchies, and (b) the hierarchy of caste categories. This congruence is achieved by the definition of invariant and imperative constellations of statuses.

In these terms, we first described the set of caste categories in Swat, and showed the close congruence between this system and the occupational framework. Then we analysed the nature of the congruence between the political framework and caste. As a result, certain constellations of statuses became apparent: Pakhtuns are high rank, landowners, and political patrons; persons of Smith caste are lower rank, blacksmiths, and political clients, etc. We have now to analyse the nature of the congruence between the caste categories and the mutual attachment of individuals through ties of kinship. This congruence is produced in all caste systems by making an aspect of kinship the primary vehicle for the transmission of caste positions; by the ascription of caste on the basis of parentage. Where children are ascribed to the caste of their parents and castes are endogamous, all ties of kinship become concentrated within castes, and the lines of kinship cleavage coincide with the boundaries between castes.

Such perfect congruence will be disturbed wherever there is 'social mobility'. There is in fact a considerable amount of such mobility in Swat; but this in part serves to preserve, rather than disturb, the characteristic constellations of statuses defined in the caste hierarchy. The kinds of social mobility of relevance to this material fall under three headings: (1) true individual mobility, whereby a man changes his caste position during adult life; (2) hypergamy and hypogamy, whereby a woman marries into a caste different from her own; and (3) inter-generational mobility, whereby a child fails to be ascribed the caste position of his parents.

Whereas cases of (1) seem to be very rare in Swat, (2) and (3) are fairly frequent. All three processes deserve explanation and discussion.

1 Individual caste mobility

There is an oft-cited popular saying in the Peshawar district, to the effect that 'last year I was a Julaha (weaver); this year I am a Shekh (disciple); next year if prices rise I shall be a Saiyad' (Ibbetson, 1916: 222). This points to what is undeniably the easiest route for individual caste mobility — that leading to Sainthood. In Peshawar city such mobility implies little more than a change in honorific title, but in Swat the transition involves change of caste, and is much harder to achieve.

The theological basis for the occasional recognition of Sainthood among non-Saints is a folk elaboration of certain Koranic suggestions regarding incarnations. Pathans believe that in every generation a certain number of very sacred persons (such as a *Ghous*, a member of the committee ruling the Heavens) are born among us, to live a pious life without disclosing their identity. Recognizing and paying respect to such persons gives religious merit.

The man who leads a pious life thus receives particular respect; he cannot make any explicit claims to Saintly status, but may in time be granted such status by others. Usually recognition does not come till after his death, and final proof of his sanctity derives from the efficacy of his grave, evaluated in a spirit of empiricism. For example, the sanctity of a minor Saint in one of the areas where I worked was discovered accidentally from the power of his grave. A shepherd boy let his goats graze between the graves; one nanny-goat disrespectfully leapt over this man's grave so that her teat brushed against it. Her udder immediately became inflamed, and the goat died shortly. The villagers realized there was power in the grave; when put further to the test it proved a potent shrine for prayers for the fertility of stock and women. The deceased man was then recognized as a Saint, and his descendants are now treated as members of the Saint caste.

But recognition may also come in the Saint's lifetime, as in the case of the Akhund of Swat, the prominent religious leader of the last century, who was originally of Tenant caste. A change of residence and a long period of seclusion seem to be invariably required in order to effect such a transition from a lower-caste status to the caste status of Saint.

The following is a summary of the career of the Akhund of Swat. Born west of the Swat river, he first supported himself as a herder; he then moved to the bank of the Indus and there retired to the life of an ascetic for twelve years, attracting pilgrims and disciples, but taking no part in secular life. In the course of this period he was recognized as a Saint. On his return to secular life he made extensive use of the special peace-making privileges of his acquired caste status so as to further his political career. After his period as a recluse he married and had sons, and his descendants are now classified as *Mians* (cf. p. 21). It should be noted that he did not return to his community of origin or re-establish contacts with collateral kin there.

This pattern of *rite de passage* can be duplicated in the careers of many less important 'created' Saints. During their period of ascetic seclusion they are referred to as *Pir*; only when they re-emerge in secular life are they reclassified as belonging to the grade of Sainthood, a position which affects the status of their descendants within the caste.

No other institutionalized pattern of caste mobility is known. Pakhtun caste status depends on descent and land ownership, both of which are unobtainable by outsiders because of the process whereby alienated land is reclassified as *siri* (see above, p. 32). Mobility between different low castes can be achieved by deception only, as when a person who has competence in the occupation of a caste other than his own travels to a distant place where he then pretends to be of that caste. Similarly, loss of caste cannot take place within a man's own lifetime. A man who was born a Pakhtun will remain a Pakhtun, even if he later loses his land, since he can maintain his claim on the pretext that alienation of land was enforced, or temporary. But such a man has no *daftar* and thus no Pakhtun status to pass on to his sons. Downward mobility thus results from a failure of succession, not from a change in the individual's own adult caste position.

The rules relating to individual social mobility thus serve to maintain the congruence between the framework of discrete castes on the one hand and the web of kinship affiliation on the other. They do this in two ways. Firstly, the possibility for individual upward mobility is blocked. In the one case where such mobility is possible, the mobile individual (would-be Saint) is required to dissociate himself entirely from his original kin, and the separation of his old and his new status is further marked by an extended intervening period of seclusion and non-participation in secular life in either capacity. Secondly, the possibility of individual downward mobility is blocked by holding over the completion of the process until the next generation.

2 Hypergamy and hypogamy

The principle of caste endogamy is usually discussed in terms of Hindu concepts of pollution rather than with reference to its structural significance; and in the former framework one is easily driven to purely scholastic explanations of the widespread phenomenon of hypergamy (e.g. Stevenson, 1954: 57). In the present discussion both hypergamy and hypogamy will be treated as special forms of social mobility which have a direct relevance to the degree of congruence which obtains between caste and kinship. Obviously, any marriage across caste lines creates kinship ties between individuals in different castes and such links persist into succeeding generations. A pattern of caste endogamy has the structural effect of preventing the development of such cross-caste kin relationships. In Swat, however, the ban on individual caste mobility for males is not reinforced by any effective check on this form of mobility for females. Although there is a clear tendency towards caste endogamy, the contrary cases are very numerous (40 per cent; see Table 2.1 p. 42).

The importance of separating kinship relationship from intercaste relationship stems from the importance of kinship in the transmission and ascription of statuses and rights. This does not imply that all social relations between castes need to be repudiated. Intimate individual ties across caste lines form an inherent part of any caste system, and are implied in the obvious complementarity of different caste roles. Strong affective ties between members of different castes are perfectly compatible with the smooth functioning of a caste system. Only those intercaste relations which would create ambiguity in the principles of status ascription are incompatible with the structural features of a caste system. It follows logically from this that a pattern of caste endogamy is vital in any system of kinship only where rights and status are transmitted to children from *both* their parents. But in the Pathan case the system of patriarchal family structure and exclusively patrilineal descent serves to make matrilineal and matrilateral kinship irrelevant to status and authority ascription, and thus obviates the need for caste endogamy. To demonstrate this fully would require considerable documentation of the ethnographic facts relating to Swat Pathan kinship and marriage, some of which can only be sketched here. The main factors to be considered are the form of marriage, descent, and the distribution of authority between kinsmen.

Pathans recognize only one form of marriage; it is made legal by a simple Islamic ceremony; and by this ceremony, and this alone, the husband obtains full and exclusive rights over the wife. Brideprice payments, often of considerable magnitude, may be necessary to make the father or marriage guardian give his legally required consent to the marriage; but their payment or non-payment in no way affects the nature or extent of the husband's rights over his wife. On marriage, all the legal rights formerly held by the father, as well as exclusive sexual access, are vested in the husband. A married woman cannot administer her own property, she may not enter any contract except with the permission of the husband, the husband has the right to demand obedience, and the right to discipline his wife to secure such obedience. For the protection of her own, limited, rights, the wife turns not to her father, but to the village headman or *Qazi*. This corresponds very closely to the Hanafi legal code.

Naturally, even though legal ties are severed, a woman's affectual ties with her parents and siblings normally persist after marriage; however, a wife must obtain her husband's permission before visiting her parents, and he has the full right to refuse her such permission and cut her off from all communication with her kin. On the death of her husband a woman's own son becomes her marriage guardian; only if she has no male issue do potestal rights revert to her father or brother. Affines, if they are friendly with each other, participate extensively in each other's associations for *rites de passage*; but when disagreements arise such participation is temporarily or permanently discontinued. There are no occasions when co-operation or even communication between affines is mandatory. This description of the authority relations within a household and of the relations between affines displays a family system which one might characterize as 'strongly patriarchal'. This pattern of authority must be distinguished from the pattern of descent, which relates to the transmission of statuses and not to the distribution of authority. While in the former case our attention centres on affines, in the latter we are concerned with distinctions between patrilateral and matrilateral relatives. Pathans combine a patriarchal family system with exclusive recognition of patrilineal descent. The greater part of the rights and obligations which define the position of a Pathan in his various spheres of activity are the subject of private contractual agreements, but all those formal positions to which there is hereditary succession are transmitted exclusively in the male line. Membership in a descent group (*khel*) is transmitted from father to son; there is no pattern of matrilateral grafting, and adoption is impossible. Chiefship in feudal states passes, in default of direct male descendants, to agnatic collaterals of the deceased chief, never to a sister's son or daughter's son, and the status of the mother — whether of chiefly birth or low birth — is immaterial. Seniority among brothers, sons of a common father, is determined by relative age, without reference to the seniority of wives, their respective mothers. Virtually all property, movable and immovable, is held by men and inherited patrilineally, without regard for Islamic laws of inheritance. Women may receive gifts and thus have possessions, or the husband may endow his wife on marriage with a special amount of property (*mahr*), but except for items of personal use such property is held by the husband on the wife's behalf and inherited by her sons. These personal possessions of a woman are inherited by Islamic law, sons each taking two shares and daughters each one share. Where a woman has such property of her own, it is transferred to her marital home upon marriage. She retains no rights in her natal home and therefore has no such rights to transmit to her children. There are thus no material interests of any kind which bind persons to their matrilateral relatives. Pathans usually have affectual ties with their mother's brothers and maternal grandparents, but such feelings have developed simply as a result of childhood visiting — subject to the father's control. Senior matrilateral relatives are shown the respect due to them by virtue of their sex and age, neither more nor less.

In sum, marriage alters the affective significance of kinship for the woman herself, but affinal relations do not create ties between households, and matrilateral kinship plays no role in the transmission of status of property, or in the distribution of authority of seniors over juniors. All status and property is held and transmitted by the male line, and all familial authority is exercised by male patrilineal relatives.

This pattern of descent and authority by itself ensures the necessary degree of structural congruence between significant kinship alignments and lines of caste cleavage: caste ascription, like all other hereditary ascription of status, is on the basis of patrilineal descent; the kinship ties of individuals, both with respect to rights and obligations and in terms of authority relations, are similarly defined on the basis of patrilineal descent alone.

The figures listed in Table 2.1 show a marked tendency towards caste endogamy, but this endogamy does not arise from any need for a precise congruence between the alignment of individuals by kinship and by caste. In the Pathan system, endogamy seems rather to relate to the hierarchical aspects of caste and to the denial of identity between castes. Pathans explicitly state that sister exchange can only take place between equals. It is appropriate for people who are alike and is a good thing as an expression of solidarity. Any kind of kin endogamy, or status endogamy, is thus approved as an overt expression of friendliness, and as a factor creating friendliness by virtue of the intervisiting which is expected to follow. But women may also be given unilaterally to unequals.

As in most of western Asia and India, women are regarded as an appropriate form of tribute from the weak man, who seeks protection, to the strong, who gives it. The value of such hypergamous marriages to the wife-givers springs, not so much from the value of the affinal relation thus established, as from the esteem acquired through giving highly valued 'tribute'. Hypergamous marriages are thus a recognized pattern; in contrast, hypogamy − the giving of a woman downwards, to inferiors − is frowned upon and considered a 'shame' for the woman's family. Claims to relative rank between castes are usually made in precisely such terms − Saints may say they receive wives from Pakhtuns, but will not give them daughters in return.

One final factor helps to obscure the effect of this explicit rule, namely the adjustable brideprice. Most of the cases of apparently hypogamous marriages which appear in Table 2.1 might, if the matter were argued properly during the marriage negotiation, be represented as marriages between near equals; any reluctance on the bride's family could then be overcome by a higher brideprice offer. Thus, in seventeen of the nineteen cases of marriage between a man of Priest caste and a woman of Pakhtun or Saint caste, the man belonged to a colony of land (*siri*) owning Priests who are established in the village of Sangota. Such men are lower in caste status than their Pakhtun fathers-in-law, yet, for the purposes of argument, they can be classified as 'fellow landowners'. Generally speaking, brideprice varies in terms of two criteria which are made quite explicit during brideprice negotiations.

1 Where husband and wife are of approximately equal status then the higher the status of the husband the higher the brideprice.

2a Where the situation is one of hypergamy the brideprice due under (1) is cancelled.

2b Where the situation is one of hypogamy the brideprice due under (1) is increased.

Table 2.1 The caste status of living spouses in four villages

Figures from villages of Sangota, Worejo, Nalkot, Biha

Man \ Woman	Saint	Pakhtun	Priest	Goldsmith	Muleteer Shopkeeper	Farmer	Craftsman	Labourer	Herder	'Unclean'
Saint	25	17	4	0	0	0	0	0	0	0
Pakhtun	6	90	5	3	7	3	4	5	1	0
Priest	8	11	29	0	0	5	3	1	4	1
Goldsmith	2	1	0	9	4	0	0	0	0	0
Muleteer Shopkeeper	0	2	1	1	16	3	4	1	0	1
Farmer	0	6	7	0	4	42	8	0	10	1
Craftsman	0	2	1	0	4	9	29	2	6	1
Labourer	0	0	0	0	0	3	4	13	6	0
Herder	0	0	0	0	0	2	1	0	17	0
'Unclean'	0	0	2	0	1	2	0	2	1	14

Total marriages 476

Marriages endogamous to caste 283 = 60%
Hypergamous marriages 110 = 23%
Hypogamous marriages 83 = 17%

The net result of such manoeuvres is that, as shown in Table 2.1, a substantial proportion of all marriages are cross-caste. Even so the tendency towards caste endogamy is quite explicit. Each caste is commonly regarded as constituting the widest order of kin group (*nasab*), that is to say it is thought of as endogamous.

3 Intergenerational caste mobility

In Swat society the rules of marriage do not, as in an orthodox Hindu system, automatically establish a congruence between the frontiers of caste and the frontiers of kin grouping, but, even so, the principle whereby caste membership is inherited by patrilineal descent does require that individual descent groups should be confined to particular castes. Although this congruence of descent grouping and caste group-ing is in fact maintained, a certain amount of intergenerational caste mobility does occur.

Pathans themselves are fully aware of such caste changes, and relate the process to occupational mobility. Thus, if the son of a Priest takes up carpentry, he will always be known as a Priest, likewise his son again. But if a man of the third generation continues as a carpenter and there are no known collateral agnates in other occupations in the village, people may say: 'his father was a carpenter, and so was his grandfather; so he is a carpenter (by caste).' Such a process is entirely consistent with the facts described above: the reclassification is done without reference to matrilateral kin, and is made possible by (a) stability of occupation in the descent line, and (b) absence of collateral agnates in other occupations. The founder of this new 'lineage' of Carpenters — the deceased ancestor who changed his occupation — may well be remembered as having been a Priest, so long as no other agnatic descendants of his are known. Under these particular circum-stances, intergenerational mobility (and retroactive reclassification of immediate ancestors) preserves rather than disturbs the characteristic constellation of statuses defined by each caste. A patrilineal descent group such as this is unconnected with other such groups, it occupies the socio-economic position characteristic of carpenters, and thus clearly belongs in the caste category 'Carpenter'.

The depth and span of patrilineal descent groups varies between castes, and to some extent within them. While Saints recognize numer-ous quite distinct lineages, some large, some small, Pakhtuns in theory, and very nearly in practice, make up a single very large patrilineage. Among Farmers and Herders some ramifying descent groups of six to eight generations' depth are found; these occasionally have an additional pedigree which links them to distant tribes of past conquerors. Car-penters, Potters, and particularly Blacksmiths, though possessing only very shallow genealogies nevertheless have a distinctive pattern of genealogical claims. An important section of these craftsmen claim descent from King David, who, in the manner of a culture hero, forged tools, using his knee as an anvil, and with these tools made a potter's wheel — thereby inventing the techniques of smithing, carpentry, and pottery-making. He taught these arts to his sons and daughter; the latter was taught pottery, but she then married and communicated her skills to her husband and son. All 'true' craftsmen claim descent through one of these siblings from King David, and occasionally claim that this is what makes them distinct from mere *kasbər* — craft-companions. However, only about one-third of the smiths in Swat seem to claim the distinction of descent from David, and the tradition is without much importance as far as members of other castes are concerned.

The process whereby, as a consequence of change of occupation by an ancestor, a whole patrilineage may 'change its caste' is relevant for the formation of new castes. The framework of occupations itself is not entirely stable — for while no traditional occupations are known to have disappeared, some new ones are definitely known to have arisen. New castes may form around such new occupations through hereditary transmission from father to son; alternatively a new caste may be formed through the splitting of an old one. Both processes may be seen at work today. The introduction of the sewing-machine some seventy years ago has led to the emergence of a new, as yet small and not fully formed, caste of 'Tailors', recruited from a variety of castes in the middle range of the hierarchy. Similarly, the invention, outside of Swat, of a form of sandal which in the course of the last thirty years has become the predominant fashion in men's shoes, has created the new occupation of 'sandal-maker'. A variety of men have adopted this occupation, and my Pathan informants expected that a caste of 'Sandal-makers' would emerge in the course of another generation or two. On the other hand, over the last sixty years improved communications have led to a wide proliferation of shops. Formerly, all such shops were owned by Hindus; but recently there has developed a local Pathan caste of 'Shopkeepers'. Though it has received accretions, particularly from the Priest caste, the main body of this new caste derives from the traditional Muleteer caste, with which it is still sometimes identified. It is a reasonable presumption to expect that within a generation or so 'Shopkeepers' and 'Muleteers' will emerge as completely distinct castes.

To sum up: congruence between the boundaries of caste grouping and the boundaries of kinship obligation is maintained by confining each patrilineal descent group to a particular caste. Where social mobility occurs across caste boundaries various kinds of fission of the patrilineage may result which serve to restructure the kinship system into segregated caste compartments as before. The exclusively patrilineal emphasis among Swat Pathans implies that hereditary succession and the jural allocation of authority in terms of kinship is confined within particular patrilineages. This suffices to ensure consistency between caste roles and kinship roles. The self-sufficiency of the patrilineal principle accounts for the relaxation of the ordinary caste rule of endogamy. The existence of affinal links which cross caste boundaries has no consequences as regards jural authority over things or persons.

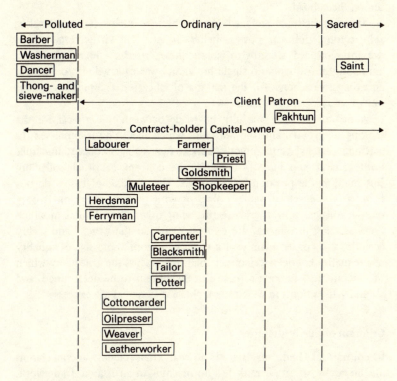

FIGURE 2.4   *The hierarchy of castes in Swat, and some criteria on which it is based*

Hierarchical aspects of caste

The main clusters of statuses that characterize each caste position in Swat should now be clear, as well as the types of relation – economic, political, and matrilateral – which exist between castes. But a caste system does not only serve to place individuals in discrete categories; like any system of social stratification it also provides for a hierarchical ordering of these categories into 'higher' and 'lower'. This hierarchical ordering may be referred to as the *ranking* of castes. The rank order of castes is made explicit in various ceremonial contexts; it may also be elicited by direct questioning of informants. The positions of the castes in the high-low axis in Figure 2.4 summarizes, to the best of my understanding, the numerous explicit and implicit statements I collected on the subject.

These evaluations are made on the basis of such criteria as wealth, skin colour, political power, belief in inherited virtue, etc. In the present section I attempt to isolate these criteria. I must stress that among my informants no single individual was ever willing to produce an exhaustive schema for the ranking of all castes. The problem is thus one of analysis and synthesis.

A distinction may usefully be made between the *criteria* for the ranking of groups, and the *idiom* in which hierarchy is expressed. In a Hindu caste system, it would appear that a single concept underlies both criteria and idiom — namely the concept of ritual pollution. But in Swat the position is less simple. The ranking of castes derives from a whole set of value scales, of which purity/pollution is only one — political power, and wealth, being others. The idioms in which these ranking differences are expressed are on the other hand highly eclectic, and consist mainly of a series of actions expressive of equality or inequality between persons. I shall first discuss the criteria by which the hierarchical ranking of castes in Swat seem to be determined, and secondly the idioms in which hierarchical differences are expressed.

Criterion of purity/pollution

In contrast to Hinduism, Islam is an egalitarian religion; and an elaborate hierarchy of ritual rank has no meaning in an Islamic framework. This is not to say that there is no development of a concept of pollution; but, according to Islam, ritual pollution, which derives from body processes such as elimination, sexual intercourse and death, applies equally to all. All men are equally cursed with such sources of pollution, and purity can only be maintained by repeated purificatory acts on the part of the individual. As a ritual system Islam is thus unsuited to produce hierarchical distinctions between social strata. However, this ideal ritual equality does not imply that Moslem societies are without ritually-based systems of social stratification.

In Swat, as in Hindu societies, the notion that pollution derives from body processes marks off certain castes as occupationally polluted.

In the case of Sweepers this pollution is so strong that the profession as such has been rejected by Pathan society. The only Sweepers to be found in Swat are members of a Panjabi caste who have been brought in and protected by prominent chiefs. The indigenous polluted castes include Washermen, Barbers (who are concerned with shaving, nail-paring, and childbirth), and Thong- and Sieve-makers (who work with the guts of animals); these three groups are everywhere despised and form the lowest stratum of society. The case of Dancers also falls in this category, since they are associated with prostitution and other morally bad practices.

These polluted castes constitute only a small percentage of the total population (cf. Fig. 2.3). There is no agreed principle whereby other occupations may be rated as more or less polluting, consequently the majority of the population remains, in this respect, undifferentiated and is of 'normal ritual status'. The concept of pollution produces no further distinctions until we reach the very top of the hierarchy, where a belief in the inherited power and holiness of the descendants of the Prophet Mohammed, or of prominent Saints, serves to set these persons apart from ordinary profane individuals. Such elevated status, however, here requires more strict observance of ritual rules, and not the abandon characteristics of Indian Sanyasis.

The criterion of purity/pollution thus gives a tripartite ranking of castes in the categories (1) *polluted*, embracing the four lowest castes, (2) *ordinary*, representing the bulk of the castes, and (3) *sacred*, represented by the highest caste, the Saints.

Criterion of political power

Political power is highly valued among Pathans; it is associated with independence and regarded as honourable and good, whereas weakness and dependence is shameful and bad. The important distinction for purposes of ranking is between *patrons* and *clients*; patrons include all Pakhtuns and Saints, clients all others. However, since Pakhtuns are politically more powerful than Saints, this introduces some ambivalence in their ranking vis-à-vis Saints, an ambivalence not unfamiliar elsewhere in India.

Politically powerful Pakhtuns can denigrate the sacred status of Saints and claim rank equality with them; Saints on the other hand are adamant in their claim that all Saints *ipso facto* rank higher than all Pakhtuns. On this issue the Saints have the support of the non-Pakhtun population.

As noted above (p. 29), the political authority of patrons over their clients depends to a considerable extent on economic control. The criterion of political power thus produces a further distinction: between (a) castes whose members are economically free, and (b) castes whose members depend on their political patrons for economic contracts. The politically more autonomous castes include the Priests, who farm or administer dedicated lands, some Farmers, who themselves own a bit of land, Goldsmiths, who have their own capital and engage on piecework only, and Shopkeepers, who do independent business on a cash or barter basis. Economic contract-holders, on the other hand, whether tenants, labourers or craftsmen, are subject to economic sanctions from their patrons. They are weaker and more dependent, and thus rank lower.

Criterion of wealth

Ranking on the basis of wealth differences tends throughout to be congruent with the ranking on the basis of pollution and political power, with two exceptions. Dancers may accumulate a fair amount of wealth, particularly in the form of pretty clothes, even though they belong in the lowest, polluted, group; on the other hand Saints cannot compete with Pakhtuns in wealth even though they claim the highest 'ritual' status. In both these cases, the criterion of purity/pollution dominates over that of wealth, so far as general ranking evaluations are concerned.

In all other respects the criterion of wealth serves to reinforce the ranking based on other criteria. In some cases it serves to intensify the differentiation between castes. Thus labourers, herdsmen, and ferrymen are all economically depressed castes, and as such they rank lower than the other craft and service castes, even though they stand higher than all the polluted groups.

The relative hierarchical positions of the castes of Swat are thus consistent with, and seem to derive from, the three widely held value criteria of purity/pollution, political power, and wealth. Each of these criteria produces one or several dichotomies, placing groups of castes in positions of inequality. In combination, these three criteria produce all the apparent rank distinctions except one, namely that between high- and low-status craftsmen: that is to say between (a) carpenter, smith, tailor and potter, who are high, and (b) cotton-carder, oil presser, weaver and leatherworker, who are low. This distinction is quite clearly recognized by Swat Pathans. Whereas carpentry, smithing, etc. are regarded as perfectly respectable occupations, weaving, oil-pressing, etc. are not respectable, and the castes associated with these latter occupations may be referred to by others as 'low' and 'unclean'. The nature of the value criterion on which this ranking is based is obscure. A similar ranking is found in North India, where it is said to be justifed in terms of the Hindu pollution concept (Stevenson, 1954: 61, but see comment by Mayer, 1956: 128 n.). Such arguments appear to be meaningless in terms of the ideas of Swat Pathans, but we may be dealing here with a direct case of cultural diffusion from India. The castes of Swat correspond to, and their members communicate with, those of the North Indian plain; and general 'snob' attitudes current in India may have been adopted in Swat without reference to the philosophic values underlying them. In all other respects, however, the ranking of castes in Swat may be seen to reflect basic values which are prevalent in Swat itself.

Hierarchical compatibility of part-statuses

I have shown above how the caste system of Swat is characterized by the principle of status clustering — groups of compatible part-statuses are associated together and thus form a single stereotyped social person characteristic for each caste. The members of the caste are then made to conform to this stereotype. As pointed out above (p. 17), this matter has two aspects:

1 Compatible statuses must imply roles that may be simultaneously satisfied by one individual.

2 In a structural sense compatible statuses must define positions that are congruent with one another. While in most of this essay I have emphasized the former aspect, I am here concerned with the latter. I seek to discover possible structural principles that govern the association of statuses in clusters.

Clearly we are concerned with rank. To be compatible, part-statuses must imply similar relative positions in the general scale of superordination/subordination. Thus a man cannot simultaneously be an economic contractholder and a political patron, since in one capacity he would rank low while in the other capacity he would rank high and be expected to exercise authority over his (economic) superiors. While such incongruities are possible in a society where the different offices and capacities of a single individual are distinguished, they are disruptive to a system where these are *not* clearly distinguished, and where individuals have intimate, face-to-face relations with each other in many different spheres of activity. Differentiation in such societies can only be maintained if individuals in their different capacities are ranked consistently. This is precisely what is achieved in a caste system by limiting the permitted combinations of part-statuses to a restricted number of constellations.

Pathans in Swat express the notion of compatibility and incompatibility of statuses in terms of a concept of shame (*sharm*). A man is 'ashamed' to assume any position or perform any action which he feels is incompatible with his caste status. Considerations of shame and its avoidance are very frequent and prominent in conversations and deliberations in Swat. In fact the concept applies in a number of different situations; it is brought into play whenever an individual's actions deviate from the norm of what is expected of him; it thus also relates to activities such as hospitality, blood feud, etc. In its relevance to caste, shame expresses precisely the notion of hierarchical incompatibility of statuses and roles, and applies equally to up- and down-grading: for example, a Carpenter refuses, from shame, to perform a polluting service like washing clothes for another, while feelings of shame similarly prevent him from trying to exercise authority over a caste superior, such as a Pakhtun or a Saint who is in debt to him. The use of this shame concept by Pathans corresponds to the use of the pollution concept among Hindus. Shame directs the choices made by individuals in assuming new part-statuses. The caste organization depends for its maintenance on the explicit recognition of this discriminating factor.

Hierarchical idioms

In Swat hierarchical differences are continually being expressed in ceremonial behaviour; but the idioms in which they are expressed are not developed into any coherent system like that of Hindu ritual. Such idioms mostly concern the relative status of pairs of actors, rather than of whole caste groups. A brief description of these idioms will help to give a fuller picture of the social implications of caste in Swat.

Economic prosperity correlates highly with caste rank, and since affluence is readily visible in dress, the style of clothing (quality, number and size of garments, cleanness, weapons carried, etc.) is used as a rough sign of caste. Only Saints, however, stand out clearly by their use of white cloth, particularly in the use of white turbans.

Saints are also marked off as a category by special deference behaviour: when any member of the saint caste enters a room, all those present rise — a sign of respect which is also shown to prominent chiefs as individuals, but not to any other whole caste group. Hierarchy is also constantly expressed in terms of address. The kinship terms *Baba* (GrFa), *Kaka* (FaBr), *Wrora* (Br) and *Haleka* (Boy/Son) are often used vocatively in a metaphorical sense, the choice of term reflecting relative status rather than age. Thus all adult males of the Saint caste are addressed as *Baba* by all others, while persons of low caste extend this term also to senior Pakhtuns and Priests. An adolescent Pakhtun, on the other hand, freely uses the term *Haleka* to older men of lower caste: for example, to craftsmen. But the most important hierarchical idioms derive from the two fundamental situations of gift-giving and commensality.

We have here to distinguish between gifts = charity, and gifts = tribute. Some kinds of goods are used in both contexts, and an observer needs to have previous knowledge of the relative statuses of the two actors to understand the meaning in each case. Thus a gift of fruits is an appropriate sign of deference, but also, inversely, it is a sign of benevolence. Other goods may be used only, or primarily, in one context. Thus gifts of money are frequently made, but only *from* a superior *to* an inferior; they are often described by the Arabic (Muslim) word for alms. Snuff, on the other hand (used by most adult males), is offered only to equals and superiors, and not to persons of inferior status.

Large feasts with multi-caste participation — which occur very frequently in Pathan men's houses — are the most characteristic setting for the expression of rank. Cooked food may appropriately be given not only to equals but also to inferiors. Hence, if a person of superior rank eats the cooked food of an inferior, he honours the latter by implying a rough equality between the two. This relates to the fact that the giving of food, particularly in the form of a meal, implies an obligation on the part of the host to protect his guest in a political sense. The host is the (political) superior of the guest. The superiority is temporary in the case of a visitor, but of indefinite duration when the recipient is a local person. Crucial political ties between allies, and between leaders and followers, are thus expressed in the joint participation in a feast.

In contrast, actual commensality, at close quarters, implies an approximate equality of rank. A feast can thus provide opportunity for the expression of a fairly complex set of relative differences and equalities. Feasting usually takes the following form: political unity, which cuts across caste boundaries, is asserted overall, but with an authority differentiation marking the host as leader and the guests as allies and dependants. The guests divide into three degrees — high-rank, commoner, and low-rank individuals; these group themselves in concentric circles, with the persons of high rank in the centre. Meals are generally served on trays each with a feeding capacity of four to eight. Several individuals of equal status seat themselves around one tray. Alternatively the three degrees of rank may be served with food in succession. Saints and Priests are sometimes isolated in one corner of the men's house and fed separately. Women never participate in such feasts; even in the home, the two sexes eat separately, particularly among the higher castes.

Conclusion

As has now been shown, the system of social stratification in Swat is a system of clearly delimited, named positions, into one or another of which all members of the community fall. The series of such positions is hierarchically ordered, and is differentiated with respect to functions and relative access to coveted goods. Each position is characterized by a cluster of statuses relevant in different sectors of life and frameworks of organization. Thus, for example, a *Pakhtun* is a *wealthy* man of the *Yusufzai descent group*, a *landowner* and a *political patron*, while a *Smith* is a man of *moderate* means, a putative *descendant of David*, *blacksmith* by profession, and a *political client*.

In other words, despite the highly complex system of differentiated statuses and division of labour within the society all members may be placed in one or another of a limited set of positions. This is possible because the incumbency of one status also necessarily implies incumbency of a series of other statuses forming the cluster characterizing that 'caste position'. By Nadel's definition, the system is highly *involute*, though this term was developed by him mainly to characterize homogeneous societies (Nadel, 1957: 67-72).

The principle of status summation seems to be the structural feature which most clearly characterizes caste as a system of social stratification. It is mainly for this reason that I have referred to the system of hierarchical positions in Swat as a caste system. I am aware that I thereby give the word a wider application than may suit many students of

Indian caste systems. However, if the concept of caste is to be useful in sociological analysis, its definition must be based on structural criteria, and not on particular features of the Hindu philosophical scheme. In this sociologically more fundamental sense, the concept of caste may be useful in the analysis of non-Indian societies.

In much of the Middle East, 'plural' societies are found, characterized by clear lines of internal segmentation, often based on ethnic criteria; such societies have a structure characterized by the summation of statuses in an involute system, in which a high degree of status differentiation is associated with a limited set of permitted status combinations. Such systems depend for their persistence on very clear criteria for status ascription. In societies other than those of extreme partriliny, this prerequisite implies a pattern of endogamy within the stratified groups — a feature often emphasized in the definition of caste. An analysis of such societies along the lines suggested here might make it possible to isolate other such prerequisites or correlates of caste.

The necessity for status summation in standardized clusters or positions, and the rigid differentiation of such positions in Swat, has been shown to be functionally related to the requirements of an elaborate system of division of labour in an essentially non-monetary economy (cf. p. 23). I would put forward the following general typology under which the features discussed here might be subsumed:

There are (1) truly homogeneous societies, in which internal differentiation is weak. Almost unlimited social substitution is possible within sex and/or age categories. Increasing status differentiation impairs this substitutability unless (2) clusters of statuses are defined. In that case the possibility of substitution remains, but only within a limited set of hierarchical categories ('castes') which are interdependent and together compose the community. Considerable complexity is possible in such a system without the development of any bureaucratic form of organization.

Finally there are (3) complex systems in which different statuses can be freely combined. Here the different capacities of the different statuses are clearly distinguished. This type of system is found associated with the use of a monetary medium which facilitates the division of labour.

Notes

1   The author did fieldwork in the Swat valley during nine months of 1954. Other aspects of the material have been discussed in Barth (1956) and Barth (1957).

2   The Malakand Agency was established by a British military expedition in 1895. The territories held by Dir were conquered by that state in the first years of this century. Swat state was founded in 1917 and recognized by British India in 1927. The changes in social organization wrought by the weak and unstable centralized governments of Dir and Swat have so far been limited, while the villages of Malakand agency have complete local autonomy.

3   No account is taken here of possible consequences of Pakistani plans to create elected bodies based on universal suffrage. Any such organization, if successful, would clearly prove fatal to the structure I have described.

3 Segmentary opposition and the Theory of Games: A study of Pathan organization

The present essay relates to the extensive discussion in the anthropological literature on the role of unilineal descent groups in politics, i.e. the theory of lineage systems (cf. Fortes, 1953). It is, however, concerned with the analysis of a divergent case: a political system in which ramifying patrilineal descent is of prominent importance in politics, yet where larger lineage groups do *not* emerge as corporate units.[1]

The case analysed is the acephalous political system of the Yusufzai Pathans of the North-west Frontier Province, Pakistan. To elucidate this case, it will be necessary to present considerable detail on their organization. This consists of field material, collected in the course of the year 1954. Further material has been, and will be, published elsewhere (Barth, 1956; Mss). In the analysis of this data, I shall utilize some of the elementary concepts and procedures of the Theory of Games (cf. Neumann and Morgenstern, 1947; Stone, 1948), as well as the relevant anthropological theory relating to descent groups and corporate groups.

The argument of the essay depends on a distinction between the purely structural arrangement of units defined by a unilineal descent charter, and the manner in which these units are made relevant in corporate action. In the description of lineage systems in the literature, this distinction is not often made. The analysis of the solidarity of unilineal descent groups usually relies on a Durkheimian conception of mechanical solidarity. In such a framework, solidarity derives from likeness. The descent charter defines a hierarchy of homologous groups, and thus directs the fusion of political interests within a merging series of such groups.

This *particular* expression of the descent group charter has been

* First published in *Journal of the Royal Anthropological Institute* 89, Pt. 1: 5-22.

incorporated into our whole conception of lineage organizations, as if it were a necessary derivative of the descent structure. The present case study describes a different political application of unilineal descent. Descent units are arranged in a recognizable manner by patrilineal genealogies, and hold joint rights to large territories. But close collaterals in the system do not join in corporate groups in opposition to more distant collaterals. The genealogical charter is none the less relevant to the structure of the corporate groups that do emerge; essentially, it defines rivals and allies in a system of two opposed political blocs. Closely related descent units are consistent rivals; each establishes a net of political alliances with the rivals of allies of their own rivals. In this fashion a pervasive factional split into two grand alliances of descent segments emerges, with close collateral segments consistently in opposite moieties.

Clearly, though this is a unilineal descent system of a kind, the analysis of the internal solidarity of the political units which emerge cannot be contained in a schema based on the concept of mechanical solidarity. Among the Yusufzai Pathans, the recruitment of corporate political units depends on the exercise of individual choices between alternative allegiances. Thus descent charters do not unequivocally define corporate units; these charters are made relevant to political action indirectly through their strategic implications for the choices of individuals. Therefore, the manner of recruitment of Pathan political groups cannot be understood directly in terms of the descent system; it requires some analysis of the bases of individual choices and the sources of the internal solidarity of the groups which do emerge. The 'Theory of Games' is designed precisely for the analysis of such strategic choices, and will be utilized in the latter part of this essay. The essay thus falls roughly into three parts: I, a descriptive and comparative account of Yusufzai Pathan unilineal descent groups and political organization; II, an attempted analysis of some of this data in some of the categories of the Theory of Games; and III, a concluding brief general discussion.

I

Lineage systems have been described in a number of societies in Africa and elsewhere. Their basic features are particularly apparent in acephalous systems, where their expression is not complicated by the existence of centralized political institutions based on other criteria. In these societies, unilineal descent through a line of ancestors defines a hierarchy of descent groups, the more remote the common ancestor, the wider the span of his group of descendants, and the larger the segment defined by his genealogical position. A political system based on this organization is described by Evans-Pritchard (in Fortes and Evans-Pritchard, 1940) as characterized by a situational balanced opposition of groups: 'although any group tends to split into opposed parts, these parts tend to fuse in relation to other groups' (p. 284). The political system thus becomes a 'system of fission and fusion, of relativity and opposition of segments' (p. 296).

According to Fortes, 'the guiding ideas in the analysis of African lineage organization have come mainly from Radcliffe-Brown's formulations[1] (in Fortes, 1953, p. 25) of the structural principles found in all kinship systems. Prominent among these are the appreciation of the structural implications of unilineal descent, and the principle of equivalence of siblings.

With a view to the particular orientation of this essay, the implications of unilineal descent may be expressed in terms of their significance for individual choices. For each 'ego' in society, unilineal descent resolves a problem of identification. Through his two parents, two different assemblages of kin have claims on his loyalty and support. Unilineal descent gives primacy, *for specified purposes* to one of these relations; it defines a bond which in these situations overrides other bonds. Thus, in a patrilineal society, sons are unambiguously identified with fathers in the culturally defined contexts in which descent is relevant.

A second principle is that of equivalence of siblings, which defines a bond ideally approaching a merging of the social personalities of siblings. We are here concerned with political organization, i.e. the groups and statuses concerned with the maintenance of order and the defence of rights to culturally valued goods in situations of conflict. The two principles of descent and equivalence of siblings combined together and given primacy for political purposes, produce a lineage system as we know it in the literature. In a patrilineal system, there is a fusion of the interests of fathers and sons, of the father with his brothers and of these brothers with their sons, and by the same token with grandfather, grandfather's brothers, and their descendants, etc. In such fashion, a charter of unilineal descent becomes a charter for the fusion of interests and progressive creation of larger corporate groups along a gradient of collateral distance.

This fusion of interests is situational; it implies an identification in situations of conflict with those more closely related by lineage bonds against those less related, or unrelated. Implicit in the framework of a lineage, then, are both identification and opposition, both fusion and fission. The opposition between near and distant collaterals, defined by their descent from two different ancestors on one level of segmentation, in one generation of the genealogy, is overridden in the case of outside threats by fusion in terms of the sibling bond which unites these two ancestors and defines a common interest for their descendants. The solidarity implicit in such a description of the political system is derived from the likeness of the groups concerned, and their egocentric conception of rights and wrongs. The implied solidarity of groups is thus a *mechanical* solidarity (Durkheim, 1947).

The Pathan kinship system forms no exception to Radcliffe-Brown's generalizations. The principles of descent and equivalence of siblings are clearly embodied in its structure. But the manner in which they are utilized in political contexts is only superficially reminiscent of African lineage organizations. Charters of unilineal descent define territorial units and administrative councils. But intertwined with this basic frame is a system of political alliances, through which individuals by their own choice align themselves in a political dual division. The groups which for most political purposes act together as corporate units are the regional branches of these two factions or blocs. Thus the corporate groups in the political system are formed by the strategic choices on the part of the participants, and do not emerge by virtue of a mechanical solidarity deriving from likeness. Such a political system may be analysed in terms of the bases on which the strategic choices are made. In the following account I shall attempt to show that the contexts in which patrilineal kinship is relevant are such as to emphasize the deep opposition of interests between collaterals, which is indeed implicit in any lineage organization. In the patrilineal descent system, the Pathan 'ego' is thus faced with a profound dilemma: the bonds between brothers and the bonds between fathers and sons are given political primacy; yet an organization based on these principles would unite 'ego' with his close agnatic collaterals, who for reasons elaborated below are his prime opponents. The political dual division develops as a direct result of the choices that individuals make in seeking a solution to this dilemma, and the political organization can thus be understood only in terms of the structure of the unilineal descent system. As the dilemma is to some extent implicit in all lineage systems, we may provisionally assume some generality for the problem, and for this pattern of its solution.

As a preparation for what follows, it is necessary to give some background to Pathan society, relating particularly to the Lower Swat Valley (Malakand Agency, North-west Frontier Province, Pakistan). In this area the acephalous system persists unmodified to this day. Yusufzai country consists in the main of fairly barren hill and mountain tracts, cut by a few fertile valleys, mainly those of the rivers Panjkora, Swat, and a section of the Indus. These valleys are very densely settled and intensively utilized, the population supporting itself by cereal agriculture, predominantly dependent on artificial irrigation, with double cropping and manuring. The entire valley bottom and a major part of the surrounding hills are under cultivation; thus there is no free land and practically no possibility of extending the cultivated area. Most cultivators are sharecroppers. Practically all land is owned by a dominant aristocracy of Pakhtuns, numbering, in different areas, from one half to one tenth of the population. These Pakhtuns trace patrilineal descent from ancestors who conquered the area in the sixteenth century. Title to land entails, in the manner of a feudal organization, jurisdiction over persons residing on this land. Except for certain persons of holy status, who may be disregarded in the present context, only the landowning Pakhtuns have independent political status; tenants, craftsmen, traders, and all other non-landowners are the political dependents, or clients, of the Pakhtun on whose land they reside. The 'persons' who occupy positions in the Pakhtun genealogical charter and who act as units in the political system thus vary greatly in the power they bring to it. One Pakhtun, with little land, represents himself only; another Pakhtun, who owns much land, represents perhaps a hundred male clients, and may figuratively be given a valency of one hundred in the political system. It should however be noted that the relation between Pakhtun and client is a reciprocal contract which may be broken at the will of either party. The relation is not one of adoption or bond serfdom, and changes in the political fortunes of a landowner are quickly reflected in the numbers of his clients. The essential asset of the Pakhtun is his title to land (which is scarce and, with irrigation and terracing, a highly capitalized resource), and only through his control of this resource can he attract the clients with which to inflate his political ego.

The landowning Yusufzai Pakhtuns claim patrilineal descent from the common apical ancestor, Yusuf. Indeed, through a genealogical charter of an additional six generations' depth, Yusuf is connected with the ancestors of other Pathan tribes to the first Pathan, Kais, who was converted to Islam and took the name Abdul Rashid.

The Yusufzai control a territory with a total population of more than a million inhabitants; but it is difficult to estimate the number of persons among these who trace lineal descent from Yusuf — they may count about one fifth of the total. The modern descendants of Yusuf are twelve to thirteen generations removed from the apical ancestor. The depth of genealogies varies mainly between different collateral lines, but also with respect to completeness as given by different informants. Pathan genealogies show a tendency to retain genealogical links which are superfluous from the point of view of the segmentation of groups, particularly among the closer ascendants. There is a distinct ideal of genealogies as historical traditions, apart from their value as charters for the internal segmentation of groups. Such genealogical information was however difficult to uncover; most informants admitted ignorance of the actual traditions, and would reconstruct outline genealogies on the expressedly post hoc argument of the names of the segments in the system. In any one level of segmentation, each descent group has only a limited number of subdivisions, usually two or three. Thus, fathers in the genealogies are generally represented as having two or three sons, though the recorded range is from one to five sons. Segmentation between groups of half-brothers is occasionally recognized, in which case the groups carry the names of their respective mothers.[2]

Rights as members of these descent groups are contingent on the additional criterion of ownership of land. The sons of a man who has 'eaten' or otherwise lost his title to the whole of his inherited land are no longer regarded as members of the group; and they are forced to establish bonds of clientage to a man who holds such title. This follows from the feudal principle on which the society is based. Descent group membership is thus connected with title to a share of the common landed estate of the group, both in the sense that only members can hold such title, and in the sense that membership lapses with loss of title. The descent group therefore of necessity becomes localized — all members have their permanent residence within the district appropriate to their group. The districts take their names from the descent groups holding title to them, and in similar fashion the whole population of the district, a majority of whom are clients of members and not themselves members, none the less refer to themselves by the name of the descent group. Unilineal descent groups, or lineage segments, form the cores of local territorial groups, or tribal segments, of larger membership, including both lineage members and their clients.

The number of levels of lineage segmentation varies, and their correspondence to territories is complicated by the pattern of land tenure, to be discussed shortly. An example might help somewhat to clarify the situation. The Nikbi lineage (*khel*) controls a side valley and a section of the west bank of the Swat river, a territory roughly fifteen by ten miles. Of a total population of perhaps 40,000, about 8,000 are Pakhtuns — lineal descendants of Nikbi, and owners of land, while the remainder are political clients — non-landowners who are tenants, craftsmen, and traders by occupation. A simplified genealogical framework of the Nikbi lineage is as follows:

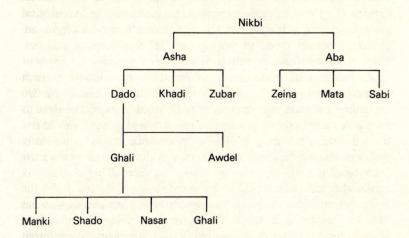

At the time of my field work, the descent segments Manki and Shado co-resided in two small villages of eight hundred inhabitants each, of whom about two hundred in each village were lineage members. The villagers all depended, directly or indirectly, on the landed estate of the Manki-Shado lineage core for their sustenance. The neighbouring villages are owned by the Ghali/Nasar and Awdel lineage segments, partly co-residing in two villages of more than 2,000 inhabitants, as well as occupying several smaller villages. The territories of the Khadi and Zubar segments lie along the river to the south, while the Aba *khel* major lineage segment occupies the main section of the tributary valley. Within each village, the local lineage segment is divided into separate households.

With the possible exception of the peculiar emphasis on title to land, and the consequent pattern of shedding of members, this formal description of the unilineal structure, its genealogical framework and territorial correlates, should fall within the limits of what is usually described in lineage systems. In other words, in its abstract structural arrangement of units, and their expression in terms of residence, the descent system of the Yusufzai Pathans belongs to the general class of lineage systems.

There is, however, wide variation between societies in terms of the contexts in which this structure it utilized, that is, in the fields of relevance of descent group membership. In this respect, the present case may represent one extreme. Thus, descent groups among Yusufzai Pathans (1) Do *not* regulate marriage through rules of exogamy of preferential choice. Islamic incest laws as to the forbidden degrees are observed; beyond them, all women are eligible as marriage partners. There is no significant statistical or ideological emphasis on any particular category of relative as a preferential spouse, though there is a strong ideology of endogamy vis-à-vis non-Pakhtun clients. (2) Do *not* define common jural responsibility in blood revenge. The right to revenge is passed on as a privilege to the person or persons who inherit from the deceased; thus, by Pathan inheritance practice, to closest male agnates and only to them. Revenge is directed against the murderer himself, or in the case of murder by hired thugs, against the person who initiated and paid for the murder.

The main relevance of agnatic descent group membership among Yusufzai Pathans is in the field of government. Members of agnatic descent groups of every recognized level of segmentation meet in councils for the purpose of governing the tribal segment of which they form the core — i.e. for the administration of their joint estate. Thus, in the example of p. 61, there may be council meetings of all of Nikbi *khel*, of the Asha *khel* major segment, of Dado *khel*, or of the members of Manki/Shado *khels* co-residing in a village. In every case, all adult males of the lineage with an individual title to land — i.e. all heads of Pakhtun households — have a right to speak in the council meeting. Such councils have formal rules of procedure, and usually a permanent employee, without vote, who serves as messenger to notify members of scheduled meetings, and who is paid a yearly rate from the fines which the council collects. This council is highly egalitarian; it does not, in fact, recognize any formal differences of rank between its members. To remove all mechanisms for the expression of precedence, the council members must sit in a circle on flat ground, away from the home of any particular member. All members have equal rights to speak, and no one may interrupt anyone else in the sense of ordering him to be quiet; although several members may speak at once. Decisions must be unanimous, in the sense that there should be no articulate objection raised to the final conclusion – there is, in fact, usually considerable mumbling by a fraction of the members. Some issues may be settled by open debate, but most settlements are arranged by 'lobbying' behind a haystack or out of earshot while the council is in session.

These councils thus look in every way like lineage councils. By their formal rules they contain the members of agnatic lineages, who meet as equals to solve the political problems of their territory, to settle conflicts between members and agree on action vis-à-vis the outside world. A hierarchy of councils is defined, corresponding in terms of their membership to a merging series of agnatic descent groups. But when members align against each other in debates, or any other form of opposition, they do *not* act in terms of such a merging series. In a meeting of a council of a wide area, there is not the fusion of interests of smaller, related segments of a minor council vis-à-vis larger segments which one would expect in a lineage system, and which is exemplified in the above citations from Evans-Pritchard (Fortes and Evans-Pritchard, 1940, p. 4). On the contrary, the opposition between small, closely related segments persists in the wider context, and these segments unite with similar small segments in a pattern of two-party opposition, not in a merging series of descent segments.

The opposition between collaterals is a structural feature of any segmentary lineage system; but where one finds a merging series of segments acting as political corporate groups, this opposition is temporarily cancelled by a fusion of interests vis-à-vis larger groups. Within the same formal architecture of a segmentary unilineal descent system, such fusion does not take place among Yusufzai Pathans. Whether or not such fusion takes place, i.e. whether the common interests of related segments, in their relations to larger units, are stronger or weaker than the opposition which divides them, would seem to be an empirical question, and depends on a great number of cultural variables. From first principles one cannot determine which interest will be the stronger. In the Pathan context, the lack of fusion is understandable in terms of the particular types of issues in which the descent is relevant, i.e. the types of issues with which the councils are mainly concerned. For the purpose of demonstrating this further empirical material must be added. But the general validity of the argument does not depend on the presence or absence of the particular cultural features which I shall describe, but on a recognition that cultural factors are effective in weighing the opposed interests in fusion or continued opposition of close collaterals.

The following section is thus ethnographically specific. The point I wish to make is that nearly all questions of administration relate to land in the Pathan system, and that the Pathan system of land tenure defines prominent lines of cleavage between agnatic collaterals. The tribal councils deal with matters which are basically of two types: the settlement of conflicts, and the co-ordination of joint or public action. Such joint public action relates to the maintenance of public roads and rights of way, and the maintenance of the joint irrigation system. Both relate prominently to land and land rights. The same is true of conflicts between individuals. Land is the *sine qua non* of Pakhtuns. From title to land springs all political power — wealth, the control of clients, and a voice in the councils. Except for questions concerning the honour of women, and revenge, all conflicts among Pathans boil down to conflicts over land.

Finally, the pattern of land tenure is itself regulated by the councils of the agnatic descent units. Yusufzai Pakhtuns hold land as individual property, but they do not own particular fields, and their tenure is subjected to a system of periodic re-allotment, known as the *wesh* (division) system, related in conception to the *musha'a* system of the Near East (cf. Patai, 1949, p. 436). This system may best be explained by the analogy of industrial shares, where a shareholder owns a specified fraction of the industrial estate by virtue of holding a certain number of shares; he does not, however, own any particular part of the factory concerned. Similarly the common estate of a descent unit is divided into an absolute number of equal shares. A Pakhtun through inheritance receives a specified fraction of the tribal estate in the form of a specified number of such shares, but no particular plot. He is allotted fields of irrigated and dry land, sand and clay, and marsh in standard proportions, corresponding to the size of his share. But as no two pieces of land are equal, the equivalence in value of each share is assured only through making this allotment temporary, and periodically redistributing the estate between the shareholders. Every fourth, fifth, or tenth year each man is allotted new fields, so through a long cycle the holders of each share exercise rights over all fields an equal length of time (cf. Baden-Powell, 1896, pp. 244 seq.).

This pattern of land tenure has been changing in the Yusufzai area during the last generation. Most of the main valley of Swat has increasingly come under the control of a recently established princely state. In this state, the ruler enforced permanent allotment twenty to thirty years ago (in a traditional ten-year cycle), with the exception of river-bank land, where continued reallotment reduces the individual hazards of erosion and undercutting by shifting river courses. In acephalous tribal area in the lower valley extensive fields are still reallotted for four-year periods. The trend towards permanent settlement is too recent and still too far from complete to invalidate the present argument.

The procedure for redistribution follows the segmentary charter of the tribal genealogy within tribal units of between 10,000 and 40,000 inhabitants. The example illustrating the genealogical framework of such a group, on p. 61 above, may also serve as an illustration of the redistribution system. Of the inhabitants of Nikbi *khel* territory, only roughly 8,000 are Pakhtuns, corresponding to a total of some 1,000 independent land-owners, all of whom are the adult male descendants of Nikbi. This group is divided into two primary segments. Similarly, the lineage territory is traditionally divided into two roughly equivalent areas, one including most of the tributary valley, the other stretching along the bank of the Swat river. Until permanent settlement was enforced twenty-eight years ago, these two segments alternated in their occupation of the two areas, each spending ten years in the side valley, and then moving some ten to fifteen miles to spend the next ten years on the river-bank. Furthermore, each of these areas is subdivided into three traditional sub-areas, corresponding to the three secondary segments of each primary segment. The council of each primary segment meets and allots one sub-area to each of its component three sub-segments, ideally in a system of rotation.

As these reallotments take place every ten years, the borders of each sub-area of the joint estate are well known to all, their equivalence in value has been established, and no great opposition of interests arises between the major descent segments in the reallotment system. The real problems arise on the lower levels of reallotment, where individuals have their eyes on particular fields, and especially where deaths and transfers change the distribution of shares from one time of allotment to the next. To pursue the present example, Dada *khel*, comprising about a hundred council members, is divided into two segments. Tensions and conflicts do arise during the division of their joint estate, since the fields granted to one segment are in fact within practical reach of members of the other segment; they are in the order of one or two miles away, and could be worked or controlled by them. But the most intense conflicts develop in the last stage of allotment, when the roughly fifty men of Ghali *khel* are competing for the actual, individual fields. There is no traditional subdivision of the village lands into the particular configuration of shares represented at that particular time; the men must meet in a council of their small segment and devise a pattern of allotment through negotiation and compromise, or force. This is a type of issue uniquely suited to generate intense factionalism between collaterals; there is an overriding opposition of interests between such groups competing for the slightly better fields. Thus at every periodic reallotment, the opposition of close agnatic collaterals is dramatized and made acute, while the opposition between segments of higher levels is routinized and involves no particular conflicts.

This opposition stops short of alienating brothers. Their landed property is not divided till after the death of the father, since he retains some measure of control of it through his life; and, even after his death, political pressure is such that few persons have the courage to split away from this minimal nucleus of agnatic kinsmen and face the hostile world completely alone.

Other factors combine to make the relation between close collaterals one of peculiar rivalry. Conflicts over inheritance inevitably involve agnates, in a modified Islamic system of exclusive patrilineal male inheritance of land. Conflicts over the borders of fields involve them, since after every new reallotment they still find themselves owning adjoining fields. Conflicts over water for irrigation, particularly intense in the last critical month before the rice harvest, involve them, since with adjoining fields they share the same irrigation channels.[3]

Such particular cultural factors combine to place close agnatic collaterals in a perpetual relation of opposition and rivalry. This negative charge on their structural relationship is clearly recognized in Yusufzai Pathan kinship terminology. Pathans distinguish between father, mother, father's brother, and mother's brother, but classify father's sister and mother's sister together. The terms for the two kinds of uncle and for aunt are extended to first and second cousins of the parents as well. Sibling terms are extended to the children of all these persons, *except* to the children of father's brother, own or classificatory (*tre*), for whom there is a special term (*tarbur*). A differentiation of kinds of 'siblings' may of course be expressed, but only by constructions such as 'aunt's son' (*da tror zoe*) or 'mother's brother's daughter' (*da mama lur*). Patrilateral parallel cousin is uniquely separated from all other cousins and siblings by a separate term. Furthermore, this term carries the subsidiary connotation of 'enemy' (cf. Morgenstierne, 1927). Thus, where friendly relations do exist, the proper term for such cousins is not used, and they are referred to as siblings by courtesy. Only those collaterals with whom one has unfriendly relations are freely referred to as *tarburan*, father's brother's sons.

This persisting opposition between collateral agnates prevents their interests from fusing even vis-à-vis outsiders. A Pakhtun's political activities are directed at gaining an advantage over his agnatic rivals, as only through their defeat can he achieve his own aggrandizement. He is not limited, as in many lineage systems, to them as his potential supporters – his clients constitute the main body of his supporters. Any loss by his collaterals means a gain for him – he wrests control of the councils from them, he encroaches on their fields, and he inherits their shares in land if they are exterminated. His political strength vis-à-vis his paternal cousins he assures by political alliances, and in the pattern of these alliances the architecture of the unilineal descent system can be recognized, as if by its very negation. Alliances are sought with small, distant collateral groups against one's close collaterals, while the latter reciprocate by allying themselves with the rivals of one's allies. Such alliances involve mutual support against the respective rivals of the partners, both in the debates of the councils, and in the case of warfare.

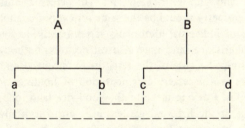

As will be seen in the figure, this means in structural terms an alliance between segments of the descent system which *cannot individually come into opposition with one another*. In other words, the alliance takes the schema of merging series of segments into account, but does so in terms of a strategic choice of allies, and by negating such merging in terms of any fusion of interests. 'a' are the rivals of 'b', and 'c' are the rivals of 'd'. 'a' and 'b' are segments of 'A', likewise 'c' and 'd' are segments of 'B'. 'a' can form an alliance, alternatively with 'c' or 'd', since there can be no occasion when they can meet either sub-segment in a simple opposition. Assume that an alliance 'a'-'d' forms. They can only meet in councils, or in any other type of situation, on a higher level where 'A' and 'B' are structurally opposed — but in this situation, 'a' and 'd' contract to combine against their respective relatives 'b' and 'c', whereby they both, if they are successful, will gain victories over their rivals.

Such alliances, if widely and consistently extended, produce a political dual division into two blocs. The Pathan blocs or alliances (*dəla*) have this pattern. Small descent segments of fathers and sons, or brothers, align under recognized leaders in a two-faction split which extends throughout the Yusufzai and bordering areas. I am suggesting that the Pathan pattern represents an alternative way of utilizing the segmentary structure defined by ramifying unilineal genealogies to build a political organization, and that the organization in this case will tend toward a consistent dual division, since the opposition between rivals leads to a dichotomization of their associates into supporters and opponents.

At this point, I should present some description of the resultant Pathan organization, before pursuing the argument further, first with regard to the political structure of the local groups in Pathan society. The group of agnatically related landowners is allotted mainly four types of property: houses in the nucleated village, irrigated garden land, irrigated rice land, and unirrigated land. The percentage distribution of each kind of property should be the same for every shareholder; but the absolute size of individual allotments varies greatly, as shares descend lineally in inheritance, and may also on occasion be bought and sold within the group. Because of the territorial concentration of each type of land, there is a necessary fragmentation of holdings, in that every share is composed of one piece of the good rice land, one piece of the bog, a corner of the irrigated garden, etc., etc. Inevitably, this inter-mixing of holdings gives scope for continual petty conflicts between adjoining opposed landowners.

With respect to residence, however, opponents separate. The village is a closely packed cluster of houses. But every village is divided in at least two wards, and political opponents occupy different wards.

Wards are in a sense miniature villages, occupied by landowners of *one* political party, and their clients. The wards, not the whole villages, are the operative political and economic units in the following contexts: there is a complex pattern of division of labour among hereditary specialists of the non-Pakhtun landless category. Such specialists perform traditional services for the sharecroppers and labourers working on the land of the pakhtuns, for which each specialist in return receives a traditional fraction of the crop. This pattern, analogous to the Hindu *jajmani* system, organizes the main occupational relations between persons, and unites them for corporate productive efforts. The units of such corporate economic action are the *wards* of a village. Correlated with the intimate economic ties within the ward is a pattern of political centralization. There is a headman or chief in every ward. The main duties pertaining to the office are to administer the communal institutions of the ward (men's house, mosque, wells), to settle disputes between members of the ward, and to co-ordinate its members in protecting their interests vis-à-vis other wards.

A full description of the role of the chief falls outside the main line of the present argument; but the existence of this office becomes important in a later connection. I should emphasize that the office is usually coveted by many pretenders. It offers great personal and strategic advantages to the incumbent. On the other hand, the incumbent can only maintain his position by constant expenditure of valuables; he must continually 'buy' the support of followers. To satisfy his men, a chief needs to control extensive rice-lands; thus, the office is invariably held by persons of inherited or achieved wealth in land.

Thus, the economic pattern of division of labour, and the presence of some essential community institutions, prevent political fission from proceeding below the level of the ward. Splits between co-residents of one ward must be solved either by a splitting of the ward into two autonomous and complete wards, or by one party moving to another ward. Of the latter I collected a series of cases; not so of the former. This might be expected, since a splitting of the ward can be achieved only if the rebels are stronger than the established chief of the united ward, in which case one would rather expect that their chief would attempt to usurp the position of the former chief as leader of the whole, undivided ward.

Wards, as geographical subdivisions of a village, are then in practice very stable units; they are conceived of as permanent fixtures by the villagers. But the composition of a ward is changeable, on account of political defections, and the system of periodic reallotment, particularly where, as in most parts, this has involved migrations of landowners. The co-residents of a ward form an alliance and pledge allegiance to the chief only till the time of the next reallotment. At that time, the landowners of a ward may move *en bloc* to occupy a common ward in their new territory; or else new alliances may form between landowners over the always fresh problems of allotment. The group of landowners who associate in a ward is thus unstable, but represents the alignment of allies that obtains in a village at any one time. Thus where a descent group containing two major segments occupies a village of two wards, there is a probability that each of the major segments will be split between two parties, and that members of both segments are found in both wards. The wards correspond to the local branches of the political blocs, while the villages of which they form parts correspond to complete descent units.

A wider, but essentially similar framework of organization is built by alliances, in two blocs, of wards of different villages, or within villages, where they contain more than two wards. Most villages contain wards belonging to both blocs, and the bloc which dominates one village or district (*bande*, 'the uppers' or 'those above') may be the weaker bloc (*lande*, 'lowers', or 'those below') for the time being in the neighbouring area. Influential men may be regarded as the leaders of blocs over wider territories, and there is considerable jostling for recognition of prominence within the bloc. Such important men mobilize large segments of their bloc in defence of their private interests.

The blocs function in protecting the interests of their members, by exerting underhand pressure, by working together in the councils, and as armies in the case of fighting. The flaring-up of actual fighting is now quite local and limited in the Swat valley, but continues on a considerable scale in neighbouring Dir and Bajaur, where a couple of thousand men may be mobilized at times. Units of comparable size are mobilized in the context of council debates in the Swat valley. While large groups of men within one bloc unite for corporate political action, whole lineages or segments seem totally unable to unite. The several attempts by the Nawab of Dir to conquer major sections of the Swat valley were invariably resisted only by the bloc in power, while their local opponents either joined the invading forces or remained neutral. United defence of the tribal estate, such as met British military efforts in the area was only achieved through the institution of holy war under the leadership of religious devotees.

The respective fields of relevance of descent groups and party groups should be summarized. Essentially, descent groups are units vested with a joint estate, while alliance blocs are units for the exercise of power in an acephalous political system. Territories and sub-territories in the administrative system are thus defined by descent units; it is the fact of shared rights to land which necessitates an administrative machinery in the form of a hierarchy of descent group councils. But whole council units never fuse for corporate action; their constituent two blocs of allies remain separate, and individually constitute the largest units which fuse politically and internally co-ordinate the actions of members. 'Agreement' in a council meeting implies the promise of passive compliance and neutrality of one bloc to the actions of the other, and not active co-operation. Apart from changes in allegiance, the alignment into blocs of allies and opponents is permanent and not situational. This is the main organizational difference from the lineage systems described in the literature, where one's opponents in one situation fuse politically with one's own group to become allies in another situation, when the dispute involves units of a higher level of segmentation. In the Pathan system of organization, members of different blocs remain opposed no matter what the situation may be. The territorial unit involved in a dispute (corresponding to a descent group council at a certain level of lineage segmentation) determines how large a part of the blocs will be mobilized, but does not affect the alignment in opposition. As a crude parallel, the opposed parties of individual counties in England persist in wider political contexts: a Labour representative from Middlesex joins the Labour members from London, and remains opposed to the Conservatives from Middlesex, even in the wider context of parliament.

The local branches of the two blocs thus emerge as corporate groups in opposition at meetings of lineage councils at every level. Through debate, threats, compromise, and occasional use of force on the part of these two blocs, the council may formally reach a decision (though often the meetings break up without any decision being reached). The implementation of this decision still depends on the action of private individuals. What may be achieved by the plaintiff in the dispute is an arrangement whereby he has the support of his own bloc in self-help, within the specified limits, while he is assured of his opponent's inability to mobilize *his* bloc in resistance. The relative strength of the opposed blocs, and the importance of the contestants to their respective allies, are more important in settling conflicts than are abstract principles of justice.

Balance between the blocs is maintained, according to the Pathan conception of the system, by the essential cupidity of politicians. The stronger bloc in an area will tend to grow in numbers and land by making good their advantage over the weaker bloc. Inevitably, however, rivalry will develop between the leaders of this growing alliance, until one such leader sees his chance to capture supreme control of the territory by seceding with his followers and joining the weaker bloc, which thereby becomes the stronger. The life histories of some prominent leaders may show one or two such changes of allegiance. But if such are the dominant attitudes, the relative stability of alliances, and the continued relatively peaceful coexistence of the two parties in most villages seems puzzling. One would rather have expected a chaos of constant realignments and a disintegration of the bloc organization. The Pathan conception of political activities as an expression of self interested opportunism on the part of their leaders appears to be contradicted by the evidence.

However, this apparent contradiction must be examined more closely. The political two-bloc system has provisionally been described as if it was derived from a system of strategic choices of allies by the individual landowners among Pathans, and as if these choices were made largely with reference to factors implicit in a relatively small number of structural features of Pathan organization. Before complicating the analysis further by the introduction of additional explanatory devices, the possibilities inherent in what has already been presented should first be exhausted. This poses, in a sense, an experiment in inductive logic: which factors are logically necessary and sufficient to produce a system like that observed in Pathan political organization?

II

For the purpose of disciplining the logical manipulations involved in this kind of argument, the 'Theory of Games' (Neumann and Morgenstern, 1947) is eminently suitable. On the basis of a limited set of assumptions the authors design concepts and procedures for the analysis of games involving strategic choices on the part of the participants. The authors state that this type of analysis is relevant to the problems of the social sciences in general; yet outside of economics it has proved difficult to apply their methods and concepts. In the following section,

I shall attempt to apply some elementary procedures borrowed from this vastly more complex and sophisticated theory. I shall endeavour to keep the somewhat frightening symbolic logic of the theory at a minimum.

In the logical framework of the Theory of Games one may regard the political manipulations of Pathans as a variety of game. This game is subject to certain rules, which embody the factors affecting the choices made by participants in the game. The crucial step in a transformation from real life to a Theory of Games model is the formulation of these rules. To be meaningful, they should express the strategic implications of those factors which one hypothecizes to be crucial in the system. In the present case, they should summarize the main points in the preceding description.

In the following I shall attempt to describe a 'game' which may serve as a model for the analysis of the Yusufzai Pathan political organization. Its rules I propose to derive from the main features of the above description. These features, I propose to show, define both the necessary and sufficient conditions for the emergence of a two-bloc system like that observed among Yusufzai Pathans. Stated briefly, they are: (1) The presence of a *persisting opposition* of interests between wards occupied by collaterals in the agnatic descent system — i.e. there is a persisting direct opposition between some units of the system. (2) The recognition by Yusufzai Pathans of relations of a patron-client type (so that no person is limited to agnatic relatives as potential supporters) and of relations of *contractual political alliance* between two or several equals, i.e. there is unrestricted freedom for the units of the system to form coalitions on the basis of strategic choices. (3) The recognition and positive value given to the status of chief of a ward and local leader of a party alliance, i.e. there is a set of indivisible 'bonuses', the distribution of which is the subject of understandings between persons.

These features correspond to Neumann's definition of a zero-sum majority game. In a zero-sum (or constant-sum) game, persons are opposed to each other, in time experience a series of victories and/or defeats, and in each case, the victory or gain of the one means a corresponding defeat or loss to his opponents. This corresponds to condition or features (1) above: there is a persisting and simple opposition of interests between opponents in Pathan politics, by virtue of their competition for control of the one basic good — land. As emphasized in the descriptive section, all tillable land is in fact under cultivation, and all other aspects of power and prestige are derived from or depend upon land. In this land tenure and administrative system, any loss to one's opponents is by necessity a gain to oneself.

Secondly, our model will be the *majority* game. In cases of opposition, the stronger party, corresponding to a 'majority' of players, gains the victory, i.e. we represent this as a simple majority game where no further restrictions or 'rules' are presumed. This expresses feature (2) above: the freedom to form majorities through strategic alliances, and the facts of an acephalous political system, where the final sanction is majority in terms of power.

Our model for this discussion is thus the zero-sum majority game, provisionally for three persons (Neumann and Morgenstern, 1947, p. 222 seq.). By its rules, each player may choose one partner. Two players who choose one another form a couple, or coalition, and are able by their simple majority to extract a value from the third player. Players 1, 2, 3 are each given a positive value a, b, c respectively, which they lose if they become outnumbered by opponents. This gives the following possibilities:

coalition 1, 2 forms: 1, 2 get c, 3 gets -c;
coalition 1, 3 forms: 1, 3 get b, 2 gets -b;
coalition 2, 3 forms: 2, 3 get a, 1 gets -a;

or no mutual choices are made, and no player gains or loses. Clearly in this game, by virtue of the rules governing it, coalitions will form for the mutual protection of the values of the coalition forming players and the extraction of a value from the minority. In other words, the emergence of coalitions in Pathan political life seems implicit in the factors as stated.

Consider next the case of a five-person majority game (Neumann and Morgenstern, 1947, pp. 332 seq.), where each player 1, 2, 3, 4, 5 for simplicity is vested with an equal value 1, which he will lose if he finds himself in minority. Each player may choose any number of allies.

One feature immediately becomes apparent: the simple nature of the opposition encourages the formation of a two-party, not a multi-party, system. In a situation where no coalitions form, no player gains any advantage. If one coalition forms, say of 2, 3, the interests of the other persons can only be defended by an opposing coalition. Thus a coalition 4, 5 can defend its members against losses. But in this situation, the third force 1 is in a desperate situation. Both coalitions can gain a victory over him, i.e. rob him with impunity, and since no further rules are presumed, this is inevitable. His advantage from holding the balance of power he can only exercise by joining a coalition. He is thus forced by the strategic implications of the rule of this game to join one or the other coalition: he is forced into the framework of a two-bloc system.

This five-person equal-value example illustrates the argument in its simplest form, but the conclusion may be seen to follow irrespective of the number of players, and also in cases where the players are vested with unequal values a, b, c . . . n respectively. The necessary conditions for the reduction of the number of coalitions to two relate to features (1) and (2) above, not to the particular numbers and values in the example. The theoretical possibility of a stalemate (i.e. an exact balance in numbers between three or more coalitions) is not considered, as it is assumed that participants are interested in completing the game, i.e. in obtaining a value.

The basic dual division in Pathan political organization would thus seem to be derived directly from the strategic implications of persisting opposition between defined groups with unrestricted possibilities for alliance-forming between these groups, i.e. an institution of contractual political alliance. The system of two blocs does not depend on a recognition of the nature or function of duality, but emerges through the separate self-interested decisions of the persons on the system.

One further consideration has a direct bearing on the relation between the two blocs in the Pathan system. In the gradual crystallization of coalitions in the above five-person game, there is a definite point at which passage from defeat to victory occurs, and thereafter a progressive reduction of the fruits of victory. Consider the situation *from the point of view of* 1:

1 stands against 2, 3, 4, 5:	1 gets	-1 value;
1, 2, stand against 3, 4, 5:	1 gets	-1 value;
1, 2, 3 stand against 4, 5:	1 gets	$\frac{1+1}{3}$ value;
1, 2, 3, 4 stand against 5:	1 gets	¼ value;
1, 2, 3, 4, 5 form coalition:	1 gets	0 value.

Every coalition of two persons will be defeated, while any overwhelming majority coalition, of four persons against one, wins a victory of limited value. This brings out one of the strategic rules of the two-bloc opposition. In terms of the simple self-interest of the persons in the winning coalition, absconders from the losing coalition will not be

welcomed, i.e. on the basis of this model one would expect the dominant bloc in Pathan politics to be hesitant about accepting absconders
and to remain moderately evenly matched in numbers with the weaker
bloc, as is indeed the case.

One final feature remains to be accounted for by the Theory of
Games model: the relatively peaceful coexistence of the blocs in one
locality, the empirical unwillingness of the stronger bloc to make the
most of its advantage and literally run the opposition out of the village.
This might of course be readily explained in terms of the numerous
bonds, e.g. of marriage and familiarity, which cross the line of opposition; yet such bonds seem surprisingly unimportant in situations
when opposition does express itself in open conflicts. All Pathans have
some matrilateral kin or affines in the opposing bloc, but in periods
of tension they are not visited, and relations with some may be permanently severed. When a man and his sister's husband or mother's
brother emerge as immediate rivals they freely oppose one another,
and attempt to ruin and even kill one another. Such bonds thus seem
insufficient as an effective check on the intensity of factionalism.
However, at least a partial answer may be found within the framework already elaborated. Perhaps not surprisingly, factor (3) above,
the presence of chiefs of wards and parties, has some relevance to this.

This introduces the problem of unequal distribution into the present
model. Imagine in the five-person game above, that the coalition 2, 4
forms, represented by 2 as chief, who thus represents the value of his
total following, b. Similarly 3, 5 forms, represented by the chief 3 of
value c. Strategically, the game is then reduced to a three-person game
of players 1, 2, 3 where 1 is the weakest person and must join either
2 or 3 in a coalition. The coalition which 1 joins will win. But 2 and 3
are 'chiefs', a position of value in terms of which they claim a special
bonus, of honour and deference, if not of the spoils, over and above
the share due to them in the coalition. This bonus is represented by
ϵ, the value attached to chieftainship. Player 1 joins whichever coalition offers him the greater advantage. If coalition 1, 2, 4 forms, 1, 2,
4 get c, 3, 5 get -c. But 2 claims his bonus ϵ, so

1 gets $\frac{c}{3} - \epsilon$ (since there are three members of the coalition and
                  1 is merely a follower)

2 gets $\frac{c}{3} + 2\epsilon$ (since he has two followers: 1 and 4, in his coalition)

3 gets -c + ϵ (since he loses, but remains chief of the opposi-
                  tion).

If coalition 1, 3, 5 forms, on the other hand:

1 gets $\frac{b}{3}$ $-\epsilon$, 2 gets $-b + \epsilon$, 3 gets $\frac{b}{3} + 2\epsilon$.

If b = c, it is indeterminate which coalition 1 joins. If on the other hand b $\neq$ c, 1 will join the *weaker* party, so that the accruing advantage to the coalition will be greatest (assuming, as we have, that it does indeed represent a majority).

Imagine that coalition 1, 2 forms. As long as b < c, i.e. as long as the fruits of a victory over 3 are greater than those of a victory over 2, 3 can entice 1 to abscond from this coalition, and join in a coalition 1, 3, only by offering him the bonus ϵ, i.e. by offering him the position as chief in the coalition. This is acceptable to 1 if his gain as a chief of the other coalition is greater than his share as a follower in his present coalition, i.e. if

$$\frac{c}{3} \cdot \epsilon < \frac{b}{3} + 2\epsilon, \qquad \text{or } 9\epsilon > c - b.$$

But 3 will offer this only if it is also to *his* advantage, i.e. if what he gets as a follower in a winning coalition is greater than what he gets as the chief of a losing coalition:

$$\frac{b}{3} \cdot \epsilon > -c + \epsilon$$
$$c > 2\epsilon - \frac{b}{3} \qquad \text{or, in the limiting case of b = c, if } c > \frac{3}{2}\epsilon.$$

In other words, 3 will offer this enticement only if his loss, - c, while remaining defeated is greater than $\frac{3}{2}$ of the value he attaches to chieftainship.

This difference defines limits of strategic importance for 2 if he wishes to retain his position as leader of the winning coalition, and thus brings out implicit restrictions on the intensity of opposition, of great interest in relation to the Pathan material. It indicates that as long as the amount which the leader of the dominant bloc extracts from his opponent does not considerably exceed the value which his opponent attaches to chieftainship, there will be no fission within the dominant bloc. For the sake of holding the bloc together, and maintaining his position, the leader of the dominant bloc is thus interested in limiting the intensity of opposition between the blocs so that it will not exceed a critical level. If he extracts too much from his weaker rival, one of his own lieutenants, who by virtue of his private following holds the balance of power, will be enticed to abscond to become the leader of the other faction. That faction thus becomes the stronger bloc, and the leader of the formerly stronger bloc will suffer a loss.

For the sake of the semi-mathematical treatment pursued, it has been necessary to leave the units such as b, c and ϵ unanalysed. In an attempt at transferring the conclusions from the Games Theory back to real life, it is necessary to clarify just what these symbols stand for in the empirical situation. The values b, c represent real gains or loot, i.e. the value of the actual amount of fines or disputed lands extracted from the opponent. In the descriptive section, I have indicated how disputes are discussed in the context of lineage councils, and how the stronger bloc utilizes its position of dominance to arrive at settlements favourable to its members. The numerical value of b, c is thus at any time a mixed function of the total value of the property of the weaker bloc, and of policy decisions by the strong bloc as to how much pressure should be applied towards the exploitation of the opponent. In the majority game model, these values are assumed to be identical or at least proportional to the weight given the players in establishing majorities, i.e. to their power, while in actual life the relation between these two variables is more complex. However, as the blocs as wholes remain fairly equally balanced through time, this discrepancy does not seriously affect the present argument.[4]

The empirical referent of the unit ϵ, the 'bonus' granted the chief, is more problematical. It does not merely represent an extra share in the loot. Some chiefs do regularly claim such an extra share, and, what is more important, all naturally direct their bloc's politics with an eye to their own material gain; on the other hand, chiefs will sometimes claim *less* than a normal share of the gains, or none at all. To be of any meaning as an expression of the value attached to chieftainship, ϵ must thus stand not merely for an inequality in the distribution of loot, but also for a less tangible inequality; for a value in terms of status differentiation. This merely implies the argument that persons will at times renounce material gains in favour of intangible gains of 'status' and 'esteem'.

Strictly speaking, ϵ is thus incommensurate with b and c, as it does not stand for a simple measure of tangible property. Yet chiefs are daily forced to reconcile such incommensurables in making decisions. Pathan leaders are by inheritance and accretion the wealthy men of their respective groups, i.e. they are vested with an initial high value in the 'game'. They constantly expend their profits through feasts and gifts in the men's houses which they control, in a pattern analogous to the potlatch in its status implications. The status as chief is thus continually being bought by expenditure of material values. The intangible value renounced by being a follower and gained by being a chief thus has, in some contexts, a tangible material value. The situation in which ε is associated with the units b and c above may legitimately be regarded as precisely one such context. Furthermore, over a longer period of time, a chief certainly expects to derive material advantage from his status.

The whole discussion of the political organization in terms of the 'strategic implications' of various structural features of the situation raises one further problem: to what extent do the actors themselves realize these implications; to what extent do they determine the choice of strategy? Implications of this type, no matter how logically significant one may demonstrate them to be, are ineffective unless realized in some form by the actors in the system.

This is a simple question of ethnographic fact, and the answer depends on observations of the types of arguments used in arriving at decisions, and the types of circumstances described in native accounts of past political events. In this particular case, the inadvisability of standing alone, outside both party alliances, is rather obvious and clearly expressed by Pathans. The question concerns mainly the degree of realization of two further strategic principles: (1) the advantage of joining the *weaker* bloc, so victory is won with a narrow margin but the value of the victory maximized and (2) the importance from the chief's point of view of restricting the intensity of opposition between blocs.

Both these principles are in fact clearly realized and expressed. Between 1917 and 1927, a major part of the Swat valley fell under the control of a prominent leader of holy descent, Miangul Gulshahzada Abdul Wadud, who founded the state of Swat. His policy is explicitly described by the politically sophisticated as one of joining the weaker bloc, thereby gaining victories over the richest chiefs, and also, by 'tipping the scales', gaining a disproportionate influence in the bloc. His great success is attributed in part to his unique freedom to effect such changes of alliance. Having eliminated the small number of agnatic collaterals in his holy descent line, he was not hampered by persisting opposition with personal rivals, and was at any time equally acceptable as a member of either alliance.

The interest of the chiefs in limiting the opposition between the blocs is proverbial, and has been noted by British political agents, who contrast the attitudes of young warrior 'hotheads' with the more reasonable attitudes of chiefs and headmen (Wylly, 1912). Popularly, this interest in maintaining relative peace is related to a great variety of causes; its mere recognition is sufficient for the present argument.

Our 'inductive test', aided by the concepts of the Theory of Games, thus appears to support the argument that Yusufzai Pathan political organization develops as the political expression of a unilineal descent system under certain simple, specified conditions. These conditions are summarized in the premises (1)–(3) above. Features (1) and (2), the overriding opposition between collaterals, and the recognition of contractual political alliances, summarize the sufficient conditions for the emergence of a system of two opposed blocs, but do not imply any control on the intensity of opposition between blocs. Feature (3), the positive value attached to the position as chief, has implications which serve as a brake on excessive factionalism.

III

This case study of unilineal descent and political organization among Yusufzai Pathans exemplifies a pattern, not previously described in the literature, of deriving corporate political groups from a ramifying unilineal descent charter. In most lineage organizations, descent segments fuse for political action in a merging series of groups, so that opponents on one level of opposition become allies when the opposition occurs on a higher level of segmentation. Among Yusufzai Pathans, on the other hand, opposition separates small descent segments, and these fuse politically with other segments in a system of two blocs where the opposition between close collateral segments is maintained in all situations.

It might be noted that this is not a unique situation. A two-bloc alliance system of named alliances, *Gar* and *Samil*, is characteristic of southern Pathans as well (Wylly, 1912), though in this case the lineage segments which form the units of the blocs are slightly larger. A corresponding division into two factions, the *Hinawi* and *Ghafari*, runs all through Southern Arabia (e.g. Thomas, 1929, p. 98).

The analysis of the Yusufzai Pathan system relies on Radcliffe-Brown's formulation of the structural principles in kinship system (Radcliffe-Brown, 1950). Most analyses of lineage systems further depend, although this is not always stated, on a Durkheimian concept of mechanical solidarity. But the present case study requires a more general framework for the analysis of the solidarity of groups. That which is utilized is derived from Neumann and Morgenstern's 'Theory of Games' and sees groups as forming through the strategic choices of persons, i.e. the solidarity of groups springs from the advantages which persons obtain from being members of the groups.

The nature of these advantages, and the various restrictions on the choices open to individuals, depend on structural features of the total situation, which in the Theory of Games are expressed as 'rules' defining the 'game'. In such a framework, the groups which do emerge thus relate to structural features or conditions of any kind which offer the bases for the development of a community of interests of group members.

This wider conception of the bases of solidarity is not altogether a departure. It is, in part, implicit in the growing emphasis in the analysis of lineage systems on the presence of a joint estate, the importance of which was first brought out by Radcliffe-Brown (1935). However, as demonstrated by the present case study, shared rights in a joint estate need not imply a community of interests, and may in fact imply an overriding *opposition* of interests which inhibits the emergence of corporate unity. The analysis of solidarity deriving from strategic choices requires a more extensive analysis of the strategic implications of the contexts in which persons and groups are mobilized, and should prove fruitful in other instances, as well as the present.

In the case analysed here, solidarity between fathers and sons, and between full brothers, is associated with strong normative emphasis, and an incompleted division of the joint economy till some time after the death of the father. Immediate agnatic kin thus constitute politically indivisible groups. The first potential line of fission is between paternal cousins, and in the descriptive section I have attempted to document how numerous factors combine to lay the foundations for a relation of rivalry and opposition between such close agnatic collaterals. As has been demonstrated, these factors have strategic implications which define the necessary and sufficient conditions under which a two-bloc alliance system emerges. Among Pathans, the factors encouraging permanent opposition assert themselves on a very low level of genealogical segmentation. Occasionally, descent groups among them of three or four generations' depth may manage to maintain group unity, but frequently permanent opposition splits groups down to the level of paternal first cousins. I should emphasize that in other ethnographic settings, factors with similar implications may impinge on higher levels only of the descent charter. Lineage segments of any size may be the units in permanent political opposition; the point in a descent charter where fusion in a merging series stops, and bloc formation begins, depends upon the factors affecting strategic choices. The distinction between clans and lineages in the description of many African lineage systems, for example, may relate precisely to this point. On the clan level, the lack of genealogies removes the restrictions on strategic choices which presumably are implied in these particular societies by established genealogies.

Thus variable features of lineage organizations and unilineal descent group organizations in general are amenable to analysis in terms of the strategic bases for the solidarity of groups. This manner of analysing the relation between descent charters and actual political organizations, exemplified in the present essay, would seem to be particularly useful in the study of the larger, more complex societies. It is also appropriate to the study of these political systems under conditions of change.

Notes

1 The present paper was written while the author held a Wenner-Gren Pre-Doctoral Fellowship. The original field work was supported by the Norwegian Research Council.

2 Fairly complete genealogical tables representing the relations of major groups are given in Ridgeway (1918).

3 The structural opposition resulting from such a relationship is implicit in our very term *rival*, derived from the Roman custom: those who shared the water of a *rivus*, or irrigation channel (Drower, 1954, p. 521).

4 It does, however, relate significantly to the possibility for a spectacular rise to power by individuals within the system, exemplified by the great chief Malak Baba who increased his land by a factor of ten in the course of his stormy lifetime.

4 Role dilemmas and father-son dominance in Middle Eastern kinship systems

This paper attempts to show the way in which behavioral characteristics in one kinship relationship are in part constrained and determined by the existence of another, dominant kinship relationship. It seeks to explore the mechanism whereby this dominance is effected, through an analysis of role dilemmas. The main factors that are given explanatory precedence are the general values prevalent in the population concerned and the external circumstances that shape the situations in which kinship behavior takes place. In the latter part of the paper I illustrate and to some extent try to test my assertions with data from my own field work among Pathans – an agricultural people with a patrilineal and patriarchal family system – and from the literature on Cyrenaica Bedouins.

The paper thus takes up for discussion one of the many problems that arise from Hsu's stimulating development of the concept of a dominant kinship relationship. There can be no denying that this concept enables us to bring out certain regular patterns in the empirical material, and thus has great descriptive utility. But the concept of dominance entails no analytical framework for understanding and explaining these patterns. It would obviously be unsatisfactory to interpret dominance literally – that is, to give concrete behavior in one institutionalized relationship causal priority over concrete behavior in another such relationship. Hsu himself looks for sources of dominance variously in the value emphases of each culture, in the requirements for maintenance of the social and cultural system, and especially in the developmental history of socialization that is common to the members of the society. I shall take a more limited and synchronic view, and concentrate on the question of the possible interactional mechanisms whereby characteristics of one social relationship can

* First published in Francis L.K. Hsu (ed.) (1971) *Kinship and culture*, Chicago: Aldine.

determine behavior in another social relationship. Since we are dealing
with social behavior in stable institutionalized relationships, it further
seems legitimate to require any explanation to be consistent with a
general theory of social behavior, in this case the analysis of roles.
The mechanisms we look for should thus be found among the general
mechanisms of role formation.

Once this synchronic and structural framework is adopted, rather
than the developmental one, there is no a priori basis for restricting
the analysis to the kinship domain, and I shall need to consider the
connections between kinship and extra-kinship behavior. More concretely, I shall try to show how general values regarding descent,
masculinity, and sexuality are made relevant to the behavior of males
in a variety of situations in Middle Eastern societies. Furthermore,
I shall argue that these values are such as to give a prominence to the
father-son relationship that may legitimately be characterized as dominance, while other relationships, such as that between husband and
wife, become recessive so that behavior in them is strongly modified
and in part suppressed. I find the mechanisms effecting this in the
process whereby actors are led to select predominantly only a small
range of behavioral elements within their present repertoire when
shaping a social role.

To argue that behavior in a relationship is being modified or suppressed, one needs some canon by which to characterize its *un*modified
form and judge that some distortion has taken place. Hsu's development of the concept of 'intrinsic attributes' of relationships, most
simply exemplified in the employer-employee relationship (Hsu, 1965:
640), serves him in this necessary purpose: 'The intrinsic attributes
of each relationship', he writes, 'are the basic ingredients and determinants of the interactional patterns between parties to that relationship.' As I understand them, then, these 'intrinsic attributes' are the
basic specifications of the relationship which no party to that relationship can deny in his behavior without repudiating the relationship as
a whole; that is, they are the minimum specifications of the *statuses*
involved in the relationship. Hsu's view of dominant kinship relationships depends on the view that some of these attributes are naturally
determined, and thereby provide a primitive, cross-cultural canon for
judging the extent of modification of behavior in kinship relationships.

However, the connection between such minimum specifications of
statuses in dyads or larger sets, and empirical behavior, is more complex
than this model indicates. Not only is actual behavior a great deal

richer and more varied than these minimum specifications; the standardized, institutionalized behavior that emerges in the roles that an observer may record reflects these specifications only partially and imperfectly because, though it is constrained by them, it is simultaneously constrained and formed by other determinants. The following analysis depends on the recognition that a role is also constrained by the setting where behavior takes place: some forms of behavior require physical props, others become necessary only as a response to characteristics or changes in the environment, including the presence of other persons. In other words, regularities of behavior – in the present case, kinship roles – can be understood in part from the constraints that status specification impose, in part from external or 'ecological' constraints in the contexts where the behavior takes place and the role thus has to be consummated.

This view of the complex transformation from status to role derives mainly from Goffman (1959), and I have made use of it elsewhere (Barth, 1966). I wish to show here how some features of the phenomenon that Hsu describes as 'dominance' between kinship relations may be understood by means of it. Most important, it implies that when seeking to understand how behavior in one relationship affects or is affected by the actor's relationships to third parties, we need to separate two different levels on which the interconnections may be found: the level of statuses, as a distribution of rights and resources on social positions, and the level of actual behavior in role play.

One type of consistency and interdependence between the forms of behavior in different kinship relations is clear: where exclusive rights, *jus in rem* (Radcliffe-Brown, 1952) are vested in the encumbents of kinship statuses, behavior relative to these rights becomes systematized throughout the kinship system. Indeed, it follows from the very definition of such rights that they affect the behavior of third parties: they are rights as against the world to certain services from certain persons. Some of the features of 'dominance' referred to by Hsu might therefore be interpreted as the expression of such rights.

Most kinship behavior, however, derives from *in personam* rights which do not entail the same degree of systematization on the level of statuses. However, I shall argue that the domestic setting in which these rights are consummated is one that produces some degree of consistency in role playing, even where *in personam* rights are involved. This follows from the intimacy and comprehensiveness of interaction within households: alter in one relationship is audience and spectator to ego's interaction with others in other relationships. In shaping one's behavior towards one alter, one is constrained by the need to avoid repudiating that which is important in one's relationship to another, who is present though the relationship may be latent at the moment. Especially when several kinsfolk are interacting simultaneously, each person involved needs to find a pattern of behavior, and an adjustment of the various kinship roles that allows them to be pursued simultaneously.

This I feel is the main sense in which certain kin relations can become 'dominant': they are important and clear enough to take precedence over other relations and to block the use of certain idioms and the expression of certain qualities in those relations which would challenge or repudiate the 'intrinsic attributes', or status-defining characteristics, of the 'dominant' relationship. I would argue that persons, in shaping their kinship roles, in many kinship systems do act in terms of some such priorities and avoid the behavioral forms and the embarrassing situations in which key relationships and obligations might seem to be challenged or repudiated, and that the patterning of behavior that Hsu notes and describes in terms of dominance and recessivity is generated by this fact.

One advantage of this view is that it distinguishes 'strata' of determinants of behavior, and enables us to identify functional equivalents in related systems of kinship behavior. To illustrate the whole argument, including this last feature, let me discuss some material on the father-son relationship, and other kinship behavior, among tribal peoples in the Middle East.

If the criteria were clarified, I believe one could make a very good case for the father-son relationship as the dominant relationship in most Middle Eastern kinship systems. Especially in tribal areas, where political life is structured by patrilineal descent groups and productive resources are held collectively by patrilineal groups, the importance of the father-son relationship is overwhelming; and throughout the area the family system can be characterized as patrilocal and patriarchal. The attributes which Hsu lists as intrinsic to this relationship are descriptive of its form in these Middle Eastern societies. The attributes of continuity, inclusiveness, authority, and asexuality have institutional correlates in patrilineality, joint property and responsibility, paternal authority, and incest taboos embracing the spouses of close agnates. They are furthermore continually expressed and confirmed in etiquette summarized under the heading of respect behavior by the son towards the father.

This behavior is somewhat at variance with the general ideals of male behavior. Masculinity and virility are very highly valued, and are recognized and asserted in behavior that exhibits independence, aggressive courage, dominance, and the repudiation of superordinate authority in others. But in the case of father and son, this repudiation is not necessary — as agnates their masculinity and virility, their honor, is joint. The honor of the father is transmitted to the son, and the son's feats of courage and strength sustain the honor of the father, of the joint patriline.

The husband-wife relationship, on the other hand, has attributes that are discordant with those of the father-son relationship. Not only is it characterized by discontinuity and exclusiveness, creating a small realm into which a father's rights and authority do not reach; the Middle Eastern view of what is intrinsic in the relationship goes further, and particularly emphasizes sexuality in the form of male aggressiveness, dominance, enjoyment, and privilege. The husband's honor also demands that he should fully monopolize the woman; no one else should be allowed a share of the pleasures she gives by seeing her beauty or interacting with her as a woman. This aggressive monopolization of male rights over a woman is a virtue in a man; it epitomizes masculine dominance and autonomy, and no husband should repudiate it in his behavior towards his wife. Yet such behavior in its very essence is a repudiation of the virtues of obedience, discipline, and respect that are demanded from a son in the father-son relationship, and it goes against the sharing of honor, and particularly of the masculinity and aggressiveness that characterize their relationship. The 'intrinsic attributes' of these two relations, in the form which they will take within a general Middle Eastern value system, are thus highly incompatible, and provide a convenient case for the analysis of dominance between kinship relations.

The incompatibility poses behavioral dilemmas in all Middle Eastern societies. Indeed, the highly unequal and complementary view of what is intrinsically male, or virile, and female, or feminine, makes for difficulties in all public interaction between male and female. There is hardly any adequate way of shaping roles so that they allow diversified interaction between a man and a woman without highly compromising the public image of both. The impasse has been created, or is resolved, by the seclusion of women: the systematic separation of two spheres of activity — one where men interact with each other and observe each other, in public; and the other the private sphere where interaction in the husband-wife relationship is consummated, and a role can be constructed between the two which may be at variance with the public image of themselves that they each individually wish to project. But to the extent that the 'continuity' of the father-son relationship is realized, fathers and sons will be found inside the same compound walls, as potential observers of each others' interactions across the sex boundary. Thus the dilemma of the kinship roles remains.

Two forms of solution may be compared: that of sedentary, village dwelling Swat Pathans (Barth, 1959) and that of nomadic, tent dwelling Cyrenaica Bedouin (Peters, 1965).

The Swat Pathan solution depends in part on the men's house — an institution with a number of political and economic functions. Almost all men spend most of their free time in the men's house, and the man who spends much time at home is ridiculed. The institution thus provides a way of affirming publicly the priority of male life and one's relations to men over one's relations to women, no matter what the emotional realities may be. In some areas of Swat, all men sleep in the men's house; and in all of Swat, young unmarried men sleep in the men's house.

As marriage approaches, the prospective groom tries to avoid situations or behavior that confirm the impending event, but his juniors and equals try to discomfit him and he rarely avoids giving expression to his embarrassment. The father plays the active role and represents the groom in the preliminary negotiations and the legal marriage ceremony. When the marriage takes place, the groom plays no part in it at all and runs away and hides for days on end during the celebration, while heartless friends spend quite a bit of time looking for him. Consummation takes place in great secrecy, aided by female agnates. As soon as possible, the new couple establish an independent household, within the walls of which they can have privacy. Until such time, the son-and-husband spends an emphatically great deal of his time away from the home, and the newly wed spouses do not speak to each other and have no interaction when others are present. They especially avoid being simultaneously in the presence of his father (her father-in-law). In the powerful landowning families, where patrilineal extended households are the rule, rooms are allocated to the new couple into which the father would never conceive of entering, and the husband-wife relationship is in relative latency outside of these rooms, when others are present.

The later phases of a man's life cycle give an opportunity to judge relative dominance of kinship relations more concretely than by the canon of intrinsic attributes. Especially in patrilineal extended families, it is instructive to compare behavior in the husband-wife relationship where the husband is senior male in his line and has no relationship to a living father, with that of husbands who are simultaneously involved as sons in a father-son relationship. The absence of the superordinate party in the father-son relationship gives opportunity for more assertive and more public behavior in the husband-wife relationship.[1]

One major difference is a freer dominance in the senior male's behavior, contrasted with the junior male's reluctance to assert authority over his wife in front of his father. A senior male will occasionally engage in loud, demonstrative assertion of such authority, both in the presence of kinsmen and within earshot of others. He also more freely interacts with his wife as an object of sexuality and affection. Senior males are far more indulgent in pampering a young attractive wife, in favoring her and protecting her as against other women in the household, while a junior undercommunicates his interest in his wife as a sexual object and supports general household views of 'fairness' that are usually discriminatory against a young wife.

Finally, the senior male is freer to enjoy his wife at will. Though all areas of the house are open to a son, it is his responsibility not to disturb the father, and unmarried sons sleep in the men's house to avoid the shame of witnessing the intimate life of the parents. Where a married son lives in the extended household of his father, the young couple are reserved private space, as noted above; but the son cannot withdraw at will to his wife, and his obligations to give his time to his father always prevail over his obligations or enjoyment in the husband-wife relationship.

The same privilege of the superordinate male, to enjoy sex himself but monopolize the subordinate males' time and the time available to them for cross-sex interaction, is seen in public life. In areas of Swat where all men sleep in the men's house, only the chief goes publicly to enjoy his wife, while other married men wait and slip off discreetly to visit their wives unnoticed, after the chief has left and the men's house has quieted down for the night.

Compare this to the situation in an entirely different technical-ecological regime, among the Bedouin pastoral nomads of Cyrenaica. Without the paraphernalia of houses and compound walls, and engaged in tasks that require women to move in public among the men, the

Bedouin cannot achieve the same degree of privacy and segregation as the Swat Pathans. Peters (1965) gives a detailed and intriguing account of father-son and husband-wife roles in this system, and of their expression at ceremonial occasions. The pattern can be summarized as one of ritualized avoidance and fiction. At the wedding the groom tries to escape but is 'caught' by the young men and brought to the nuptial tent, whereas his father is completely inactive and feigns ignorance of the whole affair. Having established his own tent, adjoining that of his father, the son continues to play-act the role of an unmarried boy, returning to his father's tent in the morning to 'wake up' in his usual place there, eating with his father out of his father's bowl, etc. In the presence of the father, no statement or action is made that would force him to acknowledge the change in the son's position.

In other words, in the Bedouin setting where husband-wife interaction cannot be as effectively contained within a secluded, private sphere, the role dilemma is resolved by the relative latency of the husband-wife relationship, and by symbolic behavior which confirms the father-son relationship. The fictions and sterotypes of Bedouin kinship behavior provide a shelter for discrepant roles that is functionally equivalent to the compound walls of the Swat Pathans. But they do not have precisely the same effects. The complete dichotomization of secluded private life and public life that is possible in the village protects the senior male very adequately and allows him to play his different roles at the appropriate occasions; the dilemmas are concentrated in the son-and-husband combination. In the Bedouin ecology, on the other hand, the father-son dominant relationship needs to be protected by special behavior on the part both of father and son. There is no way for the senior party to prevent the intrusion of information that is discrepant with his own pose and interests; as a result he must develop a role solution that actively both over- and undercommunicates aspects of the situation and asserts the dominance of the father-son relationship.

My point of view could be summarized as follows: I believe that the empirical substance of Hsu's thesis of dominance in some kinship systems is valid and can be demonstrated. But I think that the pattern he has observed does not need to be cast in the descriptive and analytical mould that he has chosen. For the kind of data I have at my disposal, an explanatory model based on role theory appears to be both adequate and economical. It starts with the view that the distribution of rights on different statuses is never entirely integrated and harmon-

ious. Where status sets and relevant social situations are clearly differentiated, this disharmony matters little to the actors, who can then
pursue discrepant roles and project variant social personalities in
different social situations. Routinized social life will in part be shaped
by these considerations: persons will seek the situations where successful role play can be consummated and avoid the situations where
serious dilemmas keep arising — to the extent of grooms in Swat
avoiding their own weddings. In general, difficulties can be resolved
by avoiding simultaneous encounters with the parties toward whom
one has discrepant relations — by patterns such as the seclusion of
women, for example.

Where, as in the domestic unit, practically all role playing in one
relationship takes place with the parties to other relationships present,
problems arise for the actor in composing his behavior, his role, in
such a way that activity in one relationship does not repudiate obligations or qualities important in the relationship to the others who are
present. Here, one relationship may emerge as dominant over others;
it takes precedence and is relatively little modified, whereas other
relationships become latent and/or behavior in them is strongly modified, because tactical considerations of possible gains and losses are
such as to make one relationship by far the most critical. In these
cases it becomes important for the actor in shaping his role to avoid
all idioms that are discrepant with his obligations in the dominant
relationship. Thus, substantial sectors of the interaction appropriate
between parties in non-dominant relationships may become suppressed,
as between husband and wife in the presence of the husband's father in
Middle Eastern society. I would suggest that behavioral solutions to
such dilemmas may go to the extent of imposing latency on the whole
relationship — so that formal avoidance behavior may be analysed
from this perspective.

Which dilemmas will arise will depend not only on where the main
discrepancies of status obligations occur, but also on the structure of
co-resident groups, and the other institutional forms that channelize
and segment social life. Which solutions will be adopted, furthermore,
depend on the 'ecology' of the behavior in question: the setting, the
technology and the tasks required.

The perspective provided by Hsu, in conjunction with such a view of
how role-patterned behavior is generated, thus seems to bear promise of
refinement in our analysis of kinship behavior. It allows us to relate
more closely the different patterns of behavior between descriptively

separable but functionally connected kinship dyads, especially within domestic units and other high-commitment living units, and may also give an improved perspective on such institutionalized forms of behavior as avoidance and joking relationships.

Note

1   Inevitably, there are other variables that may be responsible for some of the contrasts. The husband's physiological age differs in the two situations; but I assume the 'social age' of seniority to be the more significant variable. The wife's age need not differ, as the husband's behavior is frequently directed at younger, sexually more attractive later wives as well as at an original first wife. The existence of sons should have little effect in suppressing most aspects of the husband-wife relationship, since there is a harmonious authority regime of father and husband over both son and wife.

5 Ethnic processes on the Pathan-Baluch boundary

Linguistic studies on the Indo-Iranian borderland throw light on the historical processes of ebb and flow of language areas and on the role of contagion, borrowing and linguistic sub-strata, as well as genetic processes, in language development. In his many contributions to the subject, Georg Morgenstierne has referred to the importance of social structure in these processes. Thus in an early statement (Morgenstierne, 1932) he comments on how the 'tribal system of the Baloches and Brahuis, which in contrast to that of the Pathans favours the assimilation of racially foreign elements into the tribe, has no doubt led to frequent changes of language within many Baloch and Brahui clans' (8-9). As a tribute from a non-linguist, it might perhaps be fitting for me to demonstrate the validity of this contrast, and show its relevance to trends along the Pathan-Baluch language boundary[1]. Briefly I wish to demonstrate that the recent northward spread of Baluchi at the expense of Pashto in the hill country west of the Suleiman range depends precisely on the structural differences in the tribal systems of these two peoples, to which Morgenstierne refers.

Firstly, the relationship between tribal and ethnic identity and language needs to be established. The often cited Pashto proverb that 'he is Pathan who *does* Pashto, not who *speaks* Pashto' can illustrate the absence of any necessary correlation. Yet, in the tribal areas, it is true to say that tribal membership presupposes linguistic fluency. In contrast to some other of the tribal systems of the Middle East (e.g. S. Persia, cf. Barth, 1961: 130ff.) tribal political structures constitute linguistic communities and depend on constant internal cross-communication. In the case of Pathan tribes, these structures are essentially acephalous and are constituted by lineage councils (*jirgas*) arranged in a hierarchy of inclusiveness. Within councils of every level the interests — and in the longer run, survival — of individuals and

*   Originally published in G. Redard (ed.), *Indo-Iranica*, Wiesbaden,1963.

segments can only be secured through debate, requiring the skilled use of the idiom.

Baluch tribes, on the other hand, are socially stratified and have a centralized form and the structure is composed of channels of communication through echelons of leaders. In such a system foreign language bodies might be encapsulated and communicate upwards through a bilingual leader, as do linguistic minorities in S. Persian tribes. However, in their precarious niche as nomadic mixed herders in a harsh environment, the widely dispersed Baluch camps and segments depend for survival also on another network of communication, mediating information on the availability of grazing, water, and the movements of other persons and camps rather than political decisions. This network is formalized in the Baluch institution of *hāl* — exchanges of information given in a peculiar intonation and stereotyped phrases as formal greetings whenever tribesmen meet. In both cases, in other words, membership in a tribe implies membership in a linguistic community.

In seeking the causes for the growth and expansion of Baluch-speaking tribes at the expense of Pathans, it is convenient first to discuss some of the more self-evident possibilities. Indeed a number of factors of undeniable relevance in a situation of competition between tribes seem rather to favour the Pathans. Firstly, with respect to aggregate numbers, Pathans greatly outnumber Baluchis; likewise in their overall density in their respective territories. In the zone of contact that concerns us here (Marri/Bugti vs. Panni/Tarin/Kakar/Luni/Zarkun/Powindah), the same holds true, and Pathan villages and camps are consistently larger than those of the Baluchis. Relative prosperity is also on the side of the Pathans — there is a general ecologic gradient of improvement from south to north, and this is mirrored in greater capital accumulation (in dwellings, irrigation developments, flocks, movable property and weapons) among the Pathans. Relative rates of natural population growth are difficult to assess in the absence of detailed demographic information. Doubtless both populations produce a surplus, as evidenced by their history of invasions of the plains, and the wide dispersal of both groups through contemporary labour migration. But the small door-to-door censuses I have suggest a higher rate of fertility among Pathan than Baluch, as one would expect in their better environment. Finally, in military aggressiveness the reputation of Pathan tribes exceeds that of Baluchis, both in their mutual estimation and in the judgement of third parties, though perhaps more because of the Pathans' better weapons than any difference in the value placed in the two cultures on bravery and fighting.

A number of considerations would thus lead one to expect the pressure along the boundary to be primarily from Pathan to Baluch country. In the hill regions, till recently for all practical purposes uncontrolled by any external government, one would expect these pressures to express themselves in fighting, conquest and overall expansion. There can be no doubt about the anarchy that prevailed in the area (cf. Bruce, 1900), which resulted in a complex history of conquest and local succession (Dames, 1904). Yet this very anarchy created the situation where structural features of the tribal organizations of the competing peoples become overwhelmingly important. Frequent wars and plundering forays inevitably tear numbers of people loose from their territorial and social contexts: splinter groups, fleeing survivors, and families and communities divested of their property, as well as nuclei of predators, are generated. From such processes of fragmentation and mobility, a vast pool of personnel results — persons and groups seeking social identity and membership in viable communities. The growth rates of such communities will then not depend so much on their natural fertility rates as on the capacity of their formal organization to assimilate and organize such potential personnel.

In this respect, there are striking contrasts between Pathan and Baluch tribal organization, though the difference in the cultural bases on which each is built is slight. Fundamentally, both tribal forms derive from the shared principles of *patrilineality*, *honour* and *obligation*. Let me try to sketch these common bases, and then show how the two systems derive from them.

1 The *patrilineal* principle is followed in both: political rights in the tribe and rights in the tribal estate are vested in men and transmitted in male line only. Though persons may lose status and rights because of their mother's lower status, they can never *gain* rights through their mother, only through their father. A man's political position inside his lineage and tribe is thus fixed through agnatic descent.

2 A position in the tribe implies a patrimony of *honour* which must be defended against slights from persons with whom one claims to be equal. An unrequited grievance is a blemish on one's honour which only talion or blood revenge can eliminate. A failure to revenge is an acceptance of inequality, and a loss of honour and position. From the time they are very small, Pathan boys learn to fight with their

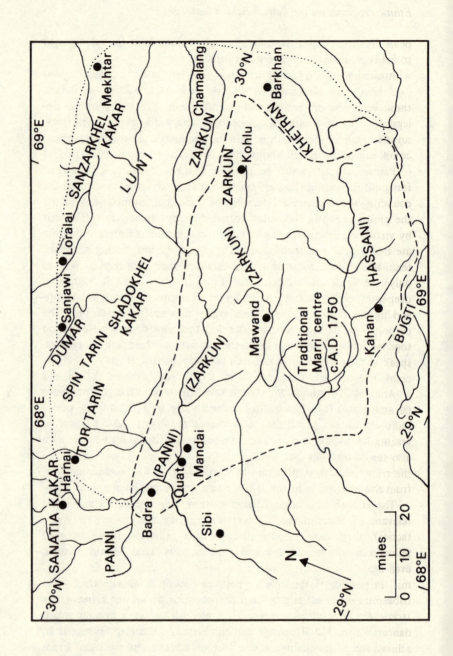

MAP 2 *Pathan-Baluch language boundary*

peers to defend their honour (*izzát*), just as the Baluch boy who fails to hit back when other boys beat him is scolded for being *beghairat* – without honour.

3 Finally, the honour of a tribesman involves an *obligation* towards those who depend on his position: his guests, his family who are his legal wards, and those who have sought his protection as clients (*ham-sayah*). Thus hospitality, patronage and physical dependence form a complex with clear political implications.

Pathan tribal organization is based on these principles, as realized for political and judicial purposes through the mechanism of the council (*jirga*). One might say that the model for the whole system is the group of brothers; independent men with separable interests, who by virtue of their common blood keep peace and can unite as a corporate body through joint decision-making on the basis of equality. Extending the notion of common blood (among patrilineal relatives only), ever-widening circles of 'brotherhood' are defined by ever-deepening genealogies, producing a hierarchy of merging segments and lineages based on common descent. Each such segment becomes corporate in the form of a council of its living male members who sit together as agnates with equal rights. It also follows that the right to speak in one small, local council implies the right to speak in every council of higher order within the merging series.

Another important feature of the Pathan tribal system is its territorial aspect. Groups and their segments hold rights to different types of joint estate. Persons thus obtain access to agricultural land and to grazing areas by virtue of agnatic status; as a result descent units are also territorial units, and localities and districts tend to be named after the tribal segment inhabiting them – names which again usually derive from the common ancestor of that descent segment.

The aspect of equality between council members indicates the relevance of honour, point 2 above, to council procedure. This has tactical implications, since acts which compromise the honour of fellow council members will lead to retaliation or blood revenge, even against superior force. For the person who is insulted cannot permit the blemish to remain – he can sit on the council and act as a tribesman only if he can defend his honour and assert his equality. It is therefore difficult for such councils to reach final decisions, and dangerous for the interested parties to use pressure on members to achieve compliance. Pathan tribes are well able to act strongly in defence of shared, short-term interests or basic values or in the pursuit of gain, but generally fail to pursue more long-term strategies, or to reach agreement on compromises requiring joint action.

Where a Pathan's honour is lost through a dishonourable act or failure to extract revenge, he loses his capacity to defend his life and interests in the council. He must then either flee the country or seek the protection of another man as noted under (3) above. Seeking the protection of one man is, however, lowering yourself before *all* the tribesmen and in most situations the unfortunate chooses emigration — so Pathans often say that 'he who leaves his tribal land has either committed incest with his mother or failed to revenge his father'. It also follows from the above that to accept *hamsayahs* is in most Pathan areas a commitment that men would prefer to avoid. In the egalitarian setting of the council, the value of clients as a fighting force is more than offset by the disputes they may cause — liabilities which fall squarely on the shoulders of their patron. Only in rich environments, where the control over a large labour force gives great economic returns, are such clients an advantage (as in e.g. Bannu in pre-administration times, and Malakand Agency today).

It should be emphasized that this description holds even where, as in many of the southern Pathan tribes, *Sardars* and *Maliks* are found. An investigation of actual decision making shows that these leaders have little authority, and political processes take place within the framework of egalitarian lineage councils. The tribal growth pattern that follows from these features is characteristic: it might be called vegetative, based on natural increase (with a certain loss through individual emigration) and tending towards a ramifying, branching form where local growth is associated with rapid segmentation.

Baluch tribal organization, though derived from the same concepts, is not based on the particular mechanism of the egalitarian council. Though defence of honour among equals is important, it thus does not become built into the *political* system as a major tactical consideration. A model for the Baluch political system is the relationship between a father and his sons — one of authority stemming from status, and common submission to this authority as the basis for joint action. Instead of working in terms of rhetoric and rallying of equals, with the ultimate sanction of talion, the Baluch political and judicial mechanism is based on *vertical* communication between ordinary men and big leaders, with communal action as the ultimate sanction. Political activity thus mainly takes place between unequals, and the important principle that is brought into play is not honour but obligation, as sketched under point 3 above. Tribal status in such a system does not require an assertion of equality, but is based on a chain of clientage and patronage between minor and major leaders in a hierarchy. A Baluch tribe as a whole becomes divided into segments in a formal pattern very much like a Pathan tribe, and membership and position in the system are ascribed on the basis of patrilineal descent; but the politically crucial aspect of the organization is the recognition of a political clientship tie to the leader of each group by its members. These leaders again work in the same 'vertical' pattern – political maneuver does not involve appeal to equals in a council, but communication with and mobilization of more influential, higher echelon leaders.

At the top of this hierarchy sits the Sardar – who has no equal, only even more influential connections: with the Khan of Kalat and the government of the plains. Sardars maintain their influence in the tribe by playing their inferiors (*waderas* and *mukadams*) off against each other, and by substantial bribes and personal favours – the patron's reciprocal to the client's request for protection.

The territorial estate of a Baluch tribe is also allocated differently from that of Pathans. Among the Marri, grazing rights to the whole tribal area are held by the Sardar and accessible to any Marri by payment of a tax (*gahl*), which has now been dispensed with. Agricultural land is held individually (till recently by leaders only) or jointly by very large tribal sections in a system of periodic reallotment. Such systems have also been common among Pathans; but among them the allocation of fields to sub-segments and families follows the schema of their genealogical relations, while among the Marri equal shares are given to all men within the section, regardless of genealogical pattern. There is thus no identity between tribal sub-units and territorial units; as might be expected, place-names in Marri area have no reference to social groups, though they sometimes derive from the personal names of prominent men, past or present.

When a man in this system is dishonoured, the consequences are of a different order from what they are for Pathans. Conflicts of honour and revenge between equals lead to fission of their immediate group, but need not in fact be resolved between the parties, since territorial separation can take place without consequences for the persons' positions in the political structure. A relationship of clientship to the same leader can thus be maintained by enemies, though the conflict may also be such as to involve the leader and thus force one faction to secede. But where a man or group does secede, this implies no important loss of rank, and a new clientship relation may be established to another leader. Again in contrast to the Pathans such seceders are welcomed in their new status: the importance and influence of a Baluch leader is roughly commensurate with the number of his effective followers, and the decision to grant new followers protection and rights lies with him, and need not be debated and accepted by a council of his equals.

The normal growth pattern that will result in such a system is in part different from that of the Pathan system. Further segmentation does not follow automatically with growth in every generation: natural growth can take place within fixed political units, merely increasing their size. And where persons secede or are expelled from one segment, they can be accommodated in an equivalent position in another segment, without loss of tribal status.

The structural differences sketched here imply clear differences in the assimilative capacities of the two forms of tribal organization. Disorganized personnel, such as is generated at a high rate during relatively anarchic periods, is readily incorporated in a Baluch tribe: persons may seek the protection of, and swear fealty to, a recognized leader within that tribe. In the case of the Marri, their tribal organization was also clearly thought of as a predatory organization, and for purposes of offence and increased loot, as well as defence, it was in everybody's interest to increase the personnel. Thus one Marri leader, himself of Pathan descent, explained to me: 'In those days there was war (*jang*) — nobody asked who is your father, brother — you joined the force (*lashkar*), moved and conquered and moved again.'

Though the same military consideration also held for Pathan tribes along the boundary, incorporation of personnel into their tribal system would either require that newcomers accept servile status or that a plenary meeting of the whole tribe agreed to accept them as equals, allotted them a compact block of land, and determined their position in the tribal schema of segmentation. Though both of these forms of incorporation have occurred, they are rare, and one would expect the growth rate by incorporation into Baluch tribes far to exceed that of Pathan tribes.

There can be little doubt that so is the case. None of the Pathan tribes along the boundary has sections or, to my knowledge persons, claiming Baluch descent, and the vast majority of tribesmen have recognized agnatic status, though some incorporation of other Pathan groups has taken place, e.g. among the Kakar and Luni (Gazetteer II:

76, 85). The tiny Zarkun tribe, partly encapsulated in Marri territory, is the only one that admits to a (rather fanciful) compound origin, explaining the name as meaning *zar koum* – 'thousand nations' – and their origin as being a defensive confederation against the Marri to which each Pathan tribe contributed one family. The presence of so many small, genealogically distant tribes along the boundary (Panni stem: Isot/Barozai; Miani stem: Luni/Jafar/Lats; Zarkun; var. Tarins, etc.) is evidence of this general failure of assimilative growth.

In the Marri tribe, on the other hand, all sections have traditions of incorporation, and many sections and subsections trace Pathan descent, often to existing Pathan tribes. Of the three main branches of the Marri, the Ghazani contains subsections of various origins, the Loharanis are half constituted by the Shiranis, tracing descent from the Pathan tribe of that name, and the Bijaranis are regarded as predominantly of Pathan origin. Among the Bijaranis the Powadhi section has had the most prolific recent growth. Mentioned in most texts (based on early and poor material) as a not particularly significant subsection, their leader is today virtually autonomous in his relation to the Bijarani leader; and the growth of the section has taken place so predominantly through incorporation of Pathans that it is referred to as 'Pathan' by other Marris, though it is uniformly Baluch-speaking.

This rapid population growth of the Marri tribe, based in large part on assimilation, has expressed itself also in territorial expansion. Growth without political subdivision has progressively tipped the military scales in favour of the Marris; over the last hundred years parts of Panni, Luni, Zarkun and Tarin land have been conquered, and the linguistic boundary moved accordingly. The broken fragments of Pathan tribes along the boundary, and the Wanechi language remnant among them, suggest that the northward trend has both considerable consistency and antiquity. Under present more peaceful conditions, increasing numbers of Marris also penetrate with their flocks into Pathan country as far north as Loralai and Mekhtar – an encroachment which the administrative authorities battle against, but are unable to stop.

The northward expansion of the Baluchi language area in the hill country west of the Suleiman range is thus an aspect of rather complex processes of incorporation and exclusion along the ethnic boundary, by which Pathans become assimilated into Baluch tribal organization, rather than a simple case of Baluch population growth and expansion. An analysis of tribal organization illuminates some of the critical factors underlying the linguistic spread.

Note

1 The discussion is based mainly on material collected during social anthropological fieldwork among Pathans in 1954 (cf. Barth, 1959a and b) and in 1960, and among the Marri by the late Robert N. Pehrson (MS) in 1955. Other sources, when used, are cited in the text.

6 Pathan identity and its maintenance

Pathans (Pashtuns, Pakhtuns, Afghans) constitute a large, highly self-aware ethnic group inhabiting adjoining areas of Afghanistan and West Pakistan, generally organized in a segmentary, replicating social system without centralized institutions.

A population of this size and organization, widely extended over an ecologically diverse area and in different regions in contact with other populations of diverse cultures, poses some interesting problems in the present context. Though the members of such an ethnic group may carry a firm conviction of identity, their knowledge of distant communities who claim to share this identity will be limited; and intercommunication within the ethnic group — though it forms an uninterrupted network — cannot lightly be assumed to disseminate adequate information to maintain a shared body of values and understandings through time. Thus, even if we can show that the maintenance of Pathan identity is an overt goal, for all members of the group, this will be a goal pursued within the limited perspective of highly discrepant local settings. Consequently the aggregate result will not automatically be the persistence of an undivided and distinctive, single ethnic group. How then can we account for the character and the boundaries of this unit? The following analysis attempts to answer this question by analysing and comparing the processes of boundary maintenance in different sectors of Pathan territory. Since our questions concern processes over time which have produced and sustained a pattern that we observe today, I shall concern myself with the traditional forms of organization which have predominated and still largely obtain in the area, and not with the recent process of penetration of some parts of Pathan country by modern administration.

Pathan communities exhibit a great range of cultural and social

* First published in Fredrik Barth (ed.) (1969) *Ethnic Groups and Boundaries*, Boston: Little Brown.

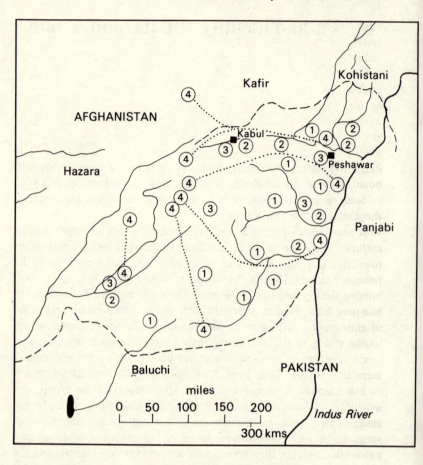

MAP 3 *Pathan area: distribution of adaptational form.*
(Digits refer to numbers in the text, see below)

forms (see map 3). 1. In a central belt of barren hills running through
most of the country we find villages of mixed agriculturalists, organized in egalitarian patrilineal descent segments with an acephalous
political form. 2. In favoured localities in the mountains, and in the
broader valleys and plains, more intensive agriculture is practised, based
on artificial irrigation; in these areas Pathans proper are landowners
or owner-cultivators, while part of the village population consists of
tenant Tajiks (south and west) or servile tenant and menial castes
(east and north). Political forms are largely based on the segmentary

organization of the Pathan descent groups, some places in acephalous systems, elsewhere integrated in quasi-feudal systems within the prevailing states and increasingly subject to bureaucratic administration. 3. Other sectors of the Pathan population live as administrators, traders, craftsmen or labourers in the towns of Afghanistan and Pakistan, as an integrated part of those two states. 4. Particularly in the south, a large sector of the ethnic group lives a pastoral nomadic life, politically organized as tribes with, in part, very great autonomy. Finally, some groups practise extensive labour or trading migrations which bring individuals and small groups periodically far outside the geographical boundaries of Pathan country.

Such diversities of life style do not appear significantly to impair the Pathans' self-image as a characteristic and distinctive ethnic unit with unambiguous social and distributional boundaries. Thus the cultural diversity which we observe between different Pathan communities, and which objectively seems to be of an order of magnitude comparable to that between any such community and neighbouring non-Pathan groups, does not provide criteria for differentiating persons in terms of ethnic identity. On the contrary, members of this society select only certain cultural traits, and make these the unambiguous criteria for ascription to the ethnic group.

Pathans appear to regard the following attributes as necessarily associated with Pathan identity (cf. Caroe, 1958; Barth, 1959a):

1 *Patrilineal descent*. All Pathans have a common ancestor, who lived 20-25 generations ago according to accepted genealogies. Though genealogical interest is considerable, knowledge of accepted genealogies varies both regionally and individually. The acceptance of a strictly patrilineal descent criterion, however, is universal.

2 *Islam*. A Pathan must be an orthodox Moslem. The putative ancestor, Qais, lived at the time of the Prophet. He sought the Prophet out in Medina, embraced the faith, and was given the name of Abdur-Rashid. Thus, Pathans have no infidel past, nor do they carry in their history the blemish of defeat and forcible conversion.

3 *Pathan custom*. Finally, a Pathan is a man who lives by a body of customs which is thought of as common and distinctive to all Pathans. The Pashto language may be included under this heading — it is a necessary and diacritical feature, but in itself not sufficient: we are not dealing simply with a linguistic group. Pathans have an explicit saying: 'He is Pathan who *does* Pashto, not (merely) who *speaks* Pashto'; and 'doing' Pashto in this sense means living by a rather exact-

ing code, in terms of which some Pashto speakers consistently fall short.

Pathan customs are imagined by the actors to be consistent with, and complementary to, Islam. Parts of this body of custom have been formalized and made overt by tribal councils and administrators as custom law, while some written and a considerable oral literature concerns itself in a normative and patriotic fashion with the distinctiveness of Pathan culture. The value orientations on which it is based emphasize male autonomy and egality, self-expression and aggressiveness in a syndrome which might be summarized under the concept of honour (*izzat*), but which differs from the meaning that this word has been given in Mediterranean studies, in ways that will become apparent as the anlysis proceeds.

Together, these characteristics may be thought of as the 'native model' (cf. Ward, 1965) of the Pathan. This model provides a Pathan with a self-image, and serves him as a general canon for evaluating behaviour on the part of himself and other Pathans. It can clearly only be maintained if it provides a practicable self-image and is moderately consistent with the sanctions that are experienced in social interaction; and some arguments in my analysis of boundary-crossing will be based on this very point. However, this 'native model' need not be a truly adequate representation of empirical facts, and for our analytic purposes I believe that Pathan custom can more usefully be depicted in a few central institutions of Pathan life. These combine central value orientations, by which performance and excellence can be judged, with fora or other organizational arrangements in which the relevant behaviour can be consummated and exhibited. The analysis of boundary-maintaining processes in different parts of the Pathan area, which will be made below, requires an understanding of three such institutions which dominate three major domains of activity: *melmastia* = hospitality, and the honourable uses of material goods; *jirga* = councils, and the honourable pursuit of public affairs; and *purdah* = seclusion, and the honourable organization of domestic life.

Hospitality involves a set of conventions whereby the person who is on home ground has obligations towards the outsider to incorporate him into the local group, temporarily be responsible for his security, and provide for his needs. The obligation is brought into play by the visitors' presenting himself in the alien setting. Accordingly, a stranger on the road who passes close to someone who is having a meal will be offered food, someone coming to a village will be greeted and helped by residents, a friend making his appearance will promptly be made welcome. In return, the guest is obligated to recognize the authority and sovereignty of the host over property and persons present. In this host-guest relation, any single encounter is temporary and the statuses thereby reversible and reciprocal, and hospitality is thus easily an idiom of equality and alliance between parties; a consistently unilateral host-guest relationship, on the other hand, entails dependence and political submission by the guest.

The appropriate forum for hospitality among Pathans varies in distinctness and scale according to local circumstances, but involves the allocation of publicly accessible space to the purpose: a special men's house, a separate guest room, or merely a place to sit. The space and occasion together may be described as a forum because they provide the opportunity to act out behaviour which can be publicly judged according to scale and quality. Specifically, it gives the host an opportunity to exhibit his competence in management, his surplus, and the reliance others place on him. More importantly, it shows the ease with which he assumes responsibility, and implies authority and assurance — basic male Pathan virtues. On a deeper level, it confirms basic premises of Pathan life: that wealth is not for amassing, but for use and is basically without importance, that only the weak man is attached to property and makes himself dependent on it, that the strong man bases his position on qualities within himself and people's recognition of these qualities, and not on control of people by the control of objects. The self-esteem of a poor hill farmer can thus be maintained in the face of the wealth and luxury of neighbouring Oriental civilizations — yet at the same time a means of converting wealth to political influence through hospitality is provided within the terms of Pathan values. While strangers are made to recognize the sovereignty of local people, local leaders can build up followings by feasting fellow villagers in a unilateral pattern. Apart from the way in which these ideas about hospitality facilitate the circulation of persons and information in anarchic territory, and protect locals from invidious comparisons with strangers, they can also further the political assimilation of servile dependents under Pathan leaders.

The *council* among Pathans is a meeting of men, called together by one or several of those present so as to arrive at a joint decision on a matter of common concern, and may thus refer to an ad hoc meeting or to an instituted tribunal. The matter of common interest may be a conflict between the parties present or the planning of a joint action.

The relationship between members of a council is one of equals, with no speaker or leader; the equality is emphasized by circular seating on the ground and the equal right of all to speak. The body does not finalize its decision in a vote: discussion and negotiation continue until the decision is unopposed, and thereby unanimous and binding as a decision by each participant. A faction which will not accept a decision can only avoid commitment by leaving the circle in protest.

The council is thus a forum where important Pathan virtues, such as courage, judgement, dependability, and morality can be acted out, while a man's influence and the respect shown him is made apparent through the procedures. On the more fundamental level, this organization of councils confirms the basic integrity and autonomy of men, and the basically voluntary nature of the social contract among Pathans. It allows groups of men to arrive at joint decisions without compromising any participant's independence; it produces binding corporate decisions about concerted action without dissembling the structure of egalitarian balanced segments through the introduction of any one's right to give commands.

Finally, *seclusion* establishes an organization of activities which allows a simultaneous emphasis on virility and the primacy of male society, and prevents the realities of performance in domestic life from affecting a man's public image. Pathan value orientations contain a number of contradictions if they are to be made relevant simultaneously in behaviour before mixed audiences. Thus, the emphasis on masculinity and virility has an aspect of sexual appetite and competence — yet eagerness to indulge oneself is 'soft' and severely ridiculed. Agnatic ideology and the emphasis on virility implies a high evaluation of males and male company over females; yet it must be through the company of females that the essence of virility is consummated. Finally, there is the problem of vulnerability through 'things' and the infringement of rights. We have seen how explicit valuations of freedom and autonomy are furthered through hospitality, through the denial of attachment and importance in things. Yet male rights in women, in sisters and wives, cannot be denied and liquidated in that way: a male is dependent on, and vulnerable through, his women.

To all these contradictions, the seclusion of women and encapsulation of domestic life is an adequate behavioural solution. It also makes possible a domestic organization that allows a realistic accommodation between spouses. The sexuality, dominance, and patriarchy demanded by public male values need not be consummated in public; the primacy of male relations can be confirmed in the public sphere without any associated sexual passivity; and at the same time the interaction between spouses need not be perverted by a male performance designed for a public male audience. The resultant pattern of domestic performance is difficult to document; but its adequacy is suggested by the relative absence among Pathans of divorce or adultery murders, by the trust placed in females by nomads and migrants who absent themselves periodically from their wives, and by the traditional view of mothers and sisters as upholders of family honour, spurring their men to bravery, etc.

These three central institutions combine to provide Pathans with the organizational mechanisms whereby they can realize core Pathan values fairly successfully, given the necessary external circumstances.

They also facilitate the maintenance of shared values and identity within an acephalous and poly-segmentary population. The public fora provide opportunities to perform and be judged by other persons regardless of residence and political allegiance; they mediate judgement and public opinion over large areas. Whenever men meet in councils, wherever guests arrive and hospitality is dispensed, core Pathan values are acted out and adequacy of performance is judged and sanctioned. Thus, agreements can be confirmed and maintained and the reality of shared identity perpetuated despite the absence of any nuclear, prototype locus or example.

Moreover, the values thus realized are shared, in general terms, by surrounding peoples: success as a Pathan implies behaviour which is also admired by non-Pathans. The ethnic identity therefore remains one that is highly valued by members also in contact situations, and is retained wherever possible. An understanding of the boundary mechanisms of the Pathan ethnic unit thus depends on an understanding of the special factors that can make it untenable or unattractive to sustain this identity. These vary in different marginal areas of Pathan country, and will be discussed in turn.

The southern Pathan boundary is one where Pathan descent groups, organized politically through lineage councils, face centrally organized Baluch tribes along a clearly demarcated territorial border. This border does not coincide with any critical ecologic difference, though there is a cline from lower and drier areas in the south to slightly wetter and more mountainous country towards the north. During recent historic times, the ethnic boundary has been moving northward through the intermittent encroachment of Baluch tribes on marginal areas.

The main factors involved in this process have been analysed else-where (chapter 5) and need only be summarized briefly. The critical factor is the difference in political structure between Baluch and Pathans. Baluch tribes are based on a contract of political submission of commoners under sub-chiefs and chiefs (Pehrson, 1966). This is a form that freely allows for reorganization and assimilation of per-sonnel, and the evidence for the historical growth of Baluch tribes through confederation and individual and small group accretion is quite conclusive.[1]

Southern Pathans on the other hand are organized in localized segmentary descent groups. Though many of them have chiefs, these are headmen of descent segments from which clients are excluded; and political decisions are made through egalitarian councils. Assimila-tion of non-descent members can only take place through clientship under persons or sections of the tribe. It involves, for the client, an inferior, non-tribesman serf status, attractive merely as a last resort. What is more, the arrangement is not very attractive to the potential patron either, for several ecologic and social reasons. A client in this area can produce only a very limited surplus from which a patron could benefit, whereas the patron's obligations to his clients are quite com-prehensive. He is not only responsible for protecting and defending him; he is also held responsible for any offence which the client may cause. And in an egalitarian society where security springs from a man's ability to rally communal support, the political advantages of control-ling a few clients are very limited. Thus, whereas Baluch chiefs compete for influence and tax income by incorporating new members into the tribe, people seeking attachment are turned away from Pathan groups due to the inability of that structure to incorporate them. Any person or small group who through war, accident, or crime is torn loose from his social moorings will thus be drawn into a *Baluch* political structure. Furthermore, as centrally led units, these are more capable of pursuing long-term strategies than are the bodies of Pathans, mobilized through fusion and ad hoc councils; and though Baluch tribes may lose battles, they tend to win wars — swelling their ranks in the process by uproot-ing fragments of personnel — and so encroach on Pathan lands.

The result is a flow of personnel from Pathan groups to Baluch groups, and not vice versa. Indeed, large parts of some Baluch tribes acknowledge Pathan origin. However, the incorporation of Pathans into Baluch type political structures goes hand in hand with a loss of Pathan ethnic identity, so the categorical dichotomy of Pathan tribes and Baluch tribes remains. The reasons for this must be sought in the clash between Pathan values and political circumstances.

Naturally, participation and success in a Baluch tribe requires facility in Baluch speech and etiquette and thus a certain assimilation of Baluch culture. However, this degree of versatility and bilingualism is widely distributed and so the external situation does not seem to require a change in identity. Rather, the critical factors are connected with the actor's own choice of identification, and all bias him in the direction of Baluch identity. I have discussed how the council provides a favoured forum for Pathan political activity, which allows Pathans to act jointly without compromising their autonomy. Membership in a centrally directed Baluch tribe, on the other hand, does irrevocably compromise this autonomy: a man must make himself the dependent, the client, of a leader and cannot speak for himself in the public forum. Judged by Pathan standards, clientship places a man among the despised failures, subordinates among independent commoners. Among Baluch, on the other hand, self-respect and recognition as an honourable commoner does not require this degree of assertion and autonomy; the costs, by Baluch standards, of being the client of a chief and nobleman are very slight. Virility and competence need not be demonstrated in the forum of political councils, to which commoners have no access, but is pursued in other fields of activity. By retaining a Pathan identity in a Baluch setting, a man would run the risk of being judged by standards in terms of which his performance is a failure, while judged by the standards current in the host group his behaviour is perfectly honourable. It is hardly surprising, then, that any one assimilated has chosen to embrace the identity that makes his situation most tolerable. As a result, changes in political membership are associated with changes in ethnic identity, and the clear dichotomy of persons and tribes is maintained despite the movement of personnel. Only one small category of people forms an exception to this: a few families and segments of Pathans who have been subjected by Baluch as serfs or slaves (cf. Pehrson, 1966: 12), and being the dependents of Baluch commoners cling to an identity which can at least offer them a claim to honourable origin, though no recognition among free Pathans.

The western margins of Pathan country exhibit a very different picture (cf. Ferdinand, 1962). Here, the adjoining area is largely occupied by Persian-speaking Hazara, and Pathan pastoral nomads and trading nomads penetrate deep into Hazara territory and settle there in increasing numbers. This is apparently a recent situation which came about only after Amir Abd-ur-Rahman of Afghanistan defeated and subjugated the Hazara. Before that, ethnic intermixture seems to have been limited. The Hazara were a poor mixed farming population of mountaineers, organized under petty chiefs and capable of defending their territory, while the Pathans held the broad valleys and plains.

The basis for this former exclusive territorialism should be sought in a combination of political and ecologic factors. As mixed farmers, the Hazara exploit both an agricultural and a pastoral niche, so both Pathan farmers and nomads constitute competitors to them. Moreover, a tribal political system of petty chieftains, as found on both sides, has very little capacity to provide for the articulation of differently organized ethnic groups in a larger system. The relationship between tribally organized Hazara and Pathan communities would thus inevitably be one of competition and mutual attempts at monopolizaton of resources along the border. The apparent stability of the border between them can be understood as a result of a balance between gains and losses: with the forms of political units that obtained, the costs of conquest and penetration of Hazara country by a Pathan tribe were greater than the expected returns.

The relative pacification that resulted from the incorporation of Hazarajat into the state structure of Afghanistan radically changed these circumstances. Competition in the exploitation of resources was freed from the concomitant costs of defence and penetration, and pastoral nomad Pathans started moving in seasonally to utilize the summer pastures. Moreover, greater freedom of movement has opened a niche for traders, and Pathans, with access to the sources of trade goods, have swiftly moved into this niche. Whereas trade in settled towns is somewhat despised and largely left to special, low ranking groups, the life as a trading nomad, who, heavily armed, penetrates foreign areas and takes large risks both personally and financially, is one that provides rich opportunities to demonstrate male qualities valued among Pathans. Through the institutional device of credit with security in land, these traders have not only been able to create a profitable volume of trade, but are also gaining control over agricultural land. As a result, there is a progressive trend towards settlement of Pathans as landowners among the Hazara.

This trend exemplifies a pattern of extension and ethnic co-residence which is characteristic of many Pathan areas. Pathan expansion northward and eastward, which has been taking place over a very long period, has certainly occasionally taken the form of migration and conquest with wholesale eviction of the previous population; but more frequently it has resulted in only a partial displacement of the non-Pathan autochthones. In these cases, Pathans have established themselves in stratified communities as a dominant, landholding group in a polyethnic system. Through much of the western area, the dichotomy is between Pashtun and Tajik, i.e. Persian-speaking serfs, while in the eastern areas, Pakhtuns are contrasted with a more highly differentiated, but largely Pashto-speaking, group of dependent castes.

One of the preconditions for these compound systems is clearly ecological. From the Pathan point of view, it is obvious that dependents will only be accepted where the disadvantages of having them, i.e. increased vulnerability, are estimated to be less than the economic and political advantages. In the barren hills of the south, I have argued that this leads to the rejection of clients. In richer agricultural areas, on the other hand, particularly where there are opportunities for artificial irrigation, farm labour produces very large surpluses so that profitable enterprises can be based on the control of land. As a result, the option of establishing oneself as a landowner and patron of others is an attractive one. Political supremacy may variously be maintained through an integration of serfs as true clients (*hamsaya*), or it may be based on the less committing obligations that follow from unilateral hospitality. Where surpluses are very large, this latter pattern is most common, as seen in the development of men's house feasting in the north (Barth, 1959a: 52ff.); and by this means Pathans can gain political influence over dependents without very greatly increasing their own vulnerability.

Pathan identity can readily be maintained under these circumstances, since they allow an adequate performance in the various fora where such an identity is validated. However, political autonomy in the system is founded on land ownership. Long-term ethnic boundary maintenance will thus presuppose mechanisms for monopolization and retention of land in Pathan hands. Persons who lose control of land must either be given reallocated fields on the basis of descent position or else denied rights as Pathan descendants and sloughed off from the group. On the other hand, land acquisition by non-Pathans must be contained and their participation in Pathan fora prevented unless they can be fully assimilated to Pathan status.

Several patterns of this are found, among them that of Swat, where those who lose their land also lose their descent position, while Saints and others who are given land are none the less excluded from participation in council meetings or in men's house hospitality. Thus conquering Pathans are able to integrate other populations in a political and social system without assimilating them; other ethnic groups and status groups can also infiltrate the system in dependent positions where niches are available, as have pastoral Gujars or trading Parachas. However, the cultural differences that go with the Pakhtun identity versus dependent group membership do tend to become reduced over time. Within the whole stratified community there is a very close and multifaceted integration that furthers this trend. Most social life can be related to a religious context of dogmatic equality. There is a constant circulation of personnel through hypergamous marriages as well as loss of land and rank. Finally, there are a multitude of contexts where a fellowship of ideals and standards are made relevant to groups that cross-cut strata: in games, in hunting, in war and bravery, non-Pakhtun and Pakhtun are joined, and judged and rewarded by the same standards of manliness.[2] As a result, the whole stratified population tends to approach a uniformly Pathan style of life as well as speech. Therefore, though the local version of the ethnic name (*Pakhtun* in the case of Swat and Peshawar) continues to indicate the dominant stratum internally, it is increasingly used collectively to designate the whole population in contrast to the population of other, non-Pashto-speaking areas. In this sense, then, the internal boundary tends to lose some of its ethnic character.

The eastern margins of Pathan country, towards the rich and populous Indus plain, illustrate a different combination of some of these factors. Repeatedly through history, tribes and groups of Pathans have swept out of the hills and conquered large or small tracts of land in the Punjab or further east, establishing themselves as landlords. Yet, here it is the conquerors who have become progressively assimilated, and the limits of Pathan country have never moved far from the foothills area, except for the almost enclosed area of the Peshawar plains. The ethnodynamics of this boundary may thus be simplified as a continuous pressure and migration of personnel from the Pathan area, balanced by a continuous absorption of the migrants into the plains population, with the rates of these two processes balancing along a line at a certain distance from the foothills. The direction and rate of assimilation must be understood in terms of the opportunity situation of Pathans settled in the plains. These plains have always been under the sway of centralized governments; for purely geographical and tactical reasons they can be controlled by armies directed from the

urban civilizations there. Any landholding, dominant group will therefore be forced, sooner or later, to come to terms with these centres
of power, or they will be destroyed. However, Pathan landlords can
only come truly to terms with such superior powers by destroying the
bases for the maintenance of their own identity: the defence of honour,
the corporation through acephalous councils, ultimately the individual
autonomy that is the basis for Pathan self-respect. Such landlords are
trapped in a social system where pursuit of Pathan virtues is consistently punished, whereas compromise, submission, and accommodation
are rewarded. Under these circumstances, Pathan descent may be
remembered but the distinctive behaviour associated with the identity
is discontinued. To the extent that such groups retain the Pashto
language, they run the risk of ridicule: they are the ones scathingly
referred to by Pathans as speaking but not doing Pashto, and retaining
the pretence of being Pathans is not rewarded.

A few less ambitious niches are, however, found in the social system
of the Indo-Pakistan area where Pathan identity can be perpetuated
on a more individual basis. As moneylenders and as nightwatchmen,
Pathans can defend and capitalize on their virtues as fearless, independent, and dominant persons, and in these capacities they are widely
dispersed through the subcontinent.

Internally, a somewhat analogous loss of identity has traditionally
taken place in the areas immediately under the control of the Afghan
(Pathan) dynasty of Afghanistan, particularly in Kabul and the other
urban centres. Here the proximity to the centralized authority is so
great that it becomes very difficult for people of any importance to
assert and exhibit the autonomy and independence that their identity
and position demand. Somewhat incongruously, the elite and urban
middle class in this purely Afghan kingdom have shown a strong tendency to Persianization in speech and culture, representing — I would
argue — a sophisticate's escape from the impossibility of successfully
consummating a Pathan identity under these circumstances. With the
more recent developments of modern Afghan nationalism, this has
changed and new processes have been set in motion.

I have analysed elsewhere (chapter 1) the ecologic factors that
determine the limits of Pathan distribution to the north: the critical
limits of double cropping, beyond which the surplus-demanding political structure based on men's house hospitality, as found in the northern
Pathan areas, cannot be sustained. North of this very clear geographical
and ethnic boundary is found a congeries of diverse tribes collectively

referred to as Kohistanis. But this boundary also is not entirely imper-
meable to the passage of personnel: several groups and segments of
Pathans are traditionally reported to have been driven out of their
territories in the south and escaped to Kohistan, while one such group
was encountered during a survey of Kohistan (Barth, 1956: 49). After
residence as a compact and independent community in the area for
four generations, this group was like neighbouring Kohistanis and
radically unlike Pathans in economy, social organization, and style of
life. It is reasonable to assume that Pashto, still used as a domestic
language among them, will soon disappear, and that other Kohistani
areas contain similar segments of genetically Pathan populations that
have been assimilated to a Kohistani ethnic identity.

That this should be so is consistent with the dynamics of assimilation elsewhere. Pathan identity, as a style of life in Kohistan, must be
compared and contrasted to the forms found in the neighbouring
valleys, where a complex system of stratification constitutes a framework within which Pakhtun landlords play prominent parts as political
leaders of corporate groups based on men's houses. By contrast, Kohistanis have a simple stratified system, with a majority of owner-
cultivator commoners and a minority stratum of dependent serfs, plus
a few Pashto-speaking craftsmen. Politically the area is highly anarchic
and fragmented.

In general value orientation, Kohistanis are not unlike Pathans;
and analogies to the institutional complexes I have described as fora
for Pathan activity are also found. Kohistani seclusion of women is
at the same time even stricter and more problematical, since women
are deeply involved in farming and thus must work more in public,
occasioning more demonstrative escape and avoidance behaviour.
Councils are limited to instituted village councils, with men seated on
benches in a square formation and grouping themselves as lineage
representatives. Finally, hospitality is very limited, for economic
reasons, and does not provide the basis for leadership: dependents are
landless serfs who are controlled through the control of land.

In the contact situation, it is a striking fact that Kohistanis over-
communicate their identity through the use of several archaic features
of dress, most strikingly footwear-puttees of poorly cured hides, and
long hair. Pathans find these rustic features very amusing, but at the
same time recognize the qualities of independence and toughness that
Kohistanis exhibit. Politically the Kohistani owner-cultivator is an
autonomous equal to the Pakhtun landowner and men's house leader,

though he speaks for a smaller group, often only his own person. Kohistanis and Pakhtuns are partners in the non-localized two-bloc alliance system that pervades the area.

Pathans who are driven off their lands in the lower valleys can escape subjection and menial rank by fleeing to Kohistan and conquering or buying land and supporting themselves as owner-cultivators. As such, they retain the autonomy which is so highly valued by Pathan and Kohistani alike. But in competition with Pathan leaders of men's houses, their performance in the fora of hospitality and gift-giving will be miserable – what they can offer there can be matched by the dependent menials of the richer areas. To maintain a claim to Pathan identity under these conditions is to condemn oneself to utter failure in performance, when by a change to Kohistani identity one can avoid being judged as a Pathan, and emphasize those features of one's situation and performance which are favourable. Just as Kohistanis find it to their advantage in contact with Pathans to emphasize their identity, so it is advantageous for Pathan migrants under these circumstances to embrace this identity. In the fragmented, anarchic area of Kohistan, with largely compatible basic value orientations, the impediments to such passing are low, and as a result the ethnic dichotomy corresponds closely to an ecologic and geographical division.

In the preceding pages, I have tried very briefly to sketch a picture of the Pathan ethnic group and its distribution. It is apparent that persons identifying themselves, and being identified by others, as Pathans live and persist under various forms of organization as members of societies constituted on rather different principles. Under these various conditions, it is not surprising that the style of life in Pathan communities should show considerable phenotypic variation. At the same time, the basic values and the social forms of Pathans are in a number of respects similar to those of other, neighbouring peoples. This raises the problem of just what is the nature of the categories and discontinuities that are referred to by ethnic names in this region: how are cultural differences made relevant as ethnic organization?

Superficially, it is true that ethnic groups are distinguished by a number of cultural traits which serve as diacritica, as overt signals of identity which persons will refer to as criteria of classification. These are specific items of custom, from style of dress to rules of inheritance. On the other hand, it is equally obvious that the ethnic dichotomies do not depend on these, so that the contrast between Pathan and Baluch would not be changed if Pathan women started wearing the embroidered tunic-fronts used among the Baluch. The analysis has attempted rather to uncover the essential characteristics of Pathans which, if changed, would change their ethnic categorization vis-à-vis one or several contrasting groups. This has meant giving special attention to boundaries and boundary maintenance.

The essential argument has been that people sustain their identity through public behaviour, which cannot be directly evaluated: first it must be interpreted with reference to the available ethnic alternatives. Ethnic identities function as categories of inclusion/exclusion and of interaction, about which both ego and alter must agree if their behaviour is to be meaningful. Signals and acceptance that one belongs to the Pathan category imply that one will be judged by a set of values which are characteristic or characteristically weighted. The most characteristic feature of Pathan values lies in giving primary emphasis to autonomy: in politics, in one's relations to material objects, in one's escape from influence and vulnerability through kin relations. This identity can be sustained only if it can be consummated moderately successfully: otherwise individuals will abandon it for other identities, or alter it through changing the criteria for the identity.

I have tried to show how different forms of Pathan organization represent various ways of consummating the identity under changing conditions. I have tried to show how individual boundary crossing, i.e. change of identity, takes place where the person's performance is poor and alternative identities are within reach, leaving the ethnic organization unchanged. I have also touched on the problems that arise when many persons experience the failure to excel, without having a contrastive identity within reach which could provide an alternative adjustment, and how this leads towards a change in the definition of the ethnic identity and thus in the organization of units and boundaries. To recapitulate in connection with the organization of the political sphere: the Pathan pattern of council organization allows men to adjust to group living without compromising their autonomy, and thus to realize and excel in a Pathan capacity. Under external constraints, as members of larger and discrepantly organized societies, Pathans seek other fora for consummating these capacities through bravery and independent confrontation with hostile forces as trading nomads, nightwatchmen and moneylenders. In some situations, however, Pathans find themselves in the position of having to make accommodations that *negate* their autonomy: they become the clients of Baluch chiefs, the vassals or taxpaying, disarmed citizens of effective centralized states, the effective dependents of landowner/hosts. Where alternative identities are available which do not give the same emphasis to the valuation of autonomy, these unfortunates embrace them and 'pass', becoming Baluch, Panjabis, or Persian-speaking townsmen. In Swat and Peshawar District, where no such contrastive identity is available, defeat and shame cannot be avoided that way. But here the fact of such wholesale failure to realize political autonomy seems to be leading towards a reinterpretation of the minimal requirements for sustaining Pathan identity, and thus to a change in the organizational potential of the Pathan ethnic identity.

We are thus led into the problem of how, and under what circumstances, the characteristics associated with an ethnic identity are maintained, and when they change. The normal social processes whereby continuity is effected are the social controls that maintain status definitions in general, through public agreement and *de facto* positive and negative sanctions. But where circumstances are such that a number of persons in a status category, *in casu* Pathans, lose their characteristics and live in a style that is discrepant from that of conventional Pathans, what happens? Are they no longer Pathans by public opinion, or are these characteristics no longer to be associated with Pathan identity?

I have tried to show that in most situations it is to the advantage of the actors themselves to change their label so as to avoid the costs of failure; and so where there is an alternative identity within reach the effect is a flow of personnel from one identity to another and *no* change in the conventional characteristics of the status. In some cases this does not happen. There is the case of the Pathan serfs of some Baluch tribal sections, where the serfs sustain a claim to Pathan identity and have this confirmed by their Baluch masters. What is actually involved in this case, however, is a kind of shame identity: the Baluch patrons enjoy the triumph of having Pathan serfs, but do explain that these people were only the serfs of the formerly dominant Pathans. The masters were defeated and driven out, and these Pashto-speakers are not in fact their descendants. And the 'Pathan' serfs do not have access to Pathan fora and would not have their identity confirmed by Pathans. Thus, the identity retains its character because *many* change their ethnic label, and only *few* are in a position where they cling to it under adverse circumstances. Only where the many choose to maintain the claim despite their failure — as where no alternative identity is accessible — or where the failure is a common and not very costly one, as in the main body of the population in Peshawar district, do the basic contents or characteristics of the identity start being modified.

The traditional version of Pathan identity has thus been one on which a population could base a feasible pattern of life under certain conditions only, and the distribution of Pathans and Pathan social forms can be understood from this. The system has been most successful, and self-maintaining, under anarchic conditions in low production areas. Producing a demographic excess under these conditions, Pathans have spread outward: extending Pathan territory northwards, north-eastward, and recently northwestward, while generating a large-scale population movement through a relatively stable ethnic boundary eastward and southward. Under changing conditions at present, with urbanization and new forms of administration, the total situation has changed so that one can expect a radical change both of Pathan culture and of the organizational relevance it is given.

Notes

1   There are also in Baluchistan some persons who are the clients of commoners or corporate groups of commoners – these are few in numbers and socially and economically deprived.
2   Except, that is, for some clearly discrepant groups like Saints, Mullahs, Dancers, etc. who recoil from or are excluded from these activities.

7　Swat Pathans reconsidered

Introduction

The preceding articles, and the monograph *Political Leadership among Swat Pathans* (1959), constitute the main body of materials I have published on Swat. Additional materials from the area have subsequently been provided by others (Fautz, 1963; Ahmed, 1976), while a considerable secondary literature, partly containing critical comments or alternative analyses to my own, has also appeared (for alternative interpretations of the data, see especially Dumont, 1967; Asad, 1972; Ahmed, op. cit.). I have also myself had the opportunity to make brief revisits to Swat in 1960, 1974, 1978 and 1979. A republication of these articles provides a welcome opportunity to review and supplement my description in view of these debates and materials, and my own changing perspectives in anthropology. In doing so, I shall try to carry my analysis of the social dynamics of Swat a few steps further. At the same time I shall attempt to put the ethnographic record straight by correcting my own mistakes and omissions, and the most serious misinterpretations and mistaken conjectures introduced by others in the course of debate.[1] At certain points the discussion can also serve to indicate the productivity of methodological and theoretical positions held by myself and others in these publications or at present.

To interpret correctly the concrete events reported from Swat (or indeed anywhere else), one must bear in mind the prevailing historical, political and environmental realities there. I shall start by emphasizing some of these, since readers seem often to have misinterpreted Swat data through carelessness in this respect. It will not do to impose thoughtlessly the assumptions and generalizations which have proved appropriate elsewhere, but for which there is no local basis. The point is that Swat — both in recent historic times and at the time of my fieldwork in 1954 — is not only a very different world from the everyday life experience of most of us; it is also quite different from the

conditions usually depicted in anthropological reports from much of
the world. This realization is not merely important to forestall the misinterpretations that might otherwise arise: data from Swat also gain
theoretical potential precisely because of their capacity to surprise,
and falsify generalizations based on other areas.

The distinctive characteristics of Swat

Swat is a secluded, inter-mountain valley of great fertility, densely
settled by a predominantly agricultural population of perhaps 300,000
in 1900, half a million in 1950 and one million today. At the time of
my fieldwork, most of the valley had been organized as a centralized
state for about thirty years. It is a notable fact that the state was an
indigenous, not a colonial creation; it reasserted previously unsuccessful
efforts of centralization during the nineteenth century and seems to
have arisen without external support and subsequently to have relied
only marginally on colonial and post-colonial national establishments.[2]
This autonomy perpetuated a distinctive feature of the preceding acephalous organization of Swat: through a turbulent history of contacts
with civilizations and empires, Swat itself had long constituted an
independent region. It was never conquered by Moghuls or Sikhs; and
despite British penetration on all sides it was never so much as seen by
European eyes till 1895-7 (Caroe, 1958: 370, 384). This isolation
and autonomy was the result, not of a centralized policy of closed
borders as in the cases of Tibet, Bhutan, or parts of Turkish Inner Asia,
but a combination of the justly reputed bellicose anarchy of the area,
which mostly kept outsiders away, and successful collective resistance
to invading armies. Such collective defence did not build on the pattern
of local leadership that normally prevailed, but sprang from the whole
population's dedicated adherence to a purist Islam, and was led when
the occasion arose by itinerant preachers (largely mullahs or faqirs,
and not Saints, cf. Barth, 1959a: 61-3), often deriving from other
Pathan hill areas and shifting their bases of operation over large parts
of Pathan country.

The singular and remarkable structure of society in Swat is pervasively shaped by these circumstances. Let us first look a moment at how
it unfolded in its traditional form up till around 1915, within the
memory of senior persons at the time of my fieldwork. We see a complex, densely populated, agrarian society based on irrigation, yet
where centralized political institutions were absent and the dominant

stratum of landowners lived a peripatetic life, moving and resettling every ten years. The population participated in the world religion of Islam, yet made up an almost totally illiterate society, to the extent that the Badshah, when he founded his state, was unable to procure the services of one single scribe (*The Story of Swat*, pp. 67-8). Production was organized by a complex system of occupational specialization and division of labour with high productivity. Yet the economy operated practically without the use of a monetary medium, and was cut off from external trade (apparently because of the internal state of anarchy) to the extent that rates of exchange for goods were entirely discrepant from those obtaining in the plains a mere 100 km away. Thus salt (an imported item) was valued as equivalent by weight to (locally produced) honey and butter-fat (cf. *The Story of Swat*, p. 47). Specialists showed a mastery of technology, including a weapons technology for producing small arms, equivalent to that found in neighbouring civilizations. Yet no instituted body or administration made any claim or attempt to control or monopolize the use of force.

In trying to understand this society, I have identified the issue of security as a major key. It is essential to recognize the extremely weak and precarious nature of security that characterized the area, not only for strangers and traders, but for its own local residents. This refers not only to life but also to property. Swat in 1915 was a social system pervasively based on individual and private ownership of wealth, land and capital items, and characterized by great and fundamental inequalities between persons with respect to their economic assets. Yet security of ownership was traditionally *neither* based on the instituted sanctions of a state organization, which did not exist, *nor* on the collective solidarity and protection which generally prevails within groups and communities of a homogeneous tribal society. Entirely different processes were involved; and their correct identification is essential for any true understanding of the society of that time (cf. below, p. 140).

What I observed in 1954, however, was a society in which a centralized state *did* try to monopolize the use of force; where insecurity was swiftly declining; where money was used for most trade (though not for most wages) and prices of most goods were sensitive to a world market; where material and social expectations were massively affected by education and by contact and communication with Pakistan and the world beyond; and where ready-made ideologies and competing interpretations of identity were being fed in from external sources.

I wished to make a synchronic study of this society, not a reconstruction of Swat society as of 1915 or 1930. But obviously what had been in that recent past provided a major fraction of people's experience, and most of their vocabulary and concepts for understanding the present. My ambition, moreover, was to depict major features of a whole large-scale, complex society, not just a village community within it. This led me to accumulate information on many different communities, and many different kinds of persons and lives. Any close demarcation of my object of study in space and time seemed only to cut me off from interesting and illuminating data, and to allow the essential features of life and society in Swat to escape my observation. But how was I, then, to conceptualize this object of study so that its complexity, large scale, and diversity could be captured and described? Clearly not by reifying any conveniently uniform bounded area as 'a society', as Radcliffe-Brown came close to recommending (Radcliffe-Brown, 1952: 193), and structural-functionalists seemed to practise, nor yet to seek escape from this by making my description of society a description of ideas or models in people's heads, as Leach seemed to invite (Leach, 1954: 8ff.). I wanted to describe society as composed of the actual events of interaction, of mingling, co-operation and strife between people, and not just their ideas about these things – i.e., I wanted to be my own sociologist in a complex society. In thinking this, I was not rejecting the perspective that has later become known as 'the social construction of reality', but I was concerned to observe this reality as faithfully and objectively as possible as a series of events. People's ideas shape their world, but are not supreme in the sense that everything which takes place is fully determined by what they think – as Leach himself showed clearly in his Kachin monograph (ibid.) and chose to give primacy in his Sinhalese study (Leach, 1961). I consciously chose to focus directly on what was actually happening in Swat, and try to construct a model containing people's ideas, *along with* all the other relevant factors which gave events this shape.

The conceptualization of 'society'

It is my understanding that my own disaffection with the structuralfunctional paradigm, and the structuralist alternative that was beginning to take shape, arose from this research focus: from the needs that such a conceptualization of the object of description and study raised, and not from a preselected theory of man as an individualist or a maximizer, as some critics have suggested (e.g. Ahmed, 1976: 59).

Let me try today to formulate this conceptualization of society which remained implicit in my writing, but which provided the impetus for the more specific theoretical positions which I developed and explicated. This I shall do by first discussing the aspects of boundedness in space and time, and then returning to the issue of what 'society' may be made up of.

From the very beginning, my material revealed major differences between villages. In the actual world any area, no matter how carefully demarcated, will exhibit a considerable variation in the form and distribution of social features. We can seek to minimize this by excluding communities, persons, or cases that seem significantly different, and seeing the relatively uniform rest as a manifested social structure, described as a set of principles embodied in the institutionalized relations of persons in a demarcated area. This gives the 'society' of structural-functionalists: a conceptualization whereby the interrelations of the 'parts' of the society can be inspected, in terms of their logical (structural) or functional connections. The issue of variation can then be raised again as a question of representativeness: where, for how many communities can this structural model serve?

My strategy was different: not to try to identify a representative form and ascertain its geographical limits, but to *seek out* variation so as to be forced to construct a description that would encompass the complex, large-scale and variable 'society'. I took a cue from Nadel (1947) whose audacity in trying to treat patently different tribes in the Nuba mountains in the compass of one monograph I found admirable, though I recognized his failure to provide much analytic integration. In the Swat area, on the other hand, I reasoned that since there were strong traditions of common origins or history, a persistence of common social categories, and a considerable amount of contact and movement of persons, it was reasonable to suppose that no matter how great the surface differences in settlement, organization etc. between villages and regions, such differences would probably derive from variations in relatively few determining factors. Thus, rather than represent a confusing diversity (as such variation would from a structural-functional perspective), these differences would provide the *range* of variation in form which is needed to discover empirical covariation (Nadel, 1951: 229ff.), and thereby test the steps in one's construction of a generative model of society for the whole region. The analytical point in this case would neither be to delimit an area of representativeness, nor yet meticulously to map the total extant range of variation, but to obtain 'interesting' cases of co-variation. In this strategy, one should let the development of one's hypotheses guide one's choice of variants for more intensive study.

The Swat valley and adjoining regions offers a rich harvest of such variation. Firstly, in the main valley itself, closely related populations lived in 1954 under very different administrative frameworks. Most of the valley was under the rule of the Wali of Swat, but from Thana village and below it was under the political agent in Malakand as a 'protected tribal area' from 1895, and thus more archaic (and acephalous) in institutional forms, but also more closely integrated with the colonial/post-colonial establishment. In the Sebujni area the special rules of the *talgerri* system[3] were in force for reasons of local personal and factional history. Further up the valley, the proportion of Pakhtun landowners to non-Pakhtun tenants, craftsmen and workers was significantly higher than in the central areas of the Babuzai and Nikbi Khel entailing clear differences in class relations.

Other major contrasts are between valley bottom and fringes, the latter mostly unirrigated, steep, and capable of producing only one crop per year. Along the main valley, the resident landowners in these fringes are more often the descendants of Saints — because such second-rate lands were more often granted to them, but also because sometimes Saints were able to wrest them by force from Pakhtun landowners, and sustain themselves on the marginal incomes they gave. Other areas were farmed by Gujars, as vassal communities tied to Pakhtun chiefs. Smaller inter-mountain valleys to the east, and the Indus bank east of them again, were partly in the hands of Pakhtun descent groups with strong chiefs (Karna), partly controlled by prominent Saintly families (Lilauni, Puran). Some very interesting areas, to my knowledge still entirely undocumented, did not fall clearly in either of these categories but are occupied by a poorly co-ordinated population of freeholders of mixed descent (parts of Ghorband and Chakesar). These could provide valuable material for an understanding of the bases for authority through its failure to emerge. Southeast, the Swat valley borders on Buner, the second major region of Swat state. This is a much drier area with only restricted irrigated lands, but dominated by Pakhtun tribes who are led by some chiefs of considerable importance. These again could provide tests of the effective sources of chiefly authority. I should no doubt have been more perceptive in 1954 in identifying and closely documenting more such variants of Swat Pathan organization. It is interesting, however, that the general appreciation among social anthropologists of the potential value of such comparative data is still, twenty-five years later, so limited that I have not (to my knowledge) been criticized for this failure, but rather for not having concentrated more single-mindedly on obtaining the greatest possible depth in my knowledge of one select community (e.g. Ahmed, 1976: 12-13)!

The other main dimension for delimiting the object of study is time. I wanted to make a synchronic analysis of Swat in 1954. My most vocal critics have called for more historical materials and fault me for my failure to adopt a historical perspective (Asad, 1972: 89ff.; Ahmed, 1976: 139-41). Some of my general arguments against this view have already been presented (above, Vol. 1: chapters 5 and 6). Let us look more closely at what is involved in this particular case. During my field-work in 1954 I was living among persons who naturally, in various ways, referred to past events, persons, and institutional arrangements which they felt were relevant to their current lives, and who also at my request could give more extensive and coherent accounts of the past as they remembered it, or knew traditions of it. There were also some few published accounts, and secondary sources providing historical materials on Swat (subsequently significantly enriched by Olaf Caroe's synthesizing *The Pathans*, 1958). Apart from the undistributed *History of Swat* deriving from the Badshah's own account, and subsequently published in considerably expurgated form as *The Story of Swat* (1962), these were all composed by persons only marginally familiar and concerned with Swat itself. Finally, there were, and are no doubt, partly available primary sources in documents and papers filed in the administrative offices of the state of Swat, the Pakistani government, and London.

It is generally recognized that accounts of the past can serve two very different purposes in an anthropological study. On the one hand, they may reproduce the awareness of the past held by the actors themselves, and depict how their 'consciousness' — i.e. values, rights, and world view — is moulded by that knowledge. This will not only include what anthropologists in the Malinowskian tradition have analysed as myth — i.e. putative historical accounts justified by select features of the present and serving as charters for these features; it also encompasses other embraced traditions with a more equivocal relationship to present institutional forms, but considered by the actors to contain true information about the past. On the other hand, critically

evaluated information about the past may also be used by the analyst
to establish what the events and conditions of the past really were,
thereby furthering our understanding of the influences that have in
fact affected the course of change, and, according to some, also furthering our understanding of the real character of the present.

My 1959 monograph, and the papers reproduced above, try in
practice to make this distinction but may fail to state it in sufficiently
general and explicit terms, and are mainly concerned with the first
perspective. Presumably my critics are indicating that the second
perspective should have prevailed, and that my very object of study
should have been defined as a society through a course of history.
Unless I were to abandon the methodology outlined in the above
discussion of regional variation, it seems to me that this second, truly
historical, perspective would add little of a fundamental nature to an
analysis; it simply provides an alternative way to establish the fact of
co-variation. The choice for me was mainly a technical one of which
kind of data were most accessible and reliable — and also, which kinds
of circumstances could be observed to co-vary. Geographical factors
can obviously not be held truly constant through regional comparison,
but can in a historical sequence; while certain macro-factors of external
influence are more readily observed to vary through time than in space.

But more fundamentally: if one thinks of society primarily as something which has a history, this invites a way of conceptualizing society
itself which is at odds with the one I adopted for the Swat material.
It easily leads us into the same kind of thinking as structural-
functionalism, that society is a thing and its history can be told as an
account of the development and change of its parts. Characteristically
Asad, who articulates the historical viewpoint most strongly in his
critique, proves most impervious to my shift in conceptualization of
the object of study, and repeatedly imposes macro-oriented and functionalist interpretations on my statements.[4] I definitely did not wish
to reify society in that manner, but to use it as a label for the sum total
of relationships and life circumstances of real people in Swat. As can
be seen from the above articles, and from the monograph, my questions
are concerned with these relationships and circumstances in the following way: what are their predominant patterns and how do they actually
vary; what are the major underlying factors that affect them; what are
the processes that reproduce them or marginally change them from one
encounter or day to the next? My focus was thus on endogenous processes and relatively pervasive exogenous factors; it is synchronic only

in the sense that it does not seek to provide an account of the main sequence of particularly fateful events in the valley, but rather of the interconnections between major organizational features and their causes and consequences. The models I try to construct are based on data obtained in 1954, but intended to be illuminating for the life circumstances of a variety of persons, for villages of a considerable range of size and organization, for Swat through a considerable span of history, and, in the last two of these essays, for Pathans under a wide range of circumstances. I have provided concrete descriptive data on institutional arrangements and extant social organization in a number of particular villages and areas in 1954. But I have also abstracted from these materials, not the parts of a social order within a set of geographical boundaries, but rather the recurring features of interaction in many situations and on many levels of scale. To explain these I have sought to uncover the combinations of factors which propel and constrain people to relate to their material surroundings and each other in these ways, and I have sought to identify the aggregate consequences for people of such ways of interacting. 'Society' in this perspective is not a thing, of which you tell a history or for which you show the fitness of design in how each part functions to support the other; it is, on the contrary, an epiphenomenon (and no less interesting for that reason!), i.e. 'society' is how things happen to be as a result of all manner of activities and circumstances. The thrust of analysis is not to show that it must be like this, but to show what must be since it is like this — i.e. to discover the major determining factors and processes. An essential link in these models is the part played by real people going about their lives. My perspective does not allow any shorthand language whereby patterns, lineage-systems, exploitation and class, or any other macro-feature is described as 'reproducing itself': the social events that make up such patterns are all brought to pass by *people*. The key which secures this integrity of people as actors is the concept of choice. Not free choice — indeed that is precisely what makes an analysis of choice illuminating: choices are decisions which are constrained by the perceptions of the actors, the circumstances under which persons act, and the reactions of others. These constraints also vary in severity, depending on the varying importance which actors attach to their consequences; and they are often at odds with each other or paradoxical in relation to each other given the actor's knowledge and his situation. My writings on Swat have aimed to show how differential life chances there, how political relations between 'the hungry' and 'the satisfied', how the pattern of two alliance blocs etc. etc. all emerge from processes in which people exercise judgment and act with intent under the circumstances in which they find themselves — whether the aggregate consequences of their separate and collective acts are indeed what they wished and sought, or are unwanted (perhaps even unperceived) by themselves.

I have been taken aback by some of the objections that have been made to this perspective (cf. Paine, 1974; Evens, 1977, and my discussion Vol. I, ch. 5). It seems as if the rhetoric for democracy is assumed to be entailed in the concept of 'choice'. I never indicated that I believe people are free to choose the most desired of all possible worlds. What I wished to point out, which provided the basis for my analysis, is the empirically patent fact that in Swat no adult male's political alignment in a solidary group is ascribed by birth position; likewise, no landless person has a predetermined right, or obligation, to cultivate any particular plot of land or enter into any particular labour contract. Such sources of livelihood must be secured by the person by means of the contracts he is able to negotiate: each adult male must make his own arrangements.

This is clearly different from many societies described by anthropologists where membership in primary political groups, and usufruct rights to cultivable land, are *ascribed*, and it is similar to features of Western societies (Barth, 1959a: 2). It does *not* entail that every man is provided with equal chances to achieve what he would like and what is generally most valued. The assets and impediments which persons are ascribed, or can accumulate, in Swat are many. The point is, however, that it does not follow from a person's descent, place of birth, residence, etc. that he will belong to this or that political group, production team, etc. On the other hand, if one knows a person's value orientations, attitudes and skills, one can make a fair guess on some of these matters, because his choices in the sense of what he has attempted and succeeded in arranging have been strongly influenced by such factors. The deeply religious person will seek the companionship formed in the mosque and probably remain peripheral to every chief's following. The brave and skilled rifleshot will be sought after as a close companion of the dominant chiefs, and have exceptionally good chances to obtain a Swat army contract. The most highly motivated and competent cultivator will have the best chance of obtaining a large tenancy allotment of the best land of his village. And how are these matters decided in Swat? By a process where each person is compelled to make his own contractual arrangement, and where they themselves say simply that they try to make the best of their situation. If they spoke in the idiom of everyday English, many would no doubt say: 'I have no choice' — meaning that as they see it, the risks and costs of their doing anything different from what they are doing, i.e. changing their circumstances, are greater than the benefits they expect from such change. But this seems to me to reflect nothing but their own calculus in attempting to maximize their advantages, since it does not deny that their position has come about and persists through a series of decisions that might have been different. And in this sense, landowners are constrained as well as the landless — though clearly their assets, and chances of shaping a good life for themselves, are greater. 'Society' in Swat emerges as an aggregate of all these choices, whereby persons in a wide range of dissimilar opportunity situations purposely and inadvertently shape their own life histories and those of others. Thus, their alignment in corporate groups and teams results from their own deliberations and decisions — influenced by, but not determined by — the rights and duties which are ascribed to them and which they ascribe to others.

If we look at 'society' this way, much of it is chaotic and highly variable; but some marked regularities also emerge, constituting those very patterns which we identify as macro-features. The degree of persistence through time of many of these features, despite profound changes in other circumstances, is also striking and seems to require sociological explanation. In these fields of activity, one must conclude, the actions of most people must be such that they have the effect of reproducing their own constraints — directly or indirectly, purposively or inadvertently. My analysis has aimed to identify, for each major pattern, the salient factors most responsible for the regularity. These explanatory models mainly take the form of simple schemata which depict the cultural, situational, and/or interactional binds which can generate such regularities in the behaviour of many actors.

Long separation from society in Swat, and criticisms both of my description and my analysis, took their toll over the years and gave me some doubts whether the models I had constructed of characteristic systems and processes possessed quite the force which I once thought. So, in August 1978, I chose to return to Swat for a brief revisit to check on previous understandings and observe recent changes. I proceeded directly by bus from Peshawar, and could immediately recognize Pathan ideals of masculine assertiveness in the hair-raisingly reckless driving of the bus through the motley traffic across the Peshawar plains. At Nowshera we had to make use of a long railway bridge, too narrow to accommodate meeting traffic, to cross the broad Kabul river. As we arrived, a small van had just entered the bridge from the other side; our driver none the less hurled his bus on to the tracks and raced towards a confrontation. The two vehicles came to a screeching halt, facing each other over the middle of the Kabul river. Both drivers demanded that the other should back up. Some of the bus passengers remained passive, maintaining that characteristic inward, withdrawn posture whereby Pathans mark their non-participation in public. Others involved themselves on the side of our driver. Both drivers got out and threatened each other, but were restrained from fighting by members of the growing crowd of spectators. Partisans on both sides started signalling to the vehicles further back in the meeting line to start backing up, while urging new arrivals in their own direction to move up and form a tight queue. A bridge guard finally appeared; he ascertained that the van had entered the bridge first, and urged the bus driver to back away. He refused, claiming that the bus was at least half way across the bridge and had far more passengers and a timetable to keep, and demonstrated his determination to sit it out by leaving the driver's place and sitting down crosswise on the gearbox. Finally, conciliatory voices could be heard from some of the previously uninvolved passengers, pointing out the inconvenience of the impasse and the virtues of reasonableness. A young man emerged from the back of the bus. After considerable discussion, access to the bridge was barred for further meeting traffic, and the young man took the vacant driver's seat and started reversing. The van, and the other meeting vehicles already on the bridge, followed us almost bumper to bumper. As the bus approached the end of the bridge, a train hooted behind us. Our bus took up position on the tracks beside the road at the bridgehead, allowing the van and the rest of the meeting traffic to move off the bridge, and then proceeded — with the driver again at the controls — across the bridge in front of the slowly advancing train. The whole incident took twenty minutes, and was followed by exhilarated discussion by most of the passengers in the bus, largely composed of recriminations against the young peacemaker: if we only had sat it out a few more minutes, the arriving train would have resolved the contest in our favour!

On another stage and with other purposes, these same persons would of course engage in other activities and form other concrete social organizations; but this same pattern of rivalry, mobilization, and resolution is recognizable again and again. I see it as a major task of analysis to identify its roots or causes in some basic conjunction of factors which recurrently generates such interactional sequences (cf. ch. 3 and below, pp. 158ff.). Ultimately, I see the most generalized description and analysis of society in Swat as the identification of a small set of such 'deep structures' which in different permutations and external circumstances will generate all the major variants of form which can be observed.

If the manner in which I conceptualize the object of study in these writings on Swat 'society' has now been sufficiently spelled out to be recognized, this still does not settle the question of the fruitfulness of such a perspective. That question can only be answered by judging the scope and adequacy of what it captures: the naturalism of its description, including the selectivity that enters into what is described; and the insight that it provides into how these descriptive features come about, are sustained or changed. After all, it is not just the shape of events on a bridge over the Kabul river, or some other narrow range of select situations, that concerns us, but the main outlines of the daily pursuit of life in the Swat valley.

Clientage in Swat: its changing forms

To discover the main lineaments of social life in Swat, I have identified two key questions: how people in the valley obtain for themselves a modicum of security regarding property and person, and what are the major membership groups that emerge in concrete decision-making and action. These two connected considerations are directly or indirectly at issue in most activities, and so have the effect of integrating many fields of social organization.

My purpose in focusing my main account of this on the activities of *leaders* (Barth, 1959a, cf. p. 2) has sometimes been misunderstood, and the underlying methodological principle overlooked. The outlines of a political system will emerge more clearly if the constraints and conditions of political activity are described from the point of view of those statuses most specifically concerned with politics, so long as their relations to others less concentrated on such activities are also given. To illuminate the life situation of the different categories of persons in a society, on the other hand, or the range of ideologies embraced by them, a broader but consequently also more complex account from the point of view of the whole population is appropriate. The same realities that were described from the point of view of leaders can thus also be given, though less compactly, from the point of view of those who follow. I showed how each chief 'establishes, as it were, a central island of authority . . . in a sea of politically amorphous villagers. From this centre his authority extends outwards with decreasing intensity' (ibid, p. 91, summarizing the description, pp. 71ff.). The obverse description would emphasize the multiplicity and looseness of attachments which in Swat in 1954 connected persons to their leaders and to the primary groups that secured them protection for their rights. True, within the state of Swat there was a simple territorial framework of administration and courts; but even the most cursory investigation of concrete case stories or life situations showed that these institutions alone were insufficient to provide a person with the protection he needed. A comparison with life in the stateless area (represented in my material by the village of Thana) showed the same vital substratum of connections and memberships to be the operative ones throughout the valley.

These connections arose out of every person's (or, most directly, every household head's) need to obtain (a) a residence, (b) employment and income, and (c) social support. Swat is an overwhelmingly agrarian society. With land in the hands of Pakhtuns and various families of Saints, most of the population was not given access to any of these essentials by birth or inheritance, and had to establish their access individually and contractually. Through this they were drawn into particular relationships of clientage and subjection. Depending on their own values and skills, and on local circumstance, however, connections of differing content and intensity could be established.

(a) Through *renting a house*, every non-landowner entered into a relationship with a particular landlord. Political relations in Swat were conceived in semi-feudal terms by its residents; and in a formal sense house tenancy contracts defined the primary jural-political bonds between patrons and clients (cf. Barth, 1959a: 50-2). This assumption was also built into the formal administration of Swat state (but cf. below, pp. 142, 150). However, a house tenant was in practice not assured any active protection by his patron in Swat when I did my fieldwork, nor was the houseowner able to wrest significant political services and fealty from every one of his house tenants. The potential group composed of all the house tenants of a particular landowner, or coalition of landowners, likewise never emerged at any occasion or for any joint action. This fact reflected, as I judged it, the absence of any effective sanction on the patron's part by virtue of his house-ownership: the ultimate sanction to evict a house tenant was very shameful for the owner and highly disapproved by public opinion, and therefore rarely practised. Conversely, genuine patronage from a landowner could only be obtained by a client entering into other additional relationships and commitments, and could even be obtained without the formally indicative house tenancy relationship.

(b) *Income* could be obtained by obtaining the lease of land, or by securing employment from others. We have seen the variety of occupations and attachments that were practised (ch. 2 and Barth, 1959 pp. 43ff.). Marginal drylands, especially on the valley slopes (*banda*) could be obtained with limited loss of autonomy, but at the cost of harder toil. Combining plots from several landowners also enhanced a tenant's independence, but at the cost of security, since no single landowner had a major interest in his crop and thus in his work and welfare. Obtaining land from a small vs. a big landowner likewise made a difference, depending on the force and integrity of the patron: a small landowner with a sound position among his fellow-Pakhtuns and a good relationship to the dominant chief could perhaps provide the best combination of security and autonomy for his tenants, but if he were weak or fell out with the chief he might fail to provide effective protection; so being one of many tenants under a larger land-owner could well be a better gamble, given the basic common interest of patron and client entailed in the sharecropping contract. Employment, in crafts or in transport, was obtainable variously from several landowners, combinations of landowners or single large landowners; or a man might try for greater independence as self-employed in his craft or service if he could secure (rent) the required shop. Protection against arbitrary confiscation or robbery was provided, in the latter case with reasonable certainty, by the state; but securing a sufficient volume of customers might be more difficult, whereas this came automatically with service contracts from big landowners. Employment by an agency of Swat state was highly sought after, as it provided exceptional security and independence; but it was also difficult to obtain and in most cases only provided part-time employment in the army (used also for public works) in return for modest payments in grains. Different communities in Swat represented a great range of circumstances, from small and relatively tightly organized agricultural autocracies to the impersonally competitive market conditions of the main town of Mingora. Though a certain amount of internal migration was practised by the non-landowners in search of opportunities, this was nowhere very prevalent, and migration out of Swat was generally seen as a very unattractive last resort. Swat thus exhibited the features of involution (cf. Geertz, 1971) characteristic of traditional irrigation-based systems of production.

(c) It was through his *association with a social circle* that the common man most immediately and directly could obtain and make known the source and strength of his protection. The main options, separately or in combination, were the *men's house (hujra)*, the *mosque*, and the *neighbourhood*. In 1954 houses in Swat were still the scenes of quite large-scale conversion of wealth into influence by local chiefs; this meant that there was also considerable material incentive for the propertyless to spend their time there. But their presence was also exploited: sitting in a men's house meant deferring to the chief, providing him with minor services on demand, and sustaining the risks of being his front-line men in case of sudden conflicts. The enhanced security of persons and property obtained by being a member of the chief's acknowledged faction was thus balanced by the risks of being unequivocally embroiled in the chief's own struggles. Yet the men's house was also attractive precisely because it was the centre of events, excitement, and danger; it was an arena for manly relationships and manly virtues. The mosque (or the *bētak* guest room of a local Saint's descendant) provided a very different atmosphere – of piety, calmness and righteousness, and little material incentive. It could also provide few political advantages; but it did give those who frequented it membership in a moral community of undeniable weight, and thus some protection against arbitrary injustice. Finally, persons could seek their main circle of companionship and support in the neighbourhood of rough equals that surrounded them. Such relations were based on long-standing friendship and familiarity, mutual participation in life crisis rituals, and – within the constraints of descent and caste – kinship and affinity. Given the size, composition, and authority relations in most villages, this kind of grouping was politically impotent and could only serve slightly to supplement either men's house or mosque position as a source of security; but where these institutions were locally absent, as in many of the hamlets in the hilly fringes, it could be of major importance. Likewise in Mingora, where men's houses were disappearing or serving new and different purposes and the Wali's administration was strong and perpetually present, this neighbourhood circle might, or might have to, suffice.

The particular mixture of these different relationships and commitments through which each particular person constructed his bases for security and political participation varied greatly. Besides the limitations imposed by local realities and options, it depended on the person's interests, skills, assets, and foresight. To maximize autonomy, a man could spread his land tenancy contracts and particularly avoid such contracts with his house owner; he could visit men's houses rarely and the mosque sparingly while cultivating neighbourhood relations and meticulously and conspicuously fulfilling his obligations in a Swat state army service, if he had one — or he could set up a shop on land rented from a non-Pakhtun landowner and keep to himself. On the other hand, among those who chose to be closely identified with the chief's faction, one might do so by renting one of the chief's houses, obtaining his land or employment from him or his close supporters, and spending his time in the men's house from fear of losing any of these advantages or calling the chief's displeasure down on himself. Another would be found there despite his relative economic autonomy, but because he enjoyed the excitement and self-assertion which he achieved as one of the Khan's companions. Yet others might be driven to sit in a men's house mainly to obtain the material benefits of feasts etc., and thereby reduce the pressure of poverty. This diversity of relationships, and considerable scope for choice in the arrangements effected by any particular person, naturally had implications for the position and strategies of leaders. A leader's following was volatile and liable to shrink or swell in response to what he could provide, or what promise followers could judge for his career in the close future, while at the same time this following represented the physical force on which his ownership of land depended. Thus the freedom — or, if one prefers, the individual necessity — for non-landowners to make their own individual arrangements with patrons also had the effect of counteracting gross abuses of authority (not in the particular, exceptional case, but for the majority of relationships entertained by each patron). Relative norms of what were 'reasonable' conditions of submission and exploitation in return for (a corresponding degree of) security emerged: where these were not fulfilled, the wronged client would withdraw and seek other patrons.[5] This is *not* to deny the abject dependence of the hungry (*wugge*) men on those who were propertied and satisfied (*mor*); it identifies a process whereby standards and expectations for their relationship emerged. It also identifies one of the sources of insecurity in the position of any particular leader. Finally, it shows the source of the observable looseness and diversity in the overall political alignments of followers: some closely bound to one or several leaders, others relatively outside the control of any leader. All persons had to secure some kind of platform of protection and membership; but the common man who was satisfied to have little personal property, work hard and reliably, and practise public restraint was, under most circumstances, capable of remaining relatively peripheral to the struggles and risks of politics, if he so chose. Yet none could afford entirely to ignore those persons who gave them access to house and work, or be impervious to their influence. Except in the small hill communities of Gujars and other poor and peripheral tenants, the only actual *groups* that emerged in political action were those led by major landowners – and bodies of the Wali's police and army.

For the small landowners, security was perhaps even more critical because they possessed a good – viz. land – which the mighty coveted. Loss of this land was also considered all the more serious because it meant a great loss of rank: from membership in the Pakhtun 'gentry' to that of common landless workers. The land ownership and tenure system was furthermore such (cf. ch. 3 pp. 66-9) as to militate against dependence on close kin for protection, since these comprised a person's closest rivals. This same land tenure system, in its traditional form as until 1930, also precluded the owner's entering into debt by offering his land as collateral, and thus prevent the typical Indian pattern of rural smallholder indebtedness from developing – but at the same time served to maintain a highly unitary, land-based authority system. The only practicable option for small landowners in 1954 seemed to be to join in the two-bloc system by aligning as supporters or co-owners of the men's house of a leader. In the final counting, their security against aggression or being short-changed by their own bloc also rested on their expected tenacity in fighting for their property, and in the event revenging its loss. As Pathans realistically observe: you will rather die fighting for your own land than another's.

The tactical pressures on large landowners, and the social and strategic factors that gave rise to them, have been explored in previous analyses (especially Barth, 1959a). Already in 1954, however, some big landowners had opted for a strategy of remaining 'neutral' and unaligned in either bloc – a pattern more prevalent by 1960 (cf. Vol. I, pp. 53-5). Clients of such landowners were offered the option of less stringent demands of submission and support, but also significantly less material benefits from feasting, and were provided in return with a certain amount of backing in relation to the expectedly favourably inclined state administration on which they were dependent. A precondition for this strategy on the part of landowners was clearly the increasing effectiveness of the state in maintaining peace, and the Wali's favourable attitude. All my case material indicates that this would have been a suicidal policy, never adopted by landowners, in the preceding decades.

Yet the question can be raised as to what were the cultural factors which propelled Pakhtun leaders in Swat generally to engage so strongly in the competitive pursuit of power and leadership positions. The intensity of pressures did not, after all, arise from a tactical situation alone, but had as its wellspring generally held evaluations of the desirability of such positions. Some formal definitions of politics identify it in one way or another with activities directed towards rallying supporters for desired purposes (cf. Barth, 1959a: 2). A literal reading of this would create a false impression for Swat in 1954: leaders there had generally no purposes in the sense of policies which they wished to implement, or long-range goals which they wished to reach. Nor is it a fair reading of my text, or a true picture of Swat, to imagine Pakhtun Khans as particularly ruthless and single-minded maximizers of power. Other things being equal, it is reasonable to expect that those persons who have in fact emerged as leaders in a society have, by and large, valued power more than others and therefore pursued it more vigorously. But observing those chiefs whom I knew most closely, I tend to think that what they sought above all was 'the *action*' in being leaders, the *involvement* in giving shape to the various individual lives of their followers, the *exercise* of administering the collective successfully and securing group advantage, conceptualized as 'strength', to its members. In truth, these benefits were of course allocated unequally and the leader's own interests were generally placed first; but for many practical purposes no clear distinction could be made between group advantage and personal advantage, and benefits were dispensed in accordance with shared expectations and norms of justice – not the ideal justice of the best of worlds, but the working arrangements of the existing, far-from-ideal real world.[6] I would thus be prepared to say that it is perhaps the *rank* of leader, rather than his *powers*, which constitutes the prize that most consciously motivates pretenders. The two used to be inseparable; but after the inception of the state of Swat much of the former could increasingly be achieved with little of

the latter through the option of state service. By 1954 increasing numbers of leaders were trying this option, despite the criticism and shame
which it entailed in terms of a strict, traditional code of manliness.
A common judgment made by the Wali, the chiefs themselves, and
their followers was that Khans were becoming 'soft'. Perhaps a more
penetrating observation which I once heard was the people were too
enamoured of empty and false status, which is probably most aptly
translated as that they were vainglorious. We shall return briefly below
to the dynamics whereby the more rigorous and exacting ideals of the
traditional chiefly role were conceptualized and sustained despite this
much broader and more diffuse general value attached to leadership.

If, rather than focussing on Swat in 1954, we look at the whole time
period 1915-78, we shall see a series of fundamental changes in the
character of clientship ties and the constitution of collective groups.
The changes provide important material on co-variation. Before the
establishment of the state of Swat, and in its earliest decades, a considerably more tightly instituted pattern seems to have prevailed. The formal
clientship arising from house tenancy contracts provided the basic
framework for patronage; and the *təlgerri* system (cf. note 3) assured
the political integration of each ward as unitary with respect to bloc
membership. All the landowners of the ward were united behind a
single 'elected' *malak* and a joint men's house, though the mode of providing for the expenses of the men's house could vary. As a consequence
of the *wesh* tenure system, leadership and membership automatically
came up for review in connection with migration and reallotment and
resettlement – this meant that *malaks* could only hope to retain their
rank if they had retained the confidence of a majority of the other
Pakhtuns of their group, and if no more influential alternative pretender
had arisen. The permanent residents of the village, likewise, could look
forward to a change of masters at every reallotment, and in the interim
they could cultivate or change their relationships to the different landowners within the ward freely, as these all belonged to the same bloc,
whereas any dramatic breach would have to entail moving to find
patronage in the other bloc. The general consensus is that Pakhtuns with
small shares of land wielded more influence on collective policy under
these circumstances, and that tenants for this reason may also have
been marginally more independent, whereas the higher craftsman and
trading groups (goldsmiths, particularly *paracha* traders) were much
weaker and highly exposed to arbitrary pressure and expropriation.

The role of the men's house followers, and of allies, in securing the property rights of every particular Pakhtun against rival Pakhtuns was paramount. Ahmed (pp. 61-2 and fn. 11) makes the passing claim that chiefs made important use of mercenaries as a source of physical force, without apparently realizing the implication such a datum would have. Clearly, the whole pattern of mobilization in conflict, and major aspects of politics and Pakhtun/non-Pakhtun relations, would be different if leaders maintained small companies of specialized soldiers rather than basing their force on influence through their network of contracts in the wider population and the large-scale conversion of rice into influence in men's house feasts. My own meticulous weighing of the evidence would indicate Ahmed's description to be erroneous. Prominent leaders have had fulltime companions and bodyguards (generally referred to as *tayar-khwor* shortened to *tĕrkhŏr*, literally 'eaters of ready-made food', and as men without substance held in low esteem in Swat) but these were few in number and never an important source of power for most Pakhtun leaders (see, however, their role in the Western Khanates, below p. 174). My evidence suggests that they may, on the other hand, have played a somewhat larger role in the followings of the few most prominent Saints and chiefs before the establishment of the state.

As the power and assurance of the state administration increased, changes were progressively introduced. Periodic reallotments were discontinued around 1930. The unity of the *təlgerri* system was progressively relaxed, and the position as *malak* of the ward went into abeyance. Conflicts were increasingly managed by organs of the administration, and the broader mobilization of followings by landowners was prevented. In 1954 confrontations would sometimes take place between swiftly gathered groups of between twenty and forty men, but they were reluctant to use firearms and expected to disperse on the arrival of the Wali's police. Characteristically, broader mobilization of force in such cases was forestalled by the posting of a policeman in each contestant's men's house, thereby discouraging the massing of followers and allies that would otherwise be the next move in escalation. But one must not naively conclude from this that a pugnacious show of force, demonstrating a broader following for one or another of the contestants, was without consequences for the final settlement. Particularly because the pervasive linkage in blocs extended throughout the territory, the Wali had to take account of local realities of power. This indeed provided the reason for the persistence of a grassroots political organization similar to that of pre-state times and non-state areas.

The emergence of new political alignments in Swat

The progressive integration of Swat into the wider economy, and the transport, trade, and in part local production which this entailed, opened the way for the accumulation of profits and wealth without a basis in land ownership. Together with permanent allotment, this also gave rise secondarily to a certain circulation of land by sale. Non-Pakhtuns (Saints of various categories, mullahs, carpenters and black-smiths) had long held a fraction of the land on special tenure (*siri*, cf. Barth, 1959a: 66); now they could also purchase plots. *Parachas* (muleteers and shopkeepers) and goldsmiths who obtained large cash incomes were particularly active as buyers. Such persons were already emancipated from any kind of clientship relation to Pakhtuns and were rather consistently protected and favoured by the Wali. A cumulative consequence was what Fautz (1963: 63f.) has aptly characterized as the 'ascent of the *parachas*' into the upper stratum − and of others, regardless of caste background, if they succeeded in achieving wealth or high administrative positions. During my presence in Swat in 1954 the Wali took a further step and started appointing forceful non-Pakhtuns as *malaks* in weak and divided wards; subsequently he started issuing certificates to landowners of modest size, whether Pakhtun or not, that they were '*malaks* of their own land'. This variously caused indigation or hilarity among the public and was seen as just more Pathan vainglory; the intent and probably the effect was to weaken further the foundations of locally and traditionally based leadership. Once this ground was sufficiently prepared, the Wali proceeded to undermine the bloc pattern. Till then, the alliance blocs had served the rulers as a main instrument of control through a strategy similar to that of major chiefs: by aligning with the weaker bloc the force of the state apparatus swung the scales and became a necessary factor for the minority bloc to retain its ascendancy. The Badshah had always been careful to hold the bloc together, and then switch sides before it grew so powerful as to no longer be dependent on state support. By the late 1950s, the Wali had started consciously interfering with the coalition-forming processes on which the blocs depended (cf. ch. 3 pp. 70-3). Instead of contributing to the normal pressures, enticing and forcing major defectors from one bloc to join the other bloc, he started 'making' third and fourth parties by publicly pledging support to the autonomy of defectors. Thus the whole two-bloc pattern disinte-grated − not as a conceptual scheme for actors and observers, which it still is in Swat, but as a corporate reality capable of concerted action.

The resulting picture of clientship and patronage in Swat by the mid 1960s was one where landowners as political leaders were drastically weakened, but came out strengthened in their superiority and security vis-à-vis tenants. Still overwhelmingly agrarian, productivity in Swat had not increased to keep up with growth in population and consumption needs, so there was ample cheap labour to be had for agricultural work. But landowners no longer needed their tenants' fealty for security of life and property, and so confined their relations with tenants to the economic sphere, and limited their contribution to a wage on whatever level that emerged on a labour market characterized by underemployment.

No longer locked with each other in a struggle to maintain their separate properties and security, landowners did not need to keep abreast with one another's acts or moves, nor were they constrained to cultivate their public image as leaders and adopt homologous measures to assure a following commensurate to their estate. Their life thus became for the first time in a sense private, their allocation of time, wealth and interest a matter of personal preference or taste. Some of them have, up till this very day, continued in a relatively unchanged old-fashioned Khan role — but if so, only active on the village level — while most have changed in various ways and degrees to a life more like that of members of the corresponding class in the administered territories of North Pakistan. For the first time in the history of Swat it would also be true to say, as Asad has erroneously claimed for earlier periods (Asad, 1972: 85), that the fact that the landless greatly outnumber the landowners was a source of strength for the latter: the disparity of advantage between those who need access to the production factor of land and *those who are secured it by a power outside themselves, i.e. the state* is greater, the more the land is monopolized. Yet this rendering gives only a very partial and banal account of the change. The landowner has secured his title to land only by giving up all claim to authority over his tenants outside the purely economic contract — he is no longer the *naëk* ('master') and has himself in fact to bow alongside with his former subjects before the new and greater power of the state. This loss of strength was inseparably connected with the gain of strength in security of ownership, since Swat state could only guarantee land titles by monopolizing effectively the use of force, i.e. crushing those who might wish to continue their roles as warlord *naëks*. But the state also used the carrot along with the stick: not only did the ruler himself likewise respect existing land rights and refrain from the arbitrary seizures that were previously practised; the dispensing of major and petty patronage also became increasingly important. 'Prominent' and loyal persons could obtain higher education for their sons, advantageous contracts and licenses, promotions in higher state administration, etc. And by disproportionately manning the higher echelons of the administration, many of them could – though as individuals politically emasculated compared to the chiefs of yore – have a marginal influence over the values and criteria whereby state policy on various matters was decided and executed, and so perhaps have rather more of an impact on the state of the world than they once had as autonomous leaders.

As seen from the perspective of the propertyless, this consolidation of the state provided new and unprecedented security. It gave new freedoms by eliminating the regime of semi-feudal leadership with its element of personal arbitrariness and tyranny. It also provided extensively increased facilities, such as hospitals, schools, roads and public transport, valued by all. But the new situation provided little material progress, since population growth made land increasingly scarce and men's house feasting and other chiefly patronage all but disappeared. It also contained little which could rally broader groups and foster loyalties and a sense of belonging: the process whereby leaders had formerly built and deployed their followings were not replaced by other sets of events that created excitement, a sense of importance, or commitment among participants. To sum up, through a series of swiftly incremental small steps, Swat had been transformed to a society more like that of neighbouring areas, although with a, in many ways, 'model' administration.

In 1969, external forces overtook Swat, and the state was finally integrated into Pakistan's civil administration. Shortly thereafter Pakistan itself was overtaken by the chain of events let loose by the fiery politician Zulfikar Ali Bhutto. The main changes that affected the inhabitants of Swat were briefly as follows.

With integration, what had been a small and highly centralized/ co-ordinated bureaucracy became compartmentalized into a number of separate local departments, each tied to large national ministries and agencies and not to each other. Senior personnel were mostly transferred quite swiftly in and out of Swat, and saw their work and careers in national rather than local context. As a result, administration has often worked at cross purposes and with little capacity to pursue any consistent or long-range constructive policy.

The Badshah's extensive private properties, and other large properties previously unaffected by twenty years' land reform legislation in Pakistan, were dismantled — in the case of the former the matter was particularly unclear in that final decision and settlement was postponed and had still not been arranged by autumn 1978. Most prominent members of the former state administration were retired. Thus all the previous leadership positions, based on property and/or public posts, were eliminated.

The first modern election took place in 1970. Both on that occasion and subsequently some of the previous leaders sought to obtain a new mandate for leadership and rank. In this they were generally successful; but the spectacle of former landowning chiefs, prominences of Swat state administration, and most of all the sons of the Wali himself, canvassing door-to-door in the villages and asking the propertyless for their support and vote, is reported to have been a profound and shaking experience for many erstwhile followers.

The program by which Bhutto rallied his national electorate was one of social welfare and radical change, involving a 'New Deal' for the masses, strong labour unions, fundamental land reform, etc. The rhetoric by which he swept the country with him was one which constantly reiterated the essential rights of the now propertyless, of the worker against the leisured, of the simple man against the former exploiters.

These signals also affected the courts which, besides being flooded beyond capacity with complaints and conflicts, were unsure and reluctant to act decisively, particularly in cases where they might appear to uphold privileges against progressive attack.

Responses within Swat were swift. Tenants on the land of many big landowners discontinued paying rent, whether redistribution of the land was pending or not. Claims of ownership were pressed on various bases, including that of having been the tenant-cultivator of a plot, and many conflicts were, at least provisionally, settled by fiat. Labour unions were formed, and demands articulated. Individual leaders emerged among local tenants and villagers; according to informants Gujars have been disproportionately many and prominent among them, practising an entirely new style of local 'firebrand' leadership. For the very first time, collectivities of tenants have also engaged in armed confrontation and battle against landowners (and their followers) in some areas, particularly Sebujni.

It was thus in the politically merged Swat of the mid-70s that the groups posited by Asad as being 'more important' than those making up chiefs' followings and blocs (Asad, 1972: 85) first emerged. We have seen through the preceding sketch how drastically different, in a number of respects, this society was from that of Swat in 1954 with which both Asad and I were concerned. Yet the documentation of these differences allows us to raise Asad's basic questions more fruitfully and with more hope of being answered: what was the form and importance of class consciousness in Swat at different time periods, how were the interests of the 'hungry men' variously articulated, and what appear to have been the preconditions for their leading to any kind of collective action dichotomizing asymmetric classes?

One may first speculate somewhat over how the Bhutto message could sweep so swiftly through Swat and have such profound effects. I would note the coincidence that it followed on the heels of a general demolition of the whole traditional edifice of authority; it coincided with an external administration which was indecisive and inconsistent, and with a rush of land distributions suggesting that valuable resources were 'up for grabs'; and it was accompanied by promises from Pakistan's premier and his party's activists, validated by court practice, that the common man would now be favoured. It also rested on some principles so simple as to seem self-evidently just in almost any ideology acknowledging human dignity (as Pathan culture most emphatically does): that the fruits of labour should belong to him who labours, that a cultivator should have (his own) land to cultivate, etc.

A recurrent phrase when people (of different strata) spoke to me in 1978, after Bhutto's fall, about these events and conflicts of recent years was 'you can have heard no such talk when you were here' — often followed by the assertion that, before, no man would even *think* that he had any rights to a plot just because he and his father cultivated it. To obtain people's direct and considered evaluation of the mood of those times, I tried asking how Bhutto's ideas could have spead so quickly, unless some such thoughts had already been familiar — and the answer was yes, of course pupils in Jahanzeb College heard such things, and the ideas were also more widely diffused 'below', i.e. in the administered areas of Pakistan; but at least no one would think them out loud in Swat before.

Yet this is not entirely accurate. Pathans in Swat in 1954, and I believe even more so in previous decades, were certainly not meek and subdued folk; and the inequalities of society in those times were stark. I believe I depicted this reasonably adequately and truly in the monograph which is Asad's main target for critique, and that his displeasure arises from the absence of certain Marxist terms in my description, rather than its content. Not only did I reject the functionalist assumption that institutionalized behaviour patterns are *ipso facto* normatively sanctioned, and maintain — as I have sought to clarify here (*contra* Asad) — that trying to make the best of a situation (in exercising choice) does not entail cherishing the situational constraints under which one is choosing. I also meant to show through parts of the text that life-situations were not subjectively embraced as happy and right. The imagery of *mor* and *wugge*, satisfied and hungry men (Barth, 1959a: 79), is certainly not a neutral or morally speaking consensual expression. In this connection I also remember vividly an evening by the fire in Biha village when a tenant of Swati descent, with histrionics but deep emotion, suddenly leapt up and cursed all the Yusufzai Pakhtuns for conquering this land — and his own ancestors for losing it (in the sixteenth century!), leaving him an impoverished tenant (cf. Barth, 1959a: 24f.)

There is no doubt that there was widespread and clearly expressed discontent: with poverty and toil; with subjugation — not just with the cases of bad treatment judged by local conventions, but with the very fact of having to bow to *anybody's* authority; with how the fortunate ones enjoyed wealth and privilege. We grasp the form of this discontent truly only if we see it in local cultural terms, not by renaming it class exploitation and class consciousness. I understand the key to lie in the values of pride, autonomy and assertion which are embraced by the whole Pathan population, not just by the landowning Pakhtuns or the privileged leaders among them. One indication of the importance which the common man and non-Pakhtun attaches to these values is the vigour with which he pursues them when the chance arises: on a bus across the Kabul river, as an upstart tenant activist, etc. The zest with which such persons plunge into the role, the care with which they orchestrate their performance to exhibit recklessness, autonomy, assurance and tactical shrewdness, indicate that these are properties which the person values and wishes to embody. In a life situation where such modes of expression were frustrated or could only rarely and imperfectly be realized, yet where others were given the opportunity to excel, one has no reason to doubt the strength of discontent, or the intensity of awareness of it.

But it is of course in its *mode* of conceptualization that one finds the key to how such discontent propels persons to act. Here, a concept of class interests makes analysis difficult by obfuscating, in practice, the distinction between an external and internal viewpoint, as Asad has done in his reanalysis. To understand the way people act in this situation, we need to find out what visions people may have of how to mobilize and organize collective force behind their discontent, i.e. what organizational models exist. Secondly, we have to judge these models in terms of their implications for the potential rank and file: what do they promise or entail of change in the position of all the others, those who recognize that they will be 'followers' also in the future? And, thirdly, what are the military and tactical realities, as seen by potential participants: do they see a subjective chance of success? It is a striking fact that as far as we know there was *never* a 'peasant uprising' in Swat until those skirmishes in Sebujni in the 1970s. The different forms of society which have characterized Swat up till then did not produce the kind of riots and uprisings that were a recurring accompaniment of agrarian exploitation elsewhere, e.g. in European or Chinese history. Why? Not because of an absence of discontent. My answer in the Swat monograph was in terms of the tenant's opportunity situation and the ways in which Pakhtun and Saint leaders rallied supporters and engaged in alliances and strife. With the insight provided by change and co-variation, it is worth reconsidering the issue.

Contrasting 1974 with 1954, we see so many fundamental differences that it may be difficult to identify the decisive factors in the co-variation. But clearly, there was a local power vacuum and a promise of external support, and there were new organizational models. As for the first point, gone was the danger of massive Pakhtun reaction which would put down an uprising. So as not to create a false picture of traditional society I might emphasize that there is *no* reason to assume that Pakhtuns in the old days would have acted collectively with the purpose to maintain their collective class interests. Swat was almost certainly conquered once in the sixteenth century by such a corporate army of Yusufzai Pakhtuns, but there is no evidence that Pakhtuns in Swat in the nineteenth or twentieth century had the capacity to re-create such unity or had a vision of such collective class interests. What would have happened, were the peasants to arise in any area, was that Pakhtuns with their followers would descend from other areas on the now fatefully weakened or dispossessed local Pakhtuns, seize their lands and divide the spoils. The *effect* would be the mobilization of massive force against the collective of tenants − but in pursuit of the spoils and not in defence of 'Pakhtun sovereignty' or 'social equilibrium'. As part of the peasants' consciousness of the tactical realities of the scene, however, this threat was no doubt an important deterrent. Later, the state of Swat clearly likewise served as a deterrent, having pledged to support existing land rights. The power vacuum created by the removal or immobilization of both these forces by integration of Swat into Pakistan administration, combined with the populist promises of the Bhutto regime, clearly created an entirely new situation.

Secondly, new models of organization were available. One may identify three traditional organizational patterns by which collectives capable of corporate political and military action were formed (1) a Chief (or Saint) and his following, (2) a patrilineal descent group, (3) a flock rallied by an inspired religious leader (*faqir*) for the purpose of holy war. I cannot see how any of these could provide the organizational model for a class-based uprising. The first reaffirms the existing leadership pattern and so entails no vision, or promise, of a different situation for the rank and file of tenants. A discontented and ambitious tenant might wish to spearhead such a movement, but would have little to offer to entice followers away from alternative, established leaders with resources and experience. Saints, on the other hand, seem at times to have served as rallying points for such groups of malcontents, but to have been militarily successful only in the unirrigated and peripheral hill areas, where the cost of conquest clearly exceeded the profits to be gained for potential Pakhtun reconquerors. (E.g. the uppermost Jambil valley became Saints' property in this fashion, cf. Barth, 1959a: 95). The second organizational mould, of a patrilineal descent group, was clearly not available for a coalition of disgruntled tenants of various castes and lineages. The third form, of inspired religious leadership, seems never (*pace* the main thesis of Ahmed, 1976) to have been directed inward as a millennial reformation of society in accord with a new vision of social organization. Such leaders led small conquering bands of Pathans, probably of mixed origin, into the northern and eastern Kohistani areas when these were still pagan, and in part settled the converting fighters as petty landowners in the subjugated areas. They led large, temporary armies in defence of regions against infidel (Sikh and British) threats or dominance. They also fought each other, on points of dogma and theological alignment. But there is no evidence within Swat that they ever articulated the sectorial and collective interests of a class of non-landowners.[7] It was thus not till Bhutto's sponsoring of labour unions that an alternative organizational form was introduced which clearly allowed co-ordination and leadership without the simultaneous reaffirmation of traditional land ownership patterns, and thus a potential mode of collective organization for non-landowners.

Which of these major changes provided the necessary preconditions for the emergence of collective tenants' movements, or whether the coincidence of all was necessary, cannot be determined from this historical sequence. Indeed, I believe that a true picture of the causalities involved also must emphasize more strongly that by the time the power structure of Swat state was eliminated, a resurgence or return to traditional Khan leadership had been precluded by the essential disappearance of traditional Khans. Such leaders had with justification been regarded as turning progressively 'soft' over the last generation, and had for a decade or more almost entirely defaulted on their obligations as leaders and patrons. In fact, there were attempts (instigated by the ex-Wali, according to rumour) in 1974 to rally Swati consciousness and pride behind a local 'Khans' party', but this quickly proved ineffectual. Yet in terms of the values embraced by the common man back in 1954, the idea would not seem at all impossible. I do not wish to imply by the preceding description of broad discontent that there were not also powerful other orientations at that time, co-existing with and partly negating the discontent. The 'consciousness' of a population is rarely consistent and of one piece. Admiration for strong and assertive leaders was marked (cf. Barth, 1959a: 81ff) and respect for one's *naëk*, 'master' was for many persons the predominant attitude, involving both identification of the follower's own interest with his lot, and a vicarious identification with his greatness and glory. Secondly, there was a clearly conceptualized logic and justness in the exchange on which clientage relations were based: the client obtained valued access to land, house, and security in return for loyalty and support. Finally, there may also have been a third component of some importance in the clients' self-image or identity. Villagers in the main Swat valley expressed, to my mind excessive, contempt for the culture and life of the northern neighbouring Kohistanis, associating them with backwardness, dispersed settlement, and an anarchic, chiefless freeholder organization. In contrast, Swatis took pride in identifying with what they saw as their own advanced society of big nucleated villages, bazaar markets, fertile irrigated lands, large-scale political institutions and famous leaders. I believe a more egalitarian organization was, by them, inherently associated with the impoverished and reduced social patterns of these despised peripheries and therefore, on balance, conceived as unattractive. Materials from the Pathan freeholding areas of Ghorband/Chakesar noted above (p. 126) would provide interesting perspective in this connection.

In other words, in the villages of the Swat valley in 1954, there was, as one might expect, both marked identification with existing leadership and institutions, and dissatisfaction with them. The dissatisfaction was however conceptualized *not* as an awareness of common interests with other unfortunates with a vision that suppression could be eliminated, but rather as a frustration of one's own drive to achieve influence, wealth and rank. The forms of consciousness that *did* serve as a basis for group formation and collective identities were thus the ones on which I based my analysis in the above articles, and the 1959 monograph. The key 'myth' by which economic inequality was justified (but not therefore *ipso facto* desirable, just, or obligating for the unprivileged!) was that of conquest of the valley by Yusufzai armies, giving rise to the constituting land rights. The failure of the ancestors of other groups to establish such dominance entailed the necessity for their descendants to make other arrangements to secure a living: by labour, crafts, trade etc., and other necessary accommodations by means of the exchanges and reciprocities they were able to sustain. On this fundamental basis, the leadership patterns and collective groups observable at the time and described in my publications emerged.

Stratum and caste

The gross division between the hungry and the satisfied men was thus an imagery to depict one's own (unsatisfactory) life situation, and not a schema of class identities. To conceptualize rank or stratum as social identities, Swat Pathans in 1954 employed the categories of *qoum*, i.e. caste, as described above in chapter 2. I thus maintain, *contra* Asad (1972: 83), that it is not by my analysis that 'the basic class structure of Swat is refracted through the categories of *caste* and *lineage*'; on the contrary these were the concepts whereby the Swat Pathans ordered and interpreted their existence. What they thereby participated in can well be characterized as a structure of agrarian exploitation (though not with the particular features of Asad's class construct, or the historical developments which he conjectures); but this does not make caste concepts and categories into something through which reality is 'refracted', but on the contrary establishes these concepts as significant empirical constituents of that reality.

My labelling of the *qoum* categories as 'castes' has occasioned some criticism and debate from other quarters (see esp. Leach, 1960; Dumont, 1967, 1970). My reasons for using the concept 'caste', and the sense in which it was used, are set out in chapter 2. The issue raised is essentially whether Swat *qoums* are sufficiently similar to Indian castes to be subsumed under the same label, and whether indeed any social category in the context of a culture not permeated by Hindu concepts could exhibit a sufficient number of such features. Dumont develops this line of criticism in detail (1967: 29-31, 35ff.). He is clearly correct that the Swat idea of *qoum* does not constitute a unified set of premises to anywhere like the extent which the Hindu caste concept does; likewise that the most fundamental criterion of hierarchy in Swat may be that differentiating patrons from clients, or the conceptually 'free' from the 'ruled', and not the purer from the impurer. But I have misgivings about an argument which would relegate an empirical description of one society from a typological category because of the imperfections described, and contrast it to a wide range of (Hindu) social systems represented by a highly abstracted ideal-type description only. By such strict standards as this, I doubt that many historical forms of *Hindu* caste would qualify as 'caste systems'. I doubt the empirical reality of the devaluation of secular power relations in Indian societies, on which Dumont sets such store (ibid, p. 34), particularly if we sought to marshal empirical data on the politically less moribund traditional India of a couple of centuries ago. In that comparison, I think it is in the absence of a social model entailing a *state* that we would find the main contrast between Swat and the range of Hindu systems. But perhaps more fundamentally, I believe Dumont and I are arguing from two incompatible ontological perspectives. He seems to me to be speaking entirely in terms of a (highly selective and intellectualized) native *model of* a caste society, and to ignore the problematics of transforming this, if so can be done at all, into an actors' *model for* caste behaviour. My concern, as always, was primarily directed to this latter focus, seeking to identify factors which lay behind empirical patterns and generated them.

In recent years, we have seen the emergence of a far more sophisticated insight into the cultural ideas that lie behind Indian caste behaviour, through a close interactional analysis of such behaviour and an illuminating exposition of the cultural conceptualizations of the person which canalizes this behaviour (Marriott and Inden, 1974 and elsewhere). This new perspective allows us to reformulate the issue. We no longer need to compare the social forms exhibited by Swat *qoums* and various Indian caste systems, as overt epiphenomena, and try to judge whether they are sufficiently similar to be included in one typological class of 'caste systems'. We may now rather analyse whether indeed the concepts of person which generate these forms are in themselves sufficiently similar, and the processes thereby set in motion sufficiently analogous in the two cases, to be classed together. I am not prepared to give the answer, since I lack the empirical materials from Swat which would demonstrate such similarity or difference decisively. But I judge this to be the most fertile way in which the question can now be raised. In the present text I shall continue to refer to the *qoums* of Swat by the English word 'caste'.

A basic model of Swat society

The two basic social identities or memberships on which society in Swat in 1954 was based can thus be described as (1) caste, subsuming lineage as a set of subdivisions for those castes where this is relevant; (2) bloc, subsuming for all persons a local subdivision or faction of political-economic alignment under one, or a group of identified leaders; and (3) the all-pervasive distinction of sex, debarring women from any prominent or active public role. To construct a model of Swat society with the widest possible relevance in time and space, I would compose this model of a small set of 'key dynamics' working on this basis, with variable intensity and consequences under varying parametric conditions. Under each such key dynamics, I shall show how the main institutional changes that have taken place in the present century have effected changing parameters. The most important institutional changes which I shall treat are (a) changes in the land tenure system; (b) monetization and commercialization; (c) population growth, and (d) the development of the state.

Key dynamics I: The formation of social identities

The different caste components of society in Swat are thought of, and their members think of themselves, as highly distinct and subject to distinctive standards and expectations. Yet they also share most basic cultural premises and value orientations. It is likewise obvious that the

standards and values associated with particular castes have changed
drastically in the present century, so that persons perform acts and
pursue goals which would have been rejected a generation earlier, and
vice versa. Rather than seek to construct elaborate value codes for each
caste category, and then detail the great number of cultural changes
that have taken place over the last six decades, I propose that we should
seek to grasp this situation by a model which is much simpler and,
I believe, much truer to the dynamics of the phenomena in question.
We should recognize that the different *quoms* in Swat live in intimate
co-residence, and that there are few organizational features which
would allow them to maintain distinctive subcultural traditions. Let us
therefore rather assume that they partake in a common tradition of
shared cultural values, and that these values are also relatively stable
through time. What clearly differs at different times is the *circumstances* under which these values are practised, i.e. transformed into
action, and likewise the life-situations in which different categories
of person practise them. As between persons of different castes, it
would follow that there are systematic differences in the relative feasa-
bility of different ways of acting; that there will be systematic differences in the life experiences which they will accumulate, and thus the
self-image that they will form; and that there will be systematic differences in the expectations one can reasonably direct towards persons of
different castes. Our model for social identities should thus be
composed of the salient features of life circumstances for different
castes at different times, which could generate such systematic differences in experience, expectations, and behaviour.

Let us consider first the situation before 1930, when the *wesh*
periodic land reallotments were practised. Briefly, these involved the
decennial rotation of the different segments within each branch of the
Yusufzai Pakhtuns as temporary landowners of different parts of their
joint estate (cf. Barth, 1959a: 65-5, or above ch. 3; also Fautz, 1963,
especially pp. 55-63). A necessary implication of this tenure system was
the massive migration of the whole Pakhtun population, but not the
other castes, to a new area and new villages every ten years. In view of
the confusion (and inconsistency) introduced by Ahmed on this point
(Ahmed, 1976: 40, 60, 123-4) it is important to reassert the empirical
fact that *all* Pakhtun landowners did in fact participate in these migrations: older persons who themselves had participated were definite on
this in conversations with me in 1954; no written evidence would
suggest differently; and it is also obviously impossible to reallot the

land so that relative and absolute sizes of allotments are reproduced at each new reallotment unless the land areas concerned have been standardized and *all* allotment holders move. But what are the practical, life-experience implications of this for members of different castes? The Pakhtuns were maintained as a highly distinct gentry without membership in *any* village community. Whether mighty Khans or owners of shares so small that they employed only one, or, theoretically, even no tenant of their own, they were categorically distinguished from the villagers. Their life centered on the men's house of their segment and faction, and on their contracts for organizing production and administering their temporary wards. The kin-and-neighbour associations for celebration of *gham-khadi*, sorrow and happiness – i.e. all life crisis – which to other villagers defined their circles of lifelong commitment and belonging, connected Pakhtuns with strangers for a limited period, and posed problems of felicitous cultivation and withdrawal to secure maximal support and following, rather than emotional identification. The critical and clearly conceptualized task of attracting followers and thus establishing a power platform in the (new) area, so strongly emphasized in Pakhtun consciousness of their position and particularly in their reminiscences of *wesh* times, was highly dramatized under these conditions.

Indeed, *wesh* tenure seems to have posed a number of problems which were troublesome to the landowners. Not only do they describe with amused despair the complications of transporting last year's manure to the new locale (but what did the tenant think, whose field was often not manured during the last year before *wesh* and who saw this source of plenty being carted away?), or the disincentives to develop orchards and gardens. They also seem to have disliked the hazards of having to establish new work teams and new followings among stranger villagers every ten years; and powerful families and factions tried to reduce this effect by avoiding full rotation and simply shifting every ten years between two alternative, stable residence areas: by rigging the lot-drawing that governed sub-allotments in some areas, or unilaterally demanding their old sites in the council meetings that they were able to dominate.

Permanent allotment was established by the then ruler of Swat around 1930. The true combination of purposes he had with this was probably known only to him, but the initiative apparently met little opposition, perhaps for the reasons noted above. The full effects of the change naturally were not felt till near the 1940s, when the next moves should have been effected and were not, though some orchard planting etc. had tentatively started before that. What followed progressively was an assimilation of Pakhtuns into the village community of their residence, analogous to the situation which had always prevailed for landowners of Saintly descent. The relative differences between Pakhtuns who were large or small landowners respectively became more apparent and their similarities less emphasized. Pakhtuns who lost their land were less unequivocally sloughed off from their caste, since they continued to co-reside with their descent group and most likely continued to frequent the same men's house. Leadership positions tended to become more entrenched, since there was no periodic, whole-sale reordering of Pakhtun co-residence and faction, including the institution of a new or reaffirmed *malak* for each ward (cf. above, p. 142). Thus Pakhtuns became progressively less differentiated from the other castes, but more differentiated internally, while the common features of Pakhtuns and Saints as landowners became more apparent.

A second set of circumstances is connected with the creeping monetization of labour and land. We have seen how the traditional organization of division of labour involved persons in comprehensive, unquantified functional roles in return for shares of the gross harvest. To partake in agricultural production, and certain other functions as barber, priest etc., entailed entering into a co-operating group and assuming *all* the conventional tasks of one's occupation vis-à-vis *all* members of that group. Thus one's occupational role tended naturally to merge with one's social personality. The member of a caste was in no way forced to practise his caste occupation; but that was what he was trained and skilled to do, and so castes tended to monopolize their occupational functions and remain with them to the extent that there was such employment to be had. Alternatively, a person would have to exercise all the skills and assume all the tasks of another occupation if he were to choose it — and over time become assimilated to that identity. Only cultivation represented a set of skills which was widely disseminated in the population, and open to persons as a sub-sidiary occupation since any size of plot could be taken on tenancy contract. It is consistent with this that persons of cultivator caste (*zamidari qoum*) would frequently give their identity in terms of a named descent group, and then, if they felt it was needed, explain that it was a cultivator group. For all other groups, caste seemed in 1954 still to provide the label for the *kind* of person they were, whereas village (by then also for Pakhtuns) provided the label for the community to which they belonged.

With increasing monetization, and increased circulation of land for money, I doubt that this is still the case. I am told that most products are increasingly bought item by item, as industrial goods or from craftsmen in the market, rather than being secured by service contracts. Labour for daily or monthly wages has become common; and a diversity of employment, depending in part on educational qualifications, has become accessible in government service or private enterprise. Differences in wealth and capital *within* occupational categories are reflected in specialization and diverse adaptations to markets and clientele, and are also directly transformable into real property regardless of caste. The homogeneity of life-situation and opportunity-situation that used to characterize persons of the same caste position has thus disappeared, while the differences between castes have become increasingly blurred. Some consciousness and identity still adheres to caste origins; thus non-Pakhtun members of the elite complain about the presumption of Pakhtuns in assuming themselves to be naturally more capable and fit to lead, take responsibility and dominate decisions. More generally, there is much talk about the lack of respect for authority: of the young for the old, of the common man for the person with greater knowledge or responsibility. I would see this in a slightly different perspective, and argue that 'respect for authority' was never a dominant norm among the people of Swat. But there used to be a far closer, and therefore more systematic, relationship between authority positions and respect, because what emerged as authority positions did so as the direct result of achieved positions of power, and thereby the command of effective sanctions with which to exact respect. Conversely, the person who was unable to command respect would thereby automatically see his claim to authority and position crumble. Besides, higher castes were by virtue of the various advantages they enjoyed in a position where they could in fact excel, by commonly shared standards, and thus win admiration more readily than they can today.

We can thus see a dynamic relationship between social categories, the life experiences which persons in these categories differentially accumulate, and the concrete role expectations and self-images entailed by membership. Where the actual experiences that accumulate become more equivocal, I would also argue that the categories themselves probably become less clear and less salient to the actors, as have caste

positions in Swat in recent decades. But economic and political circumstances in Swat used to be such that a relatively distinctive and shared
opportunity-situation, and life experience, characterized each caste
category. As a consequence they used to provide highly meaningful
identities for self-identification, and identification of others. Therefore we need not assume that the particular features of each caste are
predicated by basic values peculiar to each, but rather that they are
generated by the life experiences characteristic of members of each
caste, and thus susceptible to quite fundamental changes in ways which
reflect, *post facto*, changes in these experiences.

   This argument could be pursued for each of the *qoums* for which
I have reasonably much data. But I shall choose here to pursue it
particularly for Pakhtuns and Saints, as epitomized in the distinctive
leadership roles of persons from these two castes. This allows me to
develop somewhat further the thesis on leadership in Swat found in my
previous publications.

Key dynamics II: The bifurcation of leadership roles in 'lions' and 'foxes'

As I have shown elsewhere (Barth, 1959a: 71-103), we find in the Swat
valley two kinds of local political leaders: Chiefs (sing. *Khan*) who are
members of the Pakhtun caste, and senior men among the descendants
of Saints (of various particular descent categories, but generally labelled
by their largest sub-category as *Mian*). Whereas about a quarter of the
population of Swat are Pakhtuns, only about one man in fifty would
be sensibly classified as Chief; but they may be seen to realize in its
characteristic form the role most cherished and admired by Pakhtuns.
Among the (smaller) total population of descendants of Saints, a larger
proportion of persons occupy a position of seniority and exercise
leadership functions, but they still compose far from a majority of the
caste membership. As in previous publications, I shall refer to these
leading *Mians* for simplicity as Saints because of their descent status.

   The empirical focus of my interest was the fact that in Swat in 1954,
and even more in the preceding few generations, both Chiefs and Saints
wielded practical, secular power, but based this on followings of very
different structure. Chiefs drew their followers mainly from their own
tenants and dependents, and those of smaller Pakhtuns who were
aligned with them (*Zmā pa lās ke* – in my hand) within their own
ward(s) and village(s). This following they controlled and mobilized

through the men's house. Saints had smaller, but more widely dispersed, followings, consisting of scattered disciples and clients in a group of villages or even larger area. They did not keep or frequent men's houses, but were often associated with a shrine, or frequented a small mosque. Their lands were generally scattered, and not subject to *wesh* redistribution; technically known as *siri* land in contrast to the *daftar* of Pakhtuns, it did not give the right to speak in local and regional councils. The influence of a Chief would reach beyond his own following, and might allow him to dominate a local area. The influence of a Saint, on the other hand, could be much more widely diffused, and more pervasive in the population, though no doubt generally much weaker, than that of a Chief. Chiefs endeavoured to assert authority, to command and rule, in their men's house and in the local and regional councils in which they sat; and they led their followers and faction in confrontation and battle. Saints sought more to exercise moral leadership, to influence general opinion, and to serve as mediators and peacemakers in conflict. Very few of the *Mians* of Swat in 1954 were outstanding Islamic theologians or jurists, or deeply dedicated religious thinkers. Many of them, indeed, seemed no more 'religious' than the rest of the population. This may in part have been due to the founding ruler's systematic expulsion of all rival religious leaders after his election of kingship in 1917; but I also think it may have been true in earlier times and reflects the characteristic praxis adopted by *Mians*. Saints were accorded a certain respect for reasons of their association through descent with religious power; but as leaders they had to prove themselves pragmatically in everyday life.

The striking thing is that they did this in a manner very different from the other type of leader, the Chiefs. Whereas Chiefs seemed in their role performance to be concerned to project an image of forcefulness, vitality, and power, Saints were conspicuously softspoken, reflective, and controlled. Chiefs sometimes performed to excess in hospitality, noisiness and assertion; Saints were withdrawn and calm. Chiefs often dressed in pastel colours, or the grey-blue cloth associated in Swat with military uniform, or even in strong primary colours; Saints almost invariably dressed in white. These contrasts harmonized with the expectations generally directed towards the two kinds of leaders and the distinctive standards by which they were judged. On several occasions, I noted down the laudatory adjectives, used in conjunction with *sarei*, man, in spontaneous conversation about particular Chiefs and Saints respectively. The contrasts can be listed as follows:

Chief	Saint	
kha	*kha*	(good)
sam	*sam*	(fine)
ghat	-	(heavy, like a rock)
-	*loe*	(tall, like a tree)
zorawár	-	(forceful)
-	*zbərge*	(great, august)
nár	-	(male, virile)
-	*Mian*	(saintly)

With respect to the final item, we might note that the exclamation *Mian sarei*, 'Saintly fellow', is also idiomatic for 'miser'.

In my monograph (Barth, 1959a), I sought to analyse the contrasts in leadership behaviour as arising out of the different standards by which Chiefs and Saints were judged when attempting to establish and rally a following. This I will still maintain is a revealing perspective; but I may have given exaggerated prominence to the contrast in *values* between Chiefs and Saints as an irreduceable ideological source for the differences in behaviour of Chiefs and Saints. After all, the most successful person in the latter category was the Badshah of Swat himself — and he in no way epitomized the 'Saintly' mode of demeanour and action, and in some ways adopted the style of Chiefs. Likewise, if one looks at the interests, behaviour and poses of persons of the emerging new elite in 1954, the contrasts in style between members of the two castes were not very marked. Let us therefore instead attempt to develop the argument of contrasting opportunity situation *without* assuming the primacy of ideological differences as a premise for the contrast, but rather assume as we did in our discussion of caste, above, that value standards and priorities are basically homogeneous and shared unless proved otherwise. In other words, we shall assume that both courage *and* wisdom, both force *and* restraint, are valued by all and admired in leaders by all. Why then the systematic differences in behaviour?

Let me sketch the dynamics that I believe is at work to produce such a contrast. To generate life-like behaviour, we must start with the premises for action which arise in concrete circumstances, not in a theoretical vacuum. Let us choose to place ourselves in the circumstances prevailing in the unmonetized Swat valley, as for example around 1930.

Chiefs, as Pakhtuns, are members of the main landowning group.

We have seen that leadership positions among them are achieved and not ascribed, and that rank is eagerly sought after by many. Those who enter into competition for such positions naturally make use of the special assets they command, i.e. land and wealth. Thus the biggest landowners tend, unless they have a debilitating lack of other qualities, to become Chiefs, and to maintain this position against rivals and challengers by means of the advantages which this asset gives them.

The basic conversions of their feudal 'enterprise' — or the relevant processes of social reproduction, if you will — may be seen in Figure 7.1:

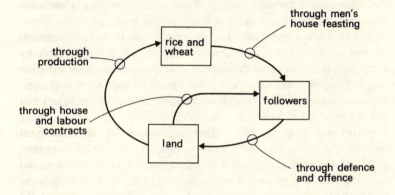

FIGURE 7.1

What can such a leader do if his position is threatened? To increase production is always desirable, but any dramatic increase is difficult to implement and not swift in its effects. It thus provides no short-term answer to a challenge. To increase his influence over followers by establishing numerous house contracts and labour contracts is always attractive to a Chief; but at any particular time all his resources will in fact be committed in such contracts and little can be won by a sudden reshuffling. To increase his men's house feasting, on the other hand, is swiftly and easily done if the Chief has any stores of rice etc. at all; and it has an immediate effect in increasing his visible and available following. Indeed this could be observed as a standard response of Chiefs during political crises in 1954; and some even secretly sold land to maintain a high level of men's house activity when they were under pressure. Finally, to intensify the use of followers in defence and offense provides an obvious strategy to increase the power and effect of a Chief's 'enterprise'. A Chief is thus in an objective position where his optimal strategy when pressed will be to 'act like lions' – to roar in his men's house, and show and use force – or, in other words, demonstrate and excel in the qualities depicted in the adjectives listed above, p. 160.

Most Saints are in rather a different opportunity situation. They are landowners, and thus autonomous and in a position as potential political leaders; but their landed properties are mostly much smaller and much less fertile, providing far more modest incomes. To compete with Chiefs in sheer mass of house- and land tenancies, or in hospitality and gift-giving in men's houses, is therefore self-defeating. Their independence, on the other hand, and their position outside the segmentary system of descent and rivalry (cf. chapter 3), give them certain tactical advantages. Their status as descendants of holy men also gives them the advantage, if not of inviolability then at least a reluctance among most people to cause them harm, and a willingness to show them respect by listening to them. These modest advantages can best be exploited in a role as negotiators and mediators between other and perhaps more powerful leaders, particularly if these are structurally prevented from entering into direct communication, or constrained in their maneuverability in negotiations. In other words, Saints are in a position where they best can win influence by 'acting like foxes', and demonstrating the qualities of wisdom and impartiality implied in the list of adjectives appropriate to them.

Unless positively *prevented* by ideological interdictions, one would thus expect Chiefs and Saints to adopt their respective standard roles for entirely practical reasons that arise from their objective circumstances. Their roles can, in other words, be generated without the benefit of any distinctive ideological demands directed differentially towards 'warlords' and 'holy men'. While analysing my first field material, I was struck by how the two statuses show very clear system properties of the kind discussed by Bateson in his early and highly perceptive paper (Bateson, 1949) under the label of 'schismogenesis' – positive reinforcement. One can readily see how competition and rivalry can arise between Chiefs, leading to 'symmetrical schismogenesis': each trying to overbid the other in increasingly excessive men's house spending and use of force. Such sequences could be observed between a few competing Chiefs in 1954, and were the theme of many stories of Chiefs in the preceding generation. Saints likewise, if they compete with each other for positions of influence, would be expected to contend by trying to excel and exceed each other in the performance of their characteristic role, though it is empirically less apparent how this was done – perhaps because seeking to outfox one another is naturally a more covert activity.

Most revealing, however, is the question of controls on such symmetrical schismogenesis, and the effects of Chiefs and Saints acting together and in competition with each other. Clearly the rivalry between Chiefs as constituted in this basic model takes on the classical features of an 'arms race' (Bateson, ibid. p. 37), which has as its only outcome either the total destruction of one or the collapse in exhaustion of both. Empirically speaking, the former outcome was the exception, and the latter difficult to identify. But the political arena in Swat contained both Chiefs and Saints, and I would argue that their interdependence was close and profound. There is no evidence for oscillation between the two types of leaders, on the pattern posited by Pareto in his theory of the circulation of the elites (Pareto, 1963). What we see instead is a clear complementarity leading to the emergence of each kind of leader as a distinctive institutionalized type. It is reasonable to imagine that the statuses Chief and Saint reinforce each other conceptually in Swat culture by virtue of the contrasts which they embody, i.e. they provide a kind of conceptual polarity of types. But more directly arising out of the preceding sketch, I would contend that they also reinforce each other functionally. The presence and activity of each allows the other to express and develop its inherent characteristics, i.e. the two are related in 'complementary schismogenesis' (Bateson, ibid. p. 36). Moreover, this complementarity has consequences for the characteristic course of events in contests and conflicts in Swat which in a functionalist framework would be described as 'adaptive'. Quite simply, it is more possible to act with heedless bravado and force when there are others present who seize the opportunity to mediate and resolve the resultant confrontation, and it is more possible to excel in moderation and morality when there are leaders who involve themselves in impasses which they wish to escape. In the improbable case that Chiefs were alone in the political field, and acted as they did in the first half of this century, life in Swat would have become very dangerous indeed; or obversely, unless Saints had been present and active in their institutionalized role, it would have been impossible for Chiefs to excel as they did by standards of 'heaviness', 'forcefulness', and 'maleness'. We are back in the bus on the bridge over the Kabul river, which in miniature illustrates the leadership dynamics, and the standard course of conflict and resolution, generated by such circumstances and values.

I thus maintain that this bifurcation and complementarity of leadership roles comes about as a dynamic process under specifiable conditions, and is not a sought organizational device deriving from a Pathan theory or ideology of legitimacy and government. The various and discrepant ideals of excellence are certainly embraced, but the system which they comprise in concert is unsought, though it is occasionally perceived by participants (cf. Barth, 1959a: 59-60 for a documented example). When conditions change, as they progressively have since the 1930s, this organization of leadership roles becomes less clear and marked – entailing a real loss of general esteem for Chiefs, who no longer excel as did the great Chiefs of yore, but no effort to reconstitute 'the system'. It is also clearly a system associated with the acephalous features of Swat organization, in which opposing groups and competing leaders established their shifting and pragmatic balances, and is distinctly at odds with ideals of responsible kingship and government in centralized states held by the population. That these are also ideas and conceptions of long standing in Pathan culture is certified by the epigram composed by the great Pashto poet Khushhal Khan Khattak (latter half of the seventeenth century) some distance from the Swat valley, but clearly within a common culture and society: 'He who has neither learning nor wisdom, if he sits on a throne, is either a lion or a fox*, or else count him as an ox or a donkey.' (* lit. *wolf*, but idiomatically more like our animal stereotype of a fox since the emphasis is on animal slyness and not voraciousness, as 'wolf' tends to be in English. Pashto text from Raverty, 1860: 5. The translation is mine.)

The concrete effects of these ideas on events and instituted forms of leadership, however, vary greatly with circumstances, as I have sought to demonstrate.

Key dynamics III: Coalitions and land circulation

My analysis of Swat society was pursued without the conventional (and questionable) axiom that society constitutes a self-correcting system, and without any theoretical or implicit assumption of equilibrium. At the same time I was fully prepared to discover that *some* empirical patterns and forms in social life could prove to be the outcome of an interplay of several processes acting in opposite directions and perhaps, at any moment, nearly neutralizing or balancing each other. One might thus discover situations where a highly dynamic set of forces generated a relatively unchanging overt result or state. Indeed, it was my expectation then, and would be still, that a fair number of the overt macro-features of a society can be expected to be generated in some such fashion, since they tend to show a considerable stability over time (or they would not be institutionalized by participants and/or recognized by us as macro-features) while being at the same time only the aggregate of such inherently volatile and changeable stuff as the understandings, acts, and fortunes of people. Thus, the rejection of the equilibrium models of structural-functionalism gives no theoretical brief for precluding that particular social phenomena can usefully be schematized in models characterized by equilibrium. Yet there is always a danger that we do so too readily, since such models show a logical closure and neatness that makes them alluring. A cornerstone in my analysis of Swat was provided by one such model, that of the balance between the blocs (cf. chapter 3), with subsidiary arguments relating to the perpetuation of the Pakhtun caste and the balance between land concentration and land fragmentation. Let us reconsider these arguments briefly.

The empirical fact that politics in Swat was patterned by an alignment of leaders in two blocs, each comprising a territorially dispersed network of alliances, in 1954 and during the preceding century, is incontrovertible. It is likewise clear that the bloc in power in any particular area tended to grow as measured in the total area of land that its members controlled and the total number of men it commanded — but not necessarily in the number of landowners that composed its membership. Furthermore, all the evidence indicates that any particular leader's alliances were not infrequently the object of negotiation and sometimes rupture, and that a recognized and practised strategy of the larger and more successful leaders was to defect from the locally dominant bloc and join the weaker, so as to reap the advantages of swinging the balance between the two blocs. It is clear that we are observing a situation where a macro-feature — the existence of two dispersed blocs in an oscillating power balance — is generated by a high level of activity and a complex interplay of events on the level of local rivalry, confrontations and leadership careers.

The essay reproduced in chapter 3 presents a model designed to capture the relevant factors and generate the patterns that were empirically observed. A careful reading of that essay will, I believe, answer

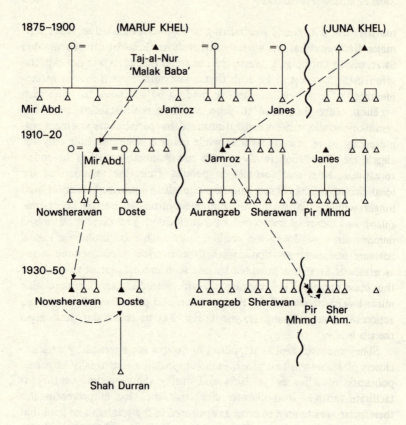

1875–1900   (MARUF KHEL)   (JUNA KHEL)

Taj-al-Nur
'Malak Baba'

Mir Abd.   Jamroz   Janes

1910–20

Mir Abd.   Jamroz   Janes

Nowsherawan   Doste   Aurangzeb Sherawan Pir Mhmd

1930–50

Nowsherawan   Doste   Aurangzeb Sherawan Pir   Sher
                                              Mhmd   Ahm.

Shah Durran

▲ leader of bloc

--→ succession to leadership

} division between blocs

FIGURE 7.2 *Some of the main leaders of blocs in Babuzai, 1875-
1960 (simplified)*

most of the criticisms subsequently made, and identifies correctly the major determinants of the two-bloc system. Subsequent changes in Swat, particularly the Wali's policy and its results (cf. above pp. 142ff.) give further evidence that the crucial factors have been correctly identified.

The political moieties in Swat are thus best understood as the *result* of the process of amalgamation of groups in alliances and not as a premise for it. At the same time the ensuing duality is certainly very clearly acknowledged in Swat as a fact of life, and serves so aptly to capture the egocentric experience of 'we-group' and 'they-group' in local rivalry that it persists as a native model even today when it is no longer empirically valid. Thus national political parties are very frequently conceptualized in two-bloc (*dəla*) terms; and local rivals demonstratively align in opposed political parties, without regard to the national platforms and ideologies of those parties: it is their function as a means to define local oppositions which is paramount. The case thus illustrates in an interesting way the complex interrelations between micro-level and aggregate, native models of society and for social action, etc., which are disguised if one tries to depict the facts using the crude opposition of ideology and praxis only.

Some further comments should be made to fit the model more closely to the full empirical complexity of Swat. Firstly, Saints as political leaders are not specifically discussed in chapter 3. This was to facilitate the schematism required in model construction; but to add their presence to the model poses no analytical problem. In focusing on Pakhtuns, the model identifies the strategic structure which amalgamates about 90 per cent of the land and the gross population in two blocs. In the hilly flank areas dominated by Saints, exactly similar factors are at work − so much so that the rival *Mians* of the hamlets of Ser and Sardarei in the Ghorband area served for a generation to personify and name the two blocs in the whole region of Middle Swat. When Saints constitute a scattered minority of landowners in the valley bottom dominated by Pakhtuns, they tend to be less tightly integrated into the blocs, since they can better capitalize on their role as mediators by retaining a modicum of neutrality. This is also compatible with the interests of those who would use them for negotiating and mediatory purposes, though strong Chiefs also try to secure the services of some Saintly 'lackeys'. But they are in fact drawn into the factions by other forces as well. In local areas where effective leadership is such that a major Chief is pitted against a prominent Saint as main rivals both will find it strategically opportune, or even necessary, to establish a close alliance with a person of the opposite category. This is because a Chief is hardly able to confront, and hope to subdue, a Saint except through the straw man provided by another Saint, who can be built up in competition with the first and hopefully divest him of the disciples and influence which no Chief could usurp or use. Likewise, though to less extent, a prominent Saint will find it convenient sometimes to act through the agency of reliable, dependent Chiefs.

This leads us to a second issue: the possible brakes on the intensity of opposition between blocs, which could explain why the dominant bloc does not resort to outright conquest and run the leaders of the weaker bloc entirely out of the village and area. Ahmed correctly observes that this did in fact take place on a few occasions in some localities in the early part of the century (Ahmed, 1976: 28): but it was definitely the exception then and never the final outcome of conflicts in 1954 or the immediately preceding decades. Why such moderation? In the Theory of Games model (above, chapter 3, pp. 72-80) I try to identify strategic factors that would generate such restraint in the intensity of predation on the weaker bloc. This analysis has been confirmed to me by Chiefs in Swat, and identifies correctly, I believe, the factors that generate an *interest* in such restraint among Pakhtun leaders. Its implementation, on the other hand, would be quite problematic for Chiefs adopting the classic courageous and reckless stance of 'lions' (cf. above pp. 160, 163). The integration of Saints into the alliance blocs solves this problem: both internally as between allied (but competing) Chiefs, and externally towards the public, there will be counsels of moderation and care articulated by allied Saints, to which strong Chiefs can 'reluctantly' assent without too great risk of showing weakness.

The essence of this whole mode of analysis is found in the careful reconstruction of the whole strategic situation, the binds and the pressures, which constitute the political reality in which leaders must act — one might even say 'are trapped'. The most important of these are the fundamental circumstances under which security of property and life must be obtained, as I have repeatedly stressed in the preceding text. Though these have been largely ignored or dismissed by some of my critics, I am still at a loss to understand how the very thrust of my argument could have been interpreted as its opposite: an imputation of individual motives (Asad, 1972: 83) entailing the view that Pakhtuns are driven by 'insatiable greed' (Asad, 1972: 88) or an 'almost insatiable compulsion' (Ahmed, 1976: 10). I can only hope that the simple reformulations offered here will make the nature of my argument clear, and preclude such misinterpretations in the future.

Two further observations should be made in fitting the Theory of Games model to the facts of Swat. The model as constructed posits an 'unrestricted freedom' of leaders to form alliances with parties of their own choosing. Though in principle true, many leaders will in fact experience certain impediments once the blocs have formed, as noted above briefly (ch. 3, p. 79): the presence of one's primary collateral rivals in an alliance bloc makes it difficult to join this bloc, even if wider considerations would make it attractive. This difficulty is sometimes overcome through negotiations within the bloc, as shown in particular case stories (e.g. Barth, 1959a: 95). Its systematic effect is not, as far as I can judge, to change the strategic structure of the situation, but only to reduce somewhat the frequency of defections between blocs. This raises the other query: why do not persons change their alliances more often? I noted that prominent leaders may make one or two such changes in a lifetime (cf. ch. 3 p. 72 and figure 7.2 p. 166). The game model gives no basis for generating this, or any other frequency of defections. Unless we are prepared to complicate this key model very considerably, however, I think we must be content to answer the query by adding circumstantial specifications only. They are, in this case, quite simple and obvious: the act of defecting from one's allies is dangerous (the risk of being double-crossed by one's former enemies, the risk of failing to swing the balance of power), particularly so for a small leader (the margins are smaller, one must trust in successful secrecy while a collective act is being negotiated).

This particular problem may thus serve to bring out a general feature of this form of analysis. The simple, logically more 'pure' analytical schemata — *in casu* the Theory of Games model — are intended to illuminate, and not replace, the ethnographic description. It makes good sense to criticize such models by showing that they depict a false dynamics because they leave out certain essential circumstances, forces or processes found in real life which interact with those depicted. It makes little sense to criticize them because they do not provide complete descriptions.

We have focused above on political events and how they affect the alliance network. If we now aggregate these same incidents of support, conflict and confrontation, not as a story of the relations between two alliance blocs but as life careers and family histories, we expose another dynamics and other, more slow-working processes with quite distinctive consequences. My analysis of these has been much more crude and incomplete, both from lack of statistical data and a failure to focus on them. Concretely, we see many Pakhtuns progressively losing their land and ultimately their position as landowners and indeed Pakhtuns. I have argued loosely that this 'sloughing-off' process counterbalances a tendency to excess population growth in the landowning class. But precisely *what* the balance has been, over the last few generations, I would be hesitant to guess. We know that roughly 400 years ago, Yusufzai Pakhtuns in a massive migration conquered a well populated area, and being entirely familiar with feudal arrangements and tenancy contracts it is most plausible that they established themselves as landowners on a pattern much like what we find in this century. Whatever proportionate changes that have taken place must in other words have been slow and relatively small. If one were to write a social history of the Swat valley, it might be quite important to know how the relative proportion of Pakhtuns to non-Pakhtuns may have changed over the centuries. To understand the politics of Swat in 1954, and the preceding decades, I know no evidence (*pace* Asad, 1972) that would point to cumulative change in the Pakhtun/non-Pakhtun ratio as a critical factor, and so I have ignored it. Absolute growth of the total population, and ensuing pressure on land, would seem to provide a far more important change of parameters. Its main impetus, however, has been in the decades *following* my study of 1954.

Another more interesting theme is that of land concentration and fragmentation. The identification of certain counterbalancing and even negative feedback processes here is quite important to my analysis, yet builds on rather sketchy foundations. In the absence of ample and definitive data one may try to conjecture; but there are dangerous pitfalls in the pursuit of simple logical reasoning if one's model of the interconnected processes is incomplete. The basic conundrum can be put like this: if one looks at the life histories of landowners, one finds examples of very swift, and in a few cases truly dramatic, growth in the personal landed property of successful leaders. Thus, for example, in the latter part of the last century Malak Baba of the central area of Babuzai increased his lands from four shares (*Rupəi*) to fifty shares in his stormy lifetime (Barth, 1959a: 113). These lands must have been taken from other landowners. Yet I maintain that there is no firm evidence for the progressive concentration of land on fewer and fewer hands, or that such careers represent steps in the growth of centralized political structures. My argument on the latter point is given briefly elsewhere (Barth, 1959a: 125ff.) and we shall return to its substance below. The former point should be discussed briefly here, since the thesis that we see an emerging oligarchy is a cornerstone of Asad's reinterpretation (Asad, 1972: 89ff.), as it provides him with the main substance for a history of developing class domination through which the structure of Swat is sought to be understood.

Let us look at some concrete materials, returning to the chart on p. 168 showing Malak Baba and his agnatic male progeny. First, we may note the growth of his line. He increased his land by a factor of twelve, but he also had ten sons, who subdivided their patrimony and joined opposite blocs to fight each other. Even so successful a career as Malak Baba's thus left the region of Babuzai with no significantly larger estate on any single hand than there was when he began.

The accounts I have of his life tell of confrontations with other big Chiefs, and give no details of land seizures from small Pakhtuns. Yet judging from the activities of more contemporary figures, there is no reason to doubt that he also dispossessed a number of small land-owners, who thereby lost their Pakhtun rank and became clients and tenants. But it is a logical *non sequitur* to conclude from a prevelance of such cases that the *category* of small landowners is declining (as in Asad, 1972: 88). These same or other events may simultaneously have other consequences entailing the creation of a number of new small landowners. If we look at the (now living) third and fourth generations of Malak Baba's line, we see how that family history has also given rise to new small landowners — in the form of its own unsuccessful branches — while eliminating others of this category. The rise and fall of other persons and families in the intervening period provides similar evidence. The body of quantified survey data which would provide us with a clear picture of the (doubtless changing) balance between these processes over time is not available; but in its absence, the more sketchy materials of life histories etc. give no indications that would support the assertion that 'land became increasingly controlled by fewer families' (Asad, 1972: 89 and following pages). His conjecture to explain such a phenomenon — the 'economic non-viability' of small landholdings — then likewise falls. Indeed, my own impression is quite to the contrary: that land ownership to a small plot gives great buoyancy to the household economy of the smallholder, and that the number of smallholders has lately probably *increased* in central areas of Swat, particularly through the ascent of many muleteers, goldsmiths,

mullahs, and members of other non-Pakhtun castes into that category
since 1930.

Key dynamics IV: Growth of centralized states

In looking at history, social anthropologists easily succumb to the
common human tendency of telescoping time. One tends to see the
changes of the most recent decades as momentous, while the preceding centuries of eventful history are collapsed into a brief prelude
to these changes. The historical interpretation proposed by Asad for the
understanding of Swat (Asad, 1972) suffers, I believe, from this distortion. There is no doubt that profound changes have issued from, or
been affected by, the emergence of a centralized state in Swat during
its fifty or so years of existence; yet in terms of the society and culture
of Swat Pathans it may none the less have equal validity to see the
emergence of this state as a kind of an epilogue (Asad, 1972: 93). On
the other hand it is not implausible that the growth of centralization
represents a key dynamic process in the area. I believe that an informed
judgment on the matter requires a comparative perspective, both
regionally and with somewhat greater historical depth. However, the
ethnography is complex and undocumented, and the history is even
more intricate and very spottily recorded. I shall summarize those
major features which I believe are necessary to give a true sense of
relationships and developments.

Note first how different historical moments and regional scopes give
the material quite opposite aspects. Swat since the mid 1930s till 1970
has been pointed to by outsiders as the most progressive and dynamic
state on the frontier, increasingly a haven of tranquillity and development. Yet from time immemorial and into the 1920s, Swat was notor-
ious for its anarchy even within one of the most turbulent corners of
the world. Which of these two characterizations captures the more
fundamental features of social dynamics in Swat? Of the frontier states,
Swat seemed distinctive and unique in that its rulers were the descendants of a Saint, in contrast to the native dynasties of Khans which
ruled the other Pathan states. But if we look at the history of the last
150 years, the Yusufzai tribes can be observed to have united in a state
under a king of Saintly descent in 1830, 1849, 1915, and 1917 − the
Mianguls were the *fourth* in a series. Thus, we need the broader perspective of region and time to identify correctly what is distinctive,

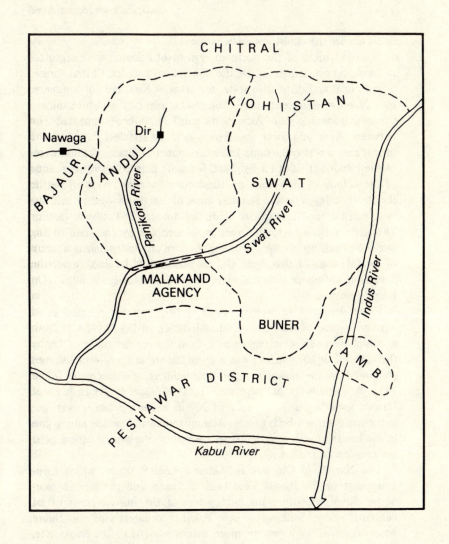

MAP 4 *Swat state and adjoining areas.*

and what are the significant co-variations.

By 1954 most of the northern regions of Pakistan were organized in local, centralized states. Of the non-Pathan peoples, Chitral formed a traditional and distinctive state, the areas of Kohistan not conquered by Pathans were uncentralized, while to the east on the Indus bank was the small Tanaoli state of Amb. Some small and rather fragmented areas between Amb and Swat states were held by stateless Pathan tribes; in this area was also the remarkable settlement of Sitana, the home area of the important Saint Pir Baba and for more than 100 years the centre of the colony of Mujahidin, or 'Hindustani Fanatics'. West of Swat in the lower valley were the stateless areas of Malakand Agency, and also in a narrow foothills strip towards the borders of Peshawar district. The main territories to the west were occupied by the state of Dir, under its Pakhtun Nawab, including the formerly independent Khanate of Jandul; west of that again was the Khanate of Nawagai, exercising a variable influence over uncentralized tribal areas surrounding it in Bajaur (see map 4).

From defectors from the Nawab of Dir's rather tyrannical rule I have an outline of the internal administration of Dir in 1954. It shows a complex mosaic of arrangements. Centring on the town of Dir, in the upper Panjkora valley, was a considerable military establishment composed of the *terkhwaro*, full-time soldiers or mercenaries (cf. p. 141). A major body of these were 1600 *ardaljan*, bodyguards of the Nawab, including an inner core of 200 *da hazur ardeljan*, private and particularly trusted bodyguards. Administrative and police duties were in the hands of appointed *naukaran*, 'servants', the central officer being the *tahsildar* of Dir town.

The Nawab of Dir was an Akhund Khel Pakhtun, which forms a segment of the Painda Khel Malizai. These, and the related group Sultan Khel, constitute the landowners of the main section of the Panjkora valley. Strikingly, these Pakhtun collaterals of the Nawab were organized in a pattern more autonomous than the Swat valley tribes, paying no tax to the Nawab and aligning in a two-bloc pattern in their internal *jirga* councils. The rest of Dir payed one tenth of all produce in *ushar* tax to the Nawab. The areas of Dir Kohistan north of Dir town are inhabited mainly by non-Pathans (Kohistanis and Gujars) and the land was the private property of the Nawab and his close relatives; it was administered through the *tahsildar* in Dir town. Other areas were organized as dependent sub-khanates, in the hands of close relatives of the Nawab or his (temporary) deputies. In previous times, the submission of the smaller khanates to the authority of the Nawab was more tenuous, and depended on the military balance of the moment. Attached to the positions as Nawab and as Khans of the subsidiary khanates, were also areas of *pargai siri* (cf. Barth, 1959: 75), i.e. impartible estates traditionally exempt from *wesh* redistribution which pass directly to successors in office.

Pathan traditions, and British sources since Elphinstone (1815), indicate that a pattern of organization in such khanates has antiquity among Yusufzai Pakhtuns. The last Nawab of Dir thus claimed to be the eleventh generation of his dynasty. But all evidence suggests that these khanates formerly had much less character of territorial states than did Dir in the present century — rather, they may most realistically be seen as local concentrations of power, centring on a nucleus of disproportionately large landed property (some of it as an impartible estate), a fortified village, and a company of paid soldiers. Such power centres participated as unequal parties in the over-all two-bloc politics of the region, and thus tended to maintain a larger area of influence, from which *ushar* revenue was often extracted. But they were often weakened by successional strife, and prone to attacks by rival pretenders supported by external, temporary coalitions. The Swat valley was distinctive in that such Khanates did *not* exist there.

The outlines of the revelant history is diagrammed in Figure 7.3. Caroe (1958) will serve as a source for most of these events. We may start around AD 1800, as the non-Moslem Sikhs became a threat to the Yusufzai Pathans of the Peshawar plain. Formerly loosely tied to the Afghan empire, the Yusufzai were not effectively supported from that side, nor could they or would they unite under any one of their own Khans. A Sayyid and Moslem notable from Hindustan, Ahmed Shah Brelwi, appeared as a leader of resistance against the infidels; and he was appointed as Badshah, i.e. king, by the Yusufzai chiefs in 1830, strongly supported by the great Saintly leader in Buner, Sayyid Akbar Shah of Sitana. Within a year, however, the Yusufzai rose against their chosen leader, and he was killed. The Peshawar plain fell under Sikh rule, and from 1846 under the British. In 1849 Akbar Shah, the sponsor of the first confederate king, was himself elected to kingship in Swat, strongly sponsored by the emerging spiritual leader there, the Akhun of Swat (cf. Barth, 1959a, especially pp. 100 and 127). Sayyid Akbar died a natural death eight years later; his son, though presenting himself as a candidate, was not appointed to succeed his father.

We must now shift briefly from these non-Pakhtun leaders to the

Khans of the western areas. Omara Khan of Jandul (a small khanate of c. 25,000 inhabitants) emerged on a career of local conquest in 1890 by surprising and seizing the town of Dir. He thereupon entered the state of Chitral as the partisan of a pretender to the throne there, and precipitated the intervention which brought British troops and overt interests into the area in 1895. The Nawab of Dir was reinstated with a British subsidy of 26,000 rupees and a commitment to protect the road (at the time a mere muletrack) connecting Chitral with Peshawar. There can be little doubt that this subsidy served to consolidate and increase the scope of the Nawab's authority. In the following years his forces repeatedly invaded major parts of the Swat valley (partly on the invitation of the weaker bloc in the areas in question); and he started asserting the kind of influence there that he had previously held only in the Panjkora valley.

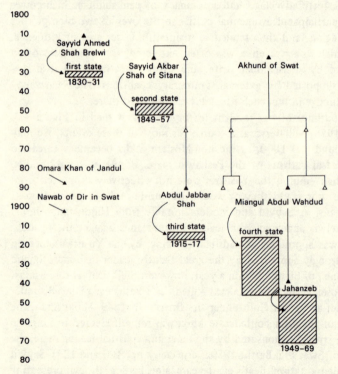

FIGURE 7.3   *Some key figures and events in Swat history, 1800-*
            1969

There were various opinions among survivors from that period whom I knew in 1954 as to where the initiative for new attempts at centralization in Swat arose. Some claim that it issued mainly from the Chiefs of Nikbi khel, who needed a coordinator for defence of their territory against the Nawab of Dir; others claim it arose among the Chiefs of Babuzai, not directly threatened, but concerned about their inability to contain the anarchy and strife arising from conflicts between the blocs. However, a great *jirga* of these and other Pakhtuns met and elected as Badshah the grandnephew of Akbar Shah, Abdul Jabbar Shah, in 1915. By 1917 he had been driven out of Swat, accused of religious heterodoxy, and the Pakhtun chiefs met again to appoint Miangul Abdul Wadud, grandson of the Akhund of Swat, as their king.

The intricate parts played by these and many other persons in the events need not concern us here; I think the main organizational features are relatively clear from what has been said. The bifurcation of leadership found in the lower echelons of political leadership also asserts itself in Yusufzai Pathan conceptions of centralized power, and has done so for centuries. Two kinds of growth can be envisaged: a khanate led by a Chief, and a kingdom led by a non-Pakhtun, impartial mediator. In a sense both forms of statehood prove unwanted in the forms which they tend to take. Khanates elicit much counteraction in defence of autonomy, building up rivals in efforts to balance and contain the authority of the leader. It is striking that the khanate nuclei have arisen with greatest strength in the marginal areas with non-Pakhtun tenant populations, whereas they have failed entirely to emerge in the broad and open valley of Swat, with large Pakhtun populations and a heavy preponderance of Pathans. The dynamics behind this have been sketched elsewhere (Barth, 1959: 125f.), and arise from the tendency, given the institutional bases that have characterized the Yusufzai, towards swifter growth of defensive alliances than that of the effective followings of single Chiefs. Only in restricted localities, and with considerable non-Pathan followings, can these negative feedbacks be overcome.

As for the 'confederate kings' which Yusufzai Pakhtuns have appointed, the immediate bone of contention is found in the limits of their authority. These are the very opposite of conquest states (*pace* Asad, 1972: 90); no doubt there was never any intention on the part of the electing chiefs to give up autonomy, only to institute a limited mechanism for coordination for specific and very necessary purposes. Efforts to contain the newly innovated authority are pursued, as in the case of khanates (cf. Barth, 1959a: 128 for how the brother of the Badshah was employed as a spearhead of an opposing faction), and a power struggle leading to the collapse of the state seems structurally portended.

The khanate nucleus of Dir probably became a true state only by virtue of the subsidies and other support of British India after 1895. How the Miangul Abdul Wadud as Badshah of Swat could succeed during those first years after 1917 without such support and sub-sidies, where others before him had failed, becomes a highly intrigu-ing question. The millenarian thesis so ramblingly argued by Ahmed (1976) will not serve, since there is neither any evidence for a dramatic message or vision on the part of the Badshah, nor any revivalist ground-swell of support for a new world on the part of the population. I would rather see the events from 1917 to 1969 as producing a cumula-tive and eventually drastic divergence from pre-existing preconditions and processes of Swat culture and society, unforeseen by all parties to the initiating event. The course of this change was influenced both by the tactical genius of the Badshah, and his son who succeeded him, and by the staggering sequence of technical, economic, and political changes impinging on Swat from the outside. The dynamics of progres-sive centralization and statehood is thus of a different order from the other key dynamics discussed above; and to seek its major lineaments in pre-established patterns, as Asad and Ahmed have attempted, is doomed to confusion and failure.

The relation of models to empirical description

In conclusion, we may reflect briefly on the nature of the description and analysis of society which has been provided in the preceding essays and most explicitly in this last chapter. The recurring feature is, on the one hand, the presentation of a relatively wide-ranging and diverse set of generalizable, empirical features of social life as it unfolds in Swat and, on the other hand, the construction of a relatively simple dynamic scheme or model to explain how these regularities come about. Each such 'key dynamics' is designed to show how the acts of people, i.e. events on the micro-level, are influenced and moulded by ubiquitous forces, or characteristics of the context, in such a way as to generate trends in behaviour that are reflected in the aggregate patterns which we identify as macro-features of the society. The models that are pro-vided for different key dynamics are not necessarily connected: I understand them to depict various independent variables which affect social forms as dependent variables, under the circumstances described. They may be of different order, and logically independent although the struggle to try to connect them logically and systematically is analytically important since it leads to the construction of more encompassing models. And they are clearly more interesting and illuminating the more encompassing they are – but also the simpler they are – thus raising the methodological need for finding a compromise between economy and comprehensiveness. The set of models presented here is not definitive or complete: other models may reveal other features, or some of the same features better, or some other combinations of features. Yet I am not resigned to say that they are arbitrary or figments of our imagination. On the contrary, I would claim that these models (schematically) identify and depict empirical processes, and could thus be falsified by a demonstration that such processes do not in fact occur, or be improved by a redesign that more faithfully mirrors these empirical processes. I understand it rather to be in their schematism, and in the selection of phenomena which they are made to embrace, that a certain degree of arbitrary induction is entailed.

Compared to the models of social structure that have been provided in the structural-functional tradition, they lack cognitively satisfying completeness, unity and closure. Indeed, they have sometimes been criticized as being partial, incomplete, and oversimplified, on the mistaken assumption that they aspire to give a persuasive representation of an assumedly bounded whole which is 'a society'. It might be helpful if I restate my position on this issue briefly. I do not see order and integration as an axiomatic or empirical feature of society. I see 'society-as-an-empirical-phenomenon' as an immensely complex conglomerate of events. Many of these events are causally connected, or interdependent in multiple ways. But the unity of the 'whole' (to the extent that we can define its boundaries – cf. above, pp. 124-30) is of an existential kind only: it arises from the fact that these events are simultaneous as parts of the life situation of a collectivity of people. 'Society-as-described', on the other hand, rests on a selection of these events, and thus purposely or inadvertently depicts a pattern or order which has been perceived as capable of characterization. To the extent that this characterization is empirically valid, it is the *degree* of regularity and generalizability of social life which is reported, exemplified by select events and characterized by generalizations, and sought to be explained by a model of the dynamics that generate it. The schematism of such a model was thus never intended to incorporate into itself the complexity of real life or the sum of described features of the society, nor to embody all the different processes that give some degree of regularity to social events in a community or region.

If such a program of description and analysis lacks some of the conceptual satisfactions of a representation of 'the social structure', it has, I feel, some compensating advantages. Not the least of these is its capacity to describe and explain features of social life in Swat in a way which makes the dramatic variation of forms, in time and space, possible and plausible, without recourse to explanatory assumptions of wholesale breakdown and reintegration of systems, and fundamental changes in the norms and cognitions of the population.

Notes

1   The temptation is strong to enter into detailed debate and rebuttal, since factual errors and unsustainable conjectures are numerous and give apparent support to interpretations and analyses at variance with my own. This is particularly true of Ahmed's monograph, where he frequently also gives the impression of commanding independent evidence. But also Asad seems to me at times to misrepresent the data I give, and certainly my intentions. For commentaries on some of these points in Ahmed, I refer to reviews by third parties in *Afghanistan Council Newsletter VII* (1) 1979, and *Reviews in Anthropology*, 1979 pp. 11-24. To avoid tiresome altercation I shall limit my corrections here to those most directly germane to the issues I raise, and ask the interested reader of Asad or Ahmed to go to my own original statements and texts to check what I actually say in context. Unless modified in the following essay, my previously published statements of observation and inference still reflect my position.

2   Cf. Barth, 1959a: 127f., Caroe, 1958: 363. Extensive data relevant to this question will be presented in a book based on autobiographical material from the Wali, *viz*, n.d.: *The Last Wali of Swat*.

3   The *telgerri* system entailed a contract between all landowners of a ward to have one men's house and one collective set of service contracts with craftsmen and labourers (cf. Barth, 1959a: 86ff.).

4   This is exemplified in his persistent understanding that mine is an equilibrium model (e.g. Asad, 1972: 87 and 91; and on this concrete issue see below, p. 178); that I should consider the study of political organization as being the study of 'the indispensable basis of social order' (ibid., p. 79 bottom, p. 91); that my assertion that actors make choices entails an assumption on my part that they consent to the circumstances which limit their choice (ibid., p. 92, cf. my 6, below); that when I observe that many tenants see the Pakhtun landlords as an unnecessary imposition I am raising the question whether landlords are necessary 'to the system' (ibid., p. 84); etc. etc.

5   We may note that these features show great constancy in Northern Pathan organization, and are understood by the participants themselves in this perspective. Thus informants explained to Elphinstone in 1809 how among the Yusufzai of the Peshawar plains 'the master is deterred from severity by the disgrace that attaches to oppression, and still more by the right of the Fakeer (poor, i.e. landless person) to remove to the lands of another Eusofzye: a right which he can always exercise, as there is a great competition for Fakeers, and many men will always be found ready to receive and protect one who is disposed to change his master' (Elphinstone, 1815: 345). In 1954, proposed reforms in this same area through the introduction of village-level democracy were judged by the public in Swat to reduce the freedom of non-landowners and not be an attractive model for them. They saw the structure as one which would enroll all members of the electorate equally behind deputed leaders, who would use their monopoly position to supress the common man further, demanding in their own idiom 'more sweet talk and more massage' (*chapi*, the tension-releasing body massage which servants provide for masters and particularly honoured guests).

6   I see Asad's attempts at interpreting such a situation, and my analysis of it, in terms of a concept of 'consent' as highly obfuscating (1972, especially pp. 82ff.). Recognizing and analysing the crucial place of choice on the part of the different participants in this political system presumes nothing about attitudes on the part of any actor of accepting or desiring the various constraints under which he makes his choice. If it were conceivable that these constraints could be removed one by one, I think the actor's choices would be changed by each step, and I have no hypotheses as to whether or when he might desire to reimpose any particular constraint. As Moslems, people of Swat embrace an ideology with an explicit image of a right and ideal society, and particular practices are often contrasted to this ideal; but people have had no experience of any society pervasively moulded by the ideal, and some practices known to be incompatible with it are indeed personally cherished. An analysis of choice and strategy need not prejudge these complicated issues of the degree to which ideologies are embraced by actors.

7   On the borders of Buner, about 50 miles south east of the Swat valley, the Mujahidin colony of 'Hindustani Fanatics' (cf. e.g. Caroe, 1958: 302-5) has been constituted on other principles. It would be extremely interesting if this colony were made the object of careful anthropological and historical investigation.

Bibliography

AHMED, AKBAR S. (1976) *Millennium and Charisma among Pathans*, London: Routledge & Kegan Paul.

ALLEE, W.C. et al. (1949) *Principles of Animal Ecology*, Philadelphia: W.B. Saunders.

ASAD, TALAL, (1972) Market model, class structure and consent: a reconsideration of Swat political organization. *Man* (NS), vol. 7, no. 1.

BADEN-POWELL, B.H. (1892) *Land Systems of British India*, Vol. III, Oxford: Frowde.

BADEN-POWELL, B.H. (1896) *The Indian Village Community*, London: Longmans.

BACON, ELIZABETH (1946) A preliminary attempt to determine the culture areas of Asia. *Southwestern Journal of Anthropology*, vol. 2, pp. 117-32.

BATESON, GREGORY (1949) Bali: The value system of a steady state, in Meyer Fortes (ed.), *Social Structure*, Oxford University Press.

BARTH, FREDRIK (1956) Indus and Swat Kohistan: an ethnographic survey, in *Studies honoring the centennial of Universitetets Etnografiske Museum*, Vol. II. Oslo.

BARTH, FREDRIK (1957) The political organization of Swat Pathans, Unpublished PhD Thesis, Cambridge University.

BARTH, FREDRIK (1959a) *Political Leadership among Swat Pathans*, London School of Economics Monographs on Social Anthropology, no. 19, London: Athlone Press.

BARTH, FREDRIK (1959b) Segmentary opposition and the Theory of Games. *Journal of the Royal Anthropological Institute*, vol. 89, pt. 1, pp. 5-22.

BARTH, FREDRIK (1961) *Nomads of South Persia*, Oslo: Norwegian Universities Press; and, Boston. Mass., Little, Brown, 1968.

BARTH, FREDRIK (1964) Capital, investment and the social structure of a pastoral nomad group in South Persia, in R. Firth and B.S. Yamey (eds), *Capital, Saving and Credit in Peasant Societies*, London: Allen & Unwin.

BARTH, FREDRIK (1966) *Models of Social Organization*, London: Royal Anthropological Institute Occasional Paper no. 23.

BARTH, FREDRIK (forthcoming) *The Last Wali of Swat*.

BARTH, FREDRIK and MORGENSTIERNE, GEORG (1957) Samples of some South Dardie dialects, *Norsk Tidsskrift for Språkvitenskap*, 18.

BLINCOW MALCOLM (1979) Islam, Social Movements, and State Formation in Swat. *Reviews in Anthropology*, Winter 1979.

BRUCE, R.I. (1900) *The Forward Policy and its Results*, London: Longmans.

CANFIELD, ROBERT L. (1979) Review of Ahmed: Millennium and Charisma in *Afghanistan Council Newsletter VII* (1).

CAROE, SIR OLAF, (1958) *The Pathans 550 B.C.-A.D. 1957*, London: Macmillan.

COON, CARLETON S. (1951) *Caravan*, New York: Henry Holt.

DAMES, M.L. (1904) *The Baloch Race*, Asiatic Society Monographs, vol. IV.

DROWER, M.S. (1954) Water-supply, irrigation and agriculture, in Charles Singer et al., *A History of Technology*, Oxford: Clarendon Press.

DUMONT, LOUIS (1967) Caste: a phenomenon of social structure or an aspect of Indian culture? *in* Antony de Reuk and Julie Knight (eds), *Caste and Race: Comparative Approaches* London: J. & A. Churchill.

DUMONT, LOUIS (1970) *Homo Hierarchicus*, London and Chicago: University of Chicago Press.

DURKHEIM, EMILE (1947) *The Division of Labour in Society*, translated by G. Simpson, Chicago: Free Press.

ELPHINSTONE, THE HON. MOUNTSTUART (1815) *An Account of the Kingdom of Caubul and its Dependencies in Persia, Tartary and India*, London: Longman, Hurst, Rees, Orme, Brown, and J. Murray.

EVENS, T.M.S. (1977) The predication of the individual in anthropological interactionism. *American Anthropologist*, vol. 79.

FAUTZ, BRUNO (1963) *Sozialstruktur und Bodennützung in der Kulturlandschaft des Swat (Nordwesthimalaya)*, Karlsruhe: Fakultät für Natur- und Geisteswissenschaften der Technischen Hochschule Karlsruhe.

FERDINAND, K. (1962) Nomadic expansion and commerce in Central Afghanistan – a sketch of some modern trend. *Folk*, vol. 4.

FORTES, M. (1953) The structure of unilineal descent groups. *American Athropologist*, vol. 55, pp. 17-41.

FORTES, M. and EVANS-PRITCHARD, E.E. (eds) (1940) *African Political Systems*, Oxford University Press.

FURNIVALL, J.S. (1944) *Netherlands India: A Study of Plural Economy*, Cambridge University Press.

GEERTZ, CLIFFORD (1971) *Agricultural Involution*, Berkeley, Cal.: University of California Press.

GERTH, H.H., and MILLS, C.W. (1947) *From Max Weber: Essays in Sociology*, London.

GOFFMANN, E. (1959) *The Presentation of Self in Everyday Life*, New York: Doubleday.

HSU, FRANCIS (1965) The effect of dominant kinship relationships on kin and non-kin behaviour. *American Anthropologist*, vol. 67, pp. 638-61.

IBBETSON, SIR DENZIL (1916) *Punjab Castes*, Lahore.

KROEBER, A.L. (1939) *Cultural and Natural Areas of Native North America*, Berkeley and Los Angeles: University of California Press.

KROEBER, A.L. (1947) Culture groupings in Asia. *Southwestern Journal of Anthropology*, vol. 3 pp. 322-30.

LEACH, E.R. (1954) *Political Systems of Highland Burma*, London: G. Bell.

LEACH, E.R. (1960) Introduction: What should one mean by caste, in E.R. Leach (ed.), *Aspects of Caste in South India, Ceylon and North-West Pakistan*, Cambridge Papers in Social Anthropology no. 2, Cambridge University Press.

LEACH, E.R. (1961) *Pul Eliya: A Village in Ceylon*, Cambridge University Press.

MARRIOTT, McKIM and RONALD B. INDEN (1974) Caste systems, in *Encyclopaedia Britannica*.

MAYER, ADRIAN C. (1956) Some hierarchical aspects of cast. *Southwestern Journal of Anthropology*, vol. 12, no. 2.

MILLER, ROBERT J. (1953) Areas and institutions in Eastern Asia. *Southwestern Journal of Anthropology*, vol. 9, pp. 203-11.

MORGENSTIERNE, GEORG (1927) *An Etymological Vocabulary of Pashto*. Det Norske Videnskaps-Akademi i Oslo II. Hist.-Filos, Kl. no. 3.

MORGENSTIERNE, G. (1932), *Report on a Linguistic Mission to North-Western India*, Oslo: Norwegian Universities Press.

NADEL, S.F. (1947) *The Nuba*, London: Oxford University Press.

NADEL, S.F. (1951) *The Foundations of Social Anthropology*, London: Cohen & West.

NADEL, S.F. (1957) *The Theory of Social Structure*, London: Cohen & West.

NEUMANN, JOHN VÓN and MORGENSTERN, OSKAR (1947) *Theory of Games and Economic Behaviour*, Princeton University Press.

PAINE, ROBERT (1974) *Second Thoughts about Barth's Models*, Royal Anthropological Institute Occasional Paper No. 32, London: Royal Anthropological Institute of Great Britain and Ireland.

PARETO, VILFREDO (1963) *The Mind and Society: A Treatise on General Sociology* (vol. 1 of 4), London: Constable.

PATAI, RAPHAEL (1949) Musha'a tenure and co-operation in Palestine. *American Anthropologist*, vol. 51, pp. 436-45.

PEHRSON, ROBERT N. (1966) *The Social Organization of the Marri Baluch*, Chicago: Aldine.

PETERS, E. (1965) Apsects of the family among the Bedouin of Cyrenaica, in M.F. Nimkoff (ed.), *Comparative Family Systems*, Boston: Houghton Mifflin.

RADCLIFFE-BROWN, A.R. (1935) Patrilineal and matrilineal success. Reprinted in *Structure and Function in Primitive Society*.

RADCLIFFE-BROWN, A.R. (1950) Introduction to A.R. Radcliffe-Brown and Daryll Forde (eds) *African Systems of Kinship and Marriage*, Oxford University Press.

RADCLIFFE-BROWN, A.R. (1952) *Structure and Function in Primitive Society*, London: Cohen & West.

RAVERTY, CPT. H.G. (1860) *A Grammar of the Pukhto, Pushto, or Language of the Afghans . . .* etc., London: Longman, Green, Longman & Roberts.

RAVERTY, H.G. (1867) *A Dictionary of the Pukhto*, London: Williams and Norgate.

REDFIELD, R., and SINGER, M. (eds) (1955) Comparative Studies of Cultures and Civilizations, *Village India* (ed. Marriott), Chicago University Press.

RIDGEWAY, MAJOR R.T.I. (1918) *Pathans*, Calcutta.

ROBERTS, FIELD MARSHAL LORD, (1898) *Forty-one Years in India*, London: Richard Betley.

SPATE, O.H.K. (1954) *India and Pakistan*, London: Methuen.

STEIN, SIR AUREL (1929) *On Alexander's Track to the Indus*, London: Macmillan.

STEVENSON, H.N.C. (1954) Status evaluation in the Hindu caste system. *Journal of the Royal Anthropological Institute* vol. 84, pp. 45-65.

STONE, J. RICHARD (1948) The Theory of Games. *Economic Journal*, vol. 58.

STUCHLIK, MILAN (ed.) (1977) *Goals and Behaviour*, Queen's University Papers in Social Anthropology Vol. 2, Belfast: Queen's University.

The Story of Swat (1962) as told by the Founder Miangul Abdul Wadud Badshah Sahib to Muhammad Asif Khan, translated by Ashruf Altaf Husain, Peshawar: Ferozsons.

THOMAS, B. (1929) Among some unknown tribes of South Arabia. *Journal of the Royal Anthropological Institute*, vol. 59, pp. 97-111.

WARD, B. (1965) Varieties of the conscious model: The fishermen of South China *in The Relevance of Models for Social Anthropology*, A.S.A. Monographs No. 1, London.

WARNER, W. LLOYD, and LUNT, PAUL S. (1942) *The Status System of a Modern Community*, Yale University Press.

WISER, W.H. (1936) *The Hindu Jajmani System*, Lucknow.

WYLLY, H.C. (1912) *From the Black Mountain to Waziristan*, London: Macmillan.

Index

Abdul Jabbar Shah, 176f
affection, 89
affinal relations, 11, 39, 76, 136
agnates, agnatic collaterals, 66ff, 81, 169f, 174
Ahmed, Akbar S., 1, 121, 125, 127, 141, 149, 154, 168f, 178, 180n
Ahmed Shah Brelwi, 175 f
Ajer, var. of Gujar, 9
Akbar Shah, 174ff
Akhund of Swat, 36f, 175ff
Akhund Sadiq Baba, 5
Allee, W.C et al., 3
ally, alliance, 56, 67f, 70ff, 140f, 142f, 164ff
alms, 27, 51
Amb state, 174
Ambeyla, 7
arena, forum, 106, 113, 116, 136
Asad, Talal, 1, 121, 127, 128, 143, 146f, 148, 151, 168, 171, 172, 177, 180n, 181n
assembly, of lineage (*jirga*), 29, 32, 62f, 70f, 93f, 97, 106, 107f, 110, 115, 116, 159, 174
assimilation, incorporation, 8, 9, 100f, 110f, 114, 116
associations (*taltole*), 28, 34, 37, 39, 136, 155
authority, 29, 39f, 87, 89, 98, 107, 134, 137, 146, 147f, 157, 177f
autonomy, 7, 87, 106, 115, 119, 135, 137, 147, 177
avoidance, 90, 91, 116

Babuzai, 126, 166, 170, 177
Bacon, Elizabeth, 3
Baden-Powell, B.H., 65
Badshah of Swat, 123, 127, 145, 159, 160, 177f
Bajaur, 70, 174

balance (between blocs), 72, 76
Baluch, 93ff, 109f, 119
Bannu, 98
barber, 20, 21, 28, 47, 156
Bateson, Gregory, 162f
Bengali origins, 20
betrothal, 28
Bhutto, Zulfikar Ali, 144ff, 150
Biha (village), 30, 42, 147
birth, 28
bloc (*dala*), 56, 58, 68, 70f, 75, 117, 138, 141, 142f, 146, 165ff, 174f, 176f
blood revenge, 62, 95f, 98f, 138
boundary, 6ff, 95ff, 103ff, 109
Brahui, 93
brideprice, including *mahr*, 39, 40, 41f
British, attitudes and activities of, 7, 54n, 70, 79, 122, 149, 175f
brotherhood, 66f, 97
Bruce, R.I., 95
Buddhism, 19
Buner, 126, 175, 181n
bureaucracy, 144

career, 165, 169ff
Caroe, Sir Olaf, 105, 122, 127, 175, 180n, 181n
carpenter, 7, 21, 22, 26, 27, 43f, 48f, 50, 142
caste, in Swat (*qoum*), 5, 16ff, 104ff, 113, 151ff
cattle, 7, 9
censuses, 22, 23, 30, 42, 61, 94
chief, 20, 29, 33, 51, 69, 76ff, 89, 110, 112, 126, 134, 136f, 139ff, 146, 149, 150, 158ff
Chitral, 174, 176
choice, 56, 129, 137, 147, 181n
circumcision, 28

186

Routledge Social Science Series

Routledge & Kegan Paul   London, Henley and Boston

39 Store Street,
London WC1E 7DD
Broadway House,
Newtown Road,
Henley-on-Thames,
Oxon RG9 1EN
9 Park Street,
Boston, Mass. 02108

Contents

*Authors wishing to submit manuscripts for any series
in this catalogue should send them to the Social Science Editor,
Routledge & Kegan Paul Ltd, 39 Store Street,
London WC1E 7DD.*
● *Books so marked are available in paperback.*
○ *Books so marked are available in paperback only.*
*All books are in metric Demy 8vo format (216 × 138mm approx.)
unless otherwise stated.*

International Library of Sociology
General Editor   John Rex

GENERAL SOCIOLOGY

Barnsley, J. H. The Social Reality of Ethics. *464 pp.*
Brown, Robert. Explanation in Social Science. *208 pp.*
● Rules and Laws in Sociology. *192 pp.*
Bruford, W. H. Chekhov and His Russia. *A Sociological Study. 244 pp.*
Burton, F. and **Carlen, P.** Official Discourse. *On Discourse Analysis, Government Publications, Ideology. About 140 pp.*
Cain, Maureen E. Society and the Policeman's Role. *326 pp.*
● **Fletcher, Colin.** Beneath the Surface. *An Account of Three Styles of Sociological Research. 221 pp.*
Gibson, Quentin. The Logic of Social Enquiry. *240 pp.*
Glassner, B. Essential Interactionism. *208 pp.*
Glucksmann, M. Structuralist Analysis in Contemporary Social Thought. *212 pp.*
Gurvitch, Georges. Sociology of Law. *Foreword by Roscoe Pound. 264 pp.*
Hinkle, R. Founding Theory of American Sociology 1881–1913. *About 350 pp.*
Homans, George C. Sentiments and Activities. *336 pp.*
Johnson, Harry M. Sociology: *A Systematic Introduction. Foreword by Robert K. Merton. 710 pp.*
● **Keat, Russell** and **Urry, John.** Social Theory as Science. *278 pp.*
Mannheim, Karl. Essays on Sociology and Social Psychology. *Edited by Paul Keckskemeti. With Editorial Note by Adolph Lowe. 344 pp.*
Martindale, Don. The Nature and Types of Sociological Theory. *292 pp.*
● **Maus, Heinz.** A Short History of Sociology. *234 pp.*
Myrdal, Gunnar. Value in Social Theory: *A Collection of Essays on Methodology. Edited by Paul Streeten. 332 pp.*
Ogburn, William F. and **Nimkoff, Meyer F.** A Handbook of Sociology. *Preface by Karl Mannheim. 656 pp. 46 figures. 35 tables.*
Parsons, Talcott and **Smelser, Neil J.** Economy and Society: *A Study in the Integration of Economic and Social Theory. 362 pp.*
Payne, G., Dingwall, R., Payne, J. and **Carter, M.** Sociology and Social Research. *About 250 pp.*
Podgórecki, A. Practical Social Sciences. *About 200 pp.*
Podgórecki, A. and **Łos, M.** Multidimensional Sociology. *268 pp.*
Raffel, S. Matters of Fact. *A Sociological Inquiry. 152 pp.*
● **Rex, John.** Key Problems of Sociological Theory. *220 pp.*
Sociology and the Demystification of the Modern World. *282 pp.*
● **Rex, John.** (Ed.) Approaches to Sociology. *Contributions by Peter Abell, Frank Bechhofer, Basil Bernstein, Ronald Fletcher, David Frisby, Miriam Glucksmann, Peter Lassman, Herminio Martins, John Rex, Roland Robertson, John Westergaard and Jock Young. 302 pp.*
Rigby, A. Alternative Realities. *352 pp.*
Roche, M. Phenomenology, Language and the Social Sciences. *374 pp.*
Sahay, A. Sociological Analysis. *220 pp.*
Strasser, Hermann. The Normative Structure of Sociology. *Conservative and Emancipatory Themes in Social Thought. About 340 pp.*
Strong, P. Ceremonial Order of the Clinic. *267 pp.*
Urry, John. Reference Groups and the Theory of Revolution. *244 pp.*
Weinberg, E. Development of Sociology in the Soviet Union. *173 pp.*

FOREIGN CLASSICS OF SOCIOLOGY

● **Gerth, H. H.** and **Mills, C. Wright.** From Max Weber: *Essays in Sociology. 502 pp.*

● **Tönnies, Ferdinand.** Community and Association *(Gemeinschaft und Gesell-schaft).\Translated and Supplemented by Charles P. Loomis. Foreword by Pitirim A. Sorokin. 334 pp.*

SOCIAL STRUCTURE

Andreski, Stanislav. Military Organization and Society. *Foreword by Professor A. R. Radcliffe-Brown. 226 pp. 1 folder.*

Broom, L., Lancaster Jones, F., McDonnell, P. and **Williams, T.** The Inheritance of Inequality. *About 180 pp.*

Carlton, Eric. Ideology and Social Order. *Foreword by Professor Philip Abrahams. About 320 pp.*

Clegg, S. and **Dunkerley, D.** Organization, Class and Control. *614 pp.*

Coontz, Sydney H. Population Theories and the Economic Interpretation. *202 pp.*

Coser, Lewis. The Functions of Social Conflict. *204 pp.*

Crook, I. and **D.** The First Years of the Yangyi Commune. *304 pp., illustrated.*

Dickie-Clark, H. F. Marginal Situation: *A Sociological Study of a Coloured Group. 240 pp. 11 tables.*

Giner, S. and **Archer, M. S.** (Eds) Contemporary Europe: *Social Structures and Cultural Patterns, 336 pp.*

● **Glaser, Barney** and **Strauss, Anselm L.** Status Passage: *A Formal Theory. 212 pp.*

Glass, D. V. (Ed.) Social Mobility in Britain. *Contributions by J. Berent, T. Bottomore, R. C. Chambers, J. Floud, D. V. Glass, J. R. Hall, H. T. Himmelweit, R. K. Kelsall, F. M. Martin, C. A. Moser, R. Mukherjee and W. Ziegel. 420 pp.*

Kelsall, R. K. Higher Civil Servants in Britain: *From 1870 to the Present Day. 268 pp. 31 tables.*

● **Lawton, Denis.** Social Class, Language and Education. *192 pp.*

McLeish, John. The Theory of Social Change: *Four Views Considered. 128 pp.*

● **Marsh, David C.** The Changing Social Structure of England and Wales, 1871–1961. *Revised edition. 288 pp.*

Menzies, Ken. Talcott Parsons and the Social Image of Man. *About 208 pp.*

● **Mouzelis, Nicos.** Organization and Bureaucracy. *An Analysis of Modern Theories. 240 pp.*

● **Ossowski, Stanislaw.** Class Structure in the Social Consciousness. *210 pp.*

● **Podgórecki, Adam.** Law and Society. *302 pp.*

Renner, Karl. Institutions of Private Law and Their Social Functions. *Edited, with an Introduction and Notes, by O. Kahn-Freud. Translated by Agnes Schwarzschild. 316 pp.*

Rex, J. and **Tomlinson, S.** Colonial Immigrants in a British City. *A Class Analysis. 368 pp.*

Smooha, S. Israel: Pluralism and Conflict. *472 pp.*

Wesolowski, W. Class, Strata and Power. *Trans. and with Introduction by G. Kolankiewicz. 160 pp.*

Zureik, E. Palestinians in Israel. *A Study in Internal Colonialism. 264 pp.*

SOCIOLOGY AND POLITICS

Acton, T. A. Gypsy Politics and Social Change. *316 pp.*

Burton, F. Politics of Legitimacy. *Struggles in a Belfast Community. 250 pp.*

Crook, I. and **D.** Revolution in a Chinese Village. *Ten Mile Inn. 216 pp., illustrated.*

Etzioni-Halevy, E. Political Manipulation and Administrative Power. *A Comparative Study. About 200 pp.*

Fielding, N. The National Front. *About 250 pp.*

● **Hechter, Michael.** Internal Colonialism. *The Celtic Fringe in British National Development, 1536–1966. 380 pp.*

Kornhauser, William. The Politics of Mass Society. *272 pp. 20 tables.*

Korpi, W. The Working Class in Welfare Capitalism. *Work, Unions and Politics in Sweden. 472 pp.*

Kroes, R. Soldiers and Students. *A Study of Right- and Left-wing Students. 174 pp.*

Martin, Roderick. Sociology of Power. *About 272 pp.*

Merquior, J. G. Rousseau and Weber. *A Study in the Theory of Legitimacy. About 288 pp.*

Myrdal, Gunnar. The Political Element in the Development of Economic Theory. *Translated from the German by Paul Streeten. 282 pp.*

Varma, B. N. The Sociology and Politics of Development. *A Theoretical Study. 236 pp.*

Wong, S.-L. Sociology and Socialism in Contemporary China. *160 pp.*

Wootton, Graham. Workers, Unions and the State. *188 pp.*

CRIMINOLOGY

Ancel, Marc. Social Defence: *A Modern Approach to Criminal Problems. Foreword by Leon Radzinowicz. 240 pp.*

Athens, L. Violent Criminal Acts and Actors. *104 pp.*

Cain, Maureen E. Society and the Policeman's Role. *326 pp.*

Cloward, Richard A. and **Ohlin, Lloyd E.** Delinquency and Opportunity: *A Theory of Delinquent Gangs. 248 pp.*

Downes, David M. The Delinquent Solution. *A Study in Subcultural Theory. 296 pp.*

Friedlander, Kate. The Psycho-Analytical Approach to Juvenile Delinquency: *Theory, Case Studies, Treatment. 320 pp.*

Gleuck, Sheldon and **Eleanor.** Family Environment and Delinquency. *With the statistical assistance of Rose W. Kneznek. 340 pp.*

Lopez-Rey, Manuel. Crime. *An Analytical Appraisal. 288 pp.*

Mannheim, Hermann. Comparative Criminology: *A Text Book. Two volumes. 442 pp. and 380 pp.*

Morris, Terence. The Criminal Area: *A Study in Social Ecology. Foreword by Hermann Mannheim. 232 pp. 25 tables. 4 maps.*

Rock, Paul. Making People Pay. *338 pp.*

● **Taylor, Ian, Walton, Paul** and **Young, Jock.** The New Criminology. *For a Social Theory of Deviance. 325 pp.*

● **Taylor, Ian, Walton, Paul** and **Young, Jock.** (Eds) Critical Criminology. *268 pp.*

SOCIAL PSYCHOLOGY

Bagley, Christopher. The Social Psychology of the Epileptic Child. *320 pp.*

Brittan, Arthur. Meanings and Situations. *224 pp.*

Carroll, J. Break-Out from the Crystal Palace. *200 pp.*

● **Fleming, C. M.** Adolescence: Its Social Psychology. *With an Introduction to recent findings from the fields of Anthropology, Physiology, Medicine, Psychometrics and Sociometry. 288 pp.*

● The Social Psychology of Education: *An Introduction and Guide to Its Study. 136 pp.*

Linton, Ralph. The Cultural Background of Personality. *132 pp.*

● **Mayo, Elton.** The Social Problems of an Industrial Civilization. *With an Appendix on the Political Problem. 180 pp.*

Ottaway, A. K. C. Learning Through Group Experience. *176 pp.*

Plummer, Ken. Sexual Stigma. *An Interactionist Account: 254 pp.*

● **Rose, Arnold M.** (Ed.) Human Behaviour and Social Processes: *an Interactionist Approach. Contributions by Arnold M. Rose, Ralph H. Turner, Anselm Strauss, Everett C. Hughes, E. Franklin Frazier, Howard S. Becker et al. 696 pp.*

Smelser, Neil J. Theory of Collective Behaviour. *448 pp.*

Stephenson, Geoffrey M. The Development of Conscience. *128 pp.*

Young, Kimball. Handbook of Social Psychology. *658 pp. 16 figures. 10 tables.*

SOCIOLOGY OF THE FAMILY

Bell, Colin R. Middle Class Families: *Social and Geographical Mobility. 224 pp.*
Burton, Lindy. Vulnerable Children. *272 pp.*
Gavron, Hannah. The Captive Wife: *Conflicts of Household Mothers. 190 pp.*
George, Victor and **Wilding, Paul.** Motherless Families. *248 pp.*
Klein, Josephine. Samples from English Cultures.
    1. Three Preliminary Studies and Aspects of Adult Life in England. *447 pp.*
    2. Child-Rearing Practices and Index. *247 pp.*
Klein, Viola. The Feminine Character. *History of an Ideology. 244 pp.*
McWhinnie, Alexina M. Adopted Children. *How They Grow Up. 304 pp.*
● **Morgan, D. H. J.** Social Theory and the Family. *About 320 pp.*
● **Myrdal, Alva** and **Klein, Viola.** Women's Two Roles: *Home and Work. 238 pp.*
    27 tables.
Parsons, Talcott and **Bales, Robert F.** Family: Socialization and Interaction Process. *In collaboration with James Olds, Morris Zelditch and Philip E. Slater. 456 pp. 50 figures and tables.*

SOCIAL SERVICES

Bastide, Roger. The Sociology of Mental Disorder. *Translated from the French by Jean McNeil. 260 pp.*
Carlebach, Julius. Caring For Children in Trouble. *266 pp.*
George, Victor. Foster Care. *Theory and Practice. 234 pp.*
  Social Security: *Beveridge and After. 258 pp.*
George, V. and **Wilding, P.** Motherless Families. *248 pp.*
● **Goetschius, George W.** Working with Community Groups. *256 pp.*
Goetschius, George W. and **Tash, Joan.** Working with Unattached Youth. *416 pp.*
Heywood, Jean S. Children in Care. *The Development of the Service for the Deprived Child. Third revised edition. 284 pp.*
King, Roy D., Ranes, Norma V. and **Tizard, Jack.** Patterns of Residential Care. *356 pp.*
Leigh, John. Young People and Leisure. *256 pp.*
● **Mays, John.** (Ed.) Penelope Hall's Social Services of England and Wales. *368 pp.*
Morris, Mary. Voluntary Work and the Welfare State. *300 pp.*
Nokes, P. L. The Professional Task in Welfare Practice. *152 pp.*
Timms, Noel. Psychiatric Social Work in Great Britain (1939–1962). *280 pp.*
●   Social Casework: *Principles and Practice. 256 pp.*

SOCIOLOGY OF EDUCATION

Banks, Olive. Parity and Prestige in English Secondary Education: a Study in Educational Sociology. *272 pp.*
● **Blyth, W. A. L.** English Primary Education. *A Sociological Description.*
    2. Background. *168 pp.*
Collier, K. G. The Social Purposes of Education: *Personal and Social Values in Education. 268 pp.*
Evans, K. M. Sociometry and Education. *158 pp.*
● **Ford, Julienne.** Social Class and the Comprehensive School. *192 pp.*
Foster, P. J. Education and Social Change in Ghana. *336 pp. 3 maps.*
Fraser, W. R. Education and Society in Modern France. *150 pp.*
Grace, Gerald R. Role Conflict and the Teacher. *150 pp.*
Hans, Nicholas. New Trends in Education in the Eighteenth Century. *278 pp. 19 tables.*
●   Comparative Education: *A Study of Educational Factors and Traditions. 360 pp.*
● **Hargreaves, David.** Interpersonal Relations and Education. *432 pp.*
●   Social Relations in a Secondary School. *240 pp.*
  School Organization and Pupil Involvement. *A Study of Secondary Schools.*

● **Mannheim, Karl** and **Stewart, W. A. C.** An Introduction to the Sociology of Education. *206 pp.*
● **Musgrove, F.** Youth and the Social Order. *176 pp.*
● **Ottaway, A. K. C.** Education and Society: An Introduction to the Sociology of Education. *With an Introduction by W. O. Lester Smith. 212 pp.*
Peers, Robert. Adult Education: *A Comparative Study. Revised edition. 398 pp.*
Stratta, Erica. The Education of Borstal Boys. *A Study of their Educational Experiences prior to, and during, Borstal Training. 256 pp.*
● **Taylor, P. H., Reid, W. A.** and **Holley, B. J.** The English Sixth Form. *A Case Study in Curriculum Research. 198 pp.*

SOCIOLOGY OF CULTURE

Eppel, E. M. and **M.** Adolescents and Morality: *A Study of some Moral Values and Dilemmas of Working Adolescents in the Context of a changing Climate of Opinion. Foreword by W. J. H. Sprott. 268 pp. 39 tables.*
● **Fromm, Erich.** The Fear of Freedom. *286 pp.*
● The Sane Society. *400 pp.*
Johnson, L. The Cultural Critics. *From Matthew Arnold to Raymond Williams. 233 pp.*
Mannheim, Karl. Essays on the Sociology of Culture. *Edited by Ernst Mannheim in co-operation with Paul Kecskemeti. Editorial Note by Adolph Lowe. 280 pp.*
Merquior, J. G. The Veil and the Mask. *Essays on Culture and Ideology. Foreword by Ernest Gellner. 140 pp.*
Zijderfeld, A. C. On Clichés. *The Supersedure of Meaning by Function in Modernity. 150 pp.*

SOCIOLOGY OF RELIGION

Argyle, Michael and **Beit-Hallahmi, Benjamin.** The Social Psychology of Religion. *256 pp.*
Glasner, Peter E. The Sociology of Secularisation. *A Critique of a Concept. 146 pp.*
Hall, J. R. The Ways Out. *Utopian Communal Groups in an Age of Babylon. 280 pp.*
Ranson, S., Hinings, B. and **Bryman, A.** Clergy, Ministers and Priests. *216 pp.*
Stark, Werner. The Sociology of Religion. *A Study of Christendom.*
Volume II. *Sectarian Religion. 368 pp.*
Volume III. *The Universal Church. 464 pp.*
Volume IV. *Types of Religious Man. 352 pp.*
Volume V. *Types of Religious Culture. 464 pp.*
Turner, B. S. Weber and Islam. *216 pp.*
Watt, W. Montgomery. Islam and the Integration of Society. *320 pp.*

SOCIOLOGY OF ART AND LITERATURE

Jarvie, Ian C. Towards a Sociology of the Cinema. *A Comparative Essay on the Structure and Functioning of a Major Entertainment Industry. 405 pp.*
Rust, Frances S. Dance in Society. *An Analysis of the Relationships between the Social Dance and Society in England from the Middle Ages to the Present Day. 256 pp. 8 pp. of plates.*
Schücking, L. L. The Sociology of Literary Taste. *112 pp.*
Wolff, Janet. Hermeneutic Philosophy and the Sociology of Art. *150 pp.*

SOCIOLOGY OF KNOWLEDGE

Diesing, P. Patterns of Discovery in the Social Sciences. *262 pp.*

● **Douglas, J. D.** (Ed.) Understanding Everyday Life. *370 pp.*
● **Hamilton, P.** Knowledge and Social Structure. *174 pp.*
Jarvie, I. C. Concepts and Society. *232 pp.*
Mannheim, Karl. Essays on the Sociology of Knowledge. *Edited by Paul Kecskemeti. Editorial Note by Adolph Lowe. 353 pp.*
Remmling, Gunter W. The Sociology of Karl Mannheim. *With a Bibliographical Guide to the Sociology of Knowledge, Ideological Analysis, and Social Planning. 255 pp.*
Remmling, Gunter W. (Ed.) Towards the Sociology of Knowledge. *Origin and Development of a Sociological Thought Style. 463 pp.*
Scheler, M. Problems of a Sociology of Knowledge. *Trans. by M. S. Frings. Edited and with an Introduction by K. Stikkers. 232 pp.*

URBAN SOCIOLOGY

Aldridge, M. The British New Towns. *A Programme Without a Policy. 232 pp.*
Ashworth, William. The Genesis of Modern British Town Planning: *A Study in Economic and Social History of the Nineteenth and Twentieth Centuries. 288 pp.*
Brittan, A. The Privatised World. *196 pp.*
Cullingworth, J. B. Housing Needs and Planning Policy: *A Restatement of the Problems of Housing Need and 'Overspill' in England and Wales. 232 pp. 44 tables. 8 maps.*
Dickinson, Robert E. City and Region: *A Geographical Interpretation. 608 pp. 125 figures.*
The West European City: *A Geographical Interpretation. 600 pp. 129 maps. 29 plates.*
Humphreys, Alexander J. New Dubliners: *Urbanization and the Irish Family. Foreword by George C. Homans. 304 pp.*
Jackson, Brian. Working Class Community: *Some General Notions raised by a Series of Studies in Northern England. 192 pp.*
● **Mann, P. H.** An Approach to Urban Sociology. *240 pp.*
Mellor, J. R. Urban Sociology in an Urbanized Society. *326 pp.*
Morris, R. N. and **Mogey, J.** The Sociology of Housing. *Studies at Berinsfield. 232 pp. 4 pp. plates.*
Mullan, R. Stevenage Ltd. *About 250 pp.*
Rex, J. and **Tomlinson, S.** Colonial Immigrants in a British City. *A Class Analysis. 368 pp.*
Rosser, C. and **Harris, C.** The Family and Social Change. *A Study of Family and Kinship in a South Wales Town. 352 pp. 8 maps.*
● **Stacey, Margaret, Batsone, Eric, Bell, Colin** and **Thurcott, Anne.** Power, Persistence and Change. *A Second Study of Banbury. 196 pp.*

RURAL SOCIOLOGY

Mayer, Adrian C. Peasants in the Pacific. *A Study of Fiji Indian Rural Society. 248 pp. 20 plates.*
Williams, W. M. The Sociology of an English Village: *Gosforth. 272 pp. 12 figures. 13 tables.*

SOCIOLOGY OF INDUSTRY AND DISTRIBUTION

Dunkerley, David. The Foreman. *Aspects of Task and Structure. 192 pp.*
Eldridge, J. E. T. Industrial Disputes. *Essays in the Sociology of Industrial Relations. 288 pp.*
Hollowell, Peter G. The Lorry Driver. *272 pp.*
● **Oxaal, I., Barnett, T.** and **Booth, D.** (Eds) Beyond the Sociology of Development.

Economy and Society in Latin America and Africa. 295 pp.

Smelser, Neil J. Social Change in the Industrial Revolution: *An Application of Theory to the Lancashire Cotton Industry, 1770–1840. 468 pp. 12 figures. 14 tables.*

Watson, T. J. The Personnel Managers. *A Study in the Sociology of Work and Employment, 262 pp.*

ANTHROPOLOGY

Brandel-Syrier, Mia. Reeftown Elite. *A Study of Social Mobility in a Modern African Community on the Reef. 376 pp.*

Dickie-Clark, H. F. The Marginal Situation. *A Sociological Study of a Coloured Group. 236 pp.*

Dube, S. C. Indian Village. *Foreword by Morris Edward Opler. 276 pp. 4 plates.* India's Changing Villages: *Human Factors in Community Development. 260 pp. 8 plates. 1 map.*

Fei, H.-T. Peasant Life in China. *A Field Study of Country Life in the Yangtze Valley. With a foreword by Bronislaw Malinowski. 328 pp. 16 pp. plates.*

Firth, Raymond. Malay Fishermen. *Their Peasant Economy. 420 pp. 17 pp. plates.*

Gulliver, P. H. Social Control in an African Society: a Study of the Arusha, Agricultural Masai of Northern Tanganyika. *320 pp. 8 plates. 10 figures.* Family Herds. *288 pp.*

Jarvie, Ian C. The Revolution in Anthropology. *268 pp.*

Little, Kenneth L. Mende of Sierra Leone. *308 pp. and folder.* Negroes in Britain. *With a New Introduction and Contemporary Study by Leonard Bloom. 320 pp.*

Tambs-Lyche, H. London Patidars. *About 180 pp.*

Madan, G. R. Western Sociologists on Indian Society. *Marx, Spencer, Weber, Durkheim, Pareto. 384 pp.*

Mayer, A. C. Peasants in the Pacific. *A Study of Fiji Indian Rural Society. 248 pp.*

Meer, Fatima. Race and Suicide in South Africa. *325 pp.*

Smith, Raymond T. The Negro Family in British Guiana: *Family Structure and Social Status in the Villages. With a Foreword by Meyer Fortes. 314 pp. 8 plates. 1 figure. 4 maps.*

SOCIOLOGY AND PHILOSOPHY

Adriaansens, H. Talcott Parsons and the Conceptual Dilemma. *About 224 pp.*

Barnsley, John H. The Social Reality of Ethics. *A Comparative Analysis of Moral Codes. 448 pp.*

Diesing, Paul. Patterns of Discovery in the Social Sciences. *362 pp.*

● **Douglas, Jack D.** (Ed.) Understanding Everyday Life. *Toward the Reconstruction of Sociological Knowledge. Contributions by Alan F. Blum, Aaron W. Cicourel, Norman K. Denzin, Jack D. Douglas, John Heeren, Peter McHugh, Peter K. Manning, Melvin Power, Matthew Speier, Roy Turner, D. Lawrence Wieder, Thomas P. Wilson and Don H. Zimmerman. 370 pp.*

Gorman, Robert A. The Dual Vision. *Alfred Schutz and the Myth of Phenomenological Social Science. 240 pp.*

Jarvie, Ian C. Concepts and Society. *216 pp.*

Kilminster, R. Praxis and Method. *A Sociological Dialogue with Lukács, Gramsci and the Early Frankfurt School. 334 pp.*

● **Pelz, Werner.** The Scope of Understanding in Sociology. *Towards a More Radical Reorientation in the Social Humanistic Sciences. 283 pp.*

Roche, Maurice. Phenomenology, Language and the Social Sciences. *371 pp.*

Sahay, Arun. Sociological Analysis. *212 pp.*

● **Slater, P.** Origin and Significance of the Frankfurt School. *A Marxist Perspective. 185 pp.*

Spurling, L. Phenomenology and the Social World. *The Philosophy of Merleau-Ponty and its Relation to the Social Sciences. 222 pp.*
Wilson, H. T. The American Ideology. *Science, Technology and Organization as Modes of Rationality. 368 pp.*

International Library of Anthropology
General Editor Adam Kuper

● **Ahmed, A. S.** Millennium and Charisma Among Pathans. *A Critical Essay in Social Anthropology. 192 pp.*
Pukhtun Economy and Society. *Traditional Structure and Economic Development. About 360 pp.*
Barth, F. Selected Essays. *Volume I. About 250 pp.* Selected Essays. *Volume II. About 250 pp.*
Brown, Paula. The Chimbu. *A Study of Change in the New Guinea Highlands. 151 pp.*
Foner, N. Jamaica Farewell. *200 pp.*
Gudeman, Stephen. Relationships, Residence and the Individual. *A Rural Panamanian Community. 288 pp. 11 plates, 5 figures, 2 maps, 10 tables.*
The Demise of a Rural Economy. *From Subsistence to Capitalism in a Latin American Village. 160 pp.*
Hamnett, Ian. Chieftainship and Legitimacy. *An Anthropological Study of Executive Law in Lesotho. 163 pp.*
Hanson, F. Allan. Meaning in Culture. *127 pp.*
Hazan, H. The Limbo People. *A Study of the Constitution of the Time Universe Among the Aged. About 192 pp.*
Humphreys, S. C. Anthropology and the Greeks. *288 pp.*
Karp, I. Fields of Change Among the Iteso of Kenya. *140 pp.*
Lloyd, P. C. Power and Independence. *Urban Africans' Perception of Social Inequality. 264 pp.*
Parry, J. P. Caste and Kinship in Kangra. *352 pp. Illustrated.*
Pettigrew, Joyce. Robber Noblemen. *A Study of the Political System of the Sikh Jats. 284 pp.*
Street, Brian V. The Savage in Literature. *Representations of 'Primitive' Society in English Fiction, 1858–1920. 207 pp.*
Van Den Berghe, Pierre L. Power and Privilege at an African University. *278 pp.*

International Library of Phenomenology and Moral Sciences
General Editor John O'Neill

Apel, K.-O. Towards a Transformation of Philosophy. *308 pp.*
Bologh, R. W. Dialectical Phenomenology. *Marx's Method. 287 pp.*
Fekete, J. The Critical Twilight. *Explorations in the Ideology of Anglo-American Literary Theory from Eliot to McLuhan. 300 pp.*
Medina, A. Reflection, Time and the Novel. *Towards a Communicative Theory of Literature. 143 pp.*

International Library of Social Policy
General Editor Kathleen Jones

Bayley, M. Mental Handicap and Community Care. *426 pp.*
Bottoms, A. E. and **McClean, J. D.** Defendants in the Criminal Process. *284 pp.*
Bradshaw, J. The Family Fund. *An Initiative in Social Policy. About 224 pp.*

Butler, J. R. Family Doctors and Public Policy. *208 pp.*
Davies, Martin. Prisoners of Society. *Attitudes and Aftercare. 204 pp.*
Gittus, Elizabeth. Flats, Families and the Under-Fives. *285 pp.*
Holman, Robert. Trading in Children. *A Study of Private Fostering. 355 pp.*
Jeffs, A. Young People and the Youth Service. *160 pp.*
Jones, Howard and Cornes, Paul. Open Prisons. *288 pp.*
Jones, Kathleen. History of the Mental Health Service. *428 pp.*
Jones, Kathleen with **Brown, John, Cunningham, W. J., Roberts, Julian** and **Williams, Peter.** Opening the Door. *A Study of New Policies for the Mentally Handicapped. 278 pp.*
Karn, Valerie. Retiring to the Seaside. *400 pp. 2 maps. Numerous tables.*
King, R. D. and **Elliot, K. W.** Albany: Birth of a Prison—End of an Era. *394 pp.*
Thomas, J. E. The English Prison Officer since 1850: *A Study in Conflict. 258 pp.*
Walton, R. G. Women in Social Work. *303 pp.*
● **Woodward, J.** To Do the Sick No Harm. *A Study of the British Voluntary Hospital System to 1875. 234 pp.*

International Library of Welfare and Philosophy
General Editors   Noel Timms and David Watson

● **McDermott, F. E.** (Ed.) Self-Determination in Social Work. *A Collection of Essays on Self-determination and Related Concepts by Philosophers and Social Work Theorists. Contributors: F. P. Biestek, S. Bernstein, A. Keith-Lucas, D. Sayer, H. H. Perelman, C. Whittington, R. F. Stalley, F. E. McDermott, I. Berlin, H. J. McCloskey, H. L. A. Hart, J. Wilson, A. I. Melden, S. I. Benn. 254 pp.*
● **Plant, Raymond.** Community and Ideology. *104 pp.*
Ragg, Nicholas M. People Not Cases. *A Philosophical Approach to Social Work. 168 pp.*
● **Timms, Noel** and **Watson, David.** (Eds) Talking About Welfare. *Readings in Philosophy and Social Policy. Contributors: T. H. Marshall, R. B. Brandt, G. H. von Wright, K. Nielsen, M. Cranston, R. M. Titmuss, R. S. Downie, E. Telfer, D. Donnison, J. Benson, P. Leonard, A. Keith-Lucas, D. Walsh, I. T. Ramsey. 320 pp.*
● Philosophy in Social Work. *250 pp.*
● **Weale, A.** Equality and Social Policy. *164 pp.*

Library of Social Work
General Editor   Noel Timms

● **Baldock, Peter.** Community Work and Social Work. *140 pp.*
○ **Beedell, Christopher.** Residential Life with Children. *210 pp. Crown 8vo.*
● **Berry, Juliet.** Daily Experience in Residential Life. *A Study of Children and their Care-givers. 202 pp.*
○ Social Work with Children. *190 pp. Crown 8vo.*
● **Brearley, C. Paul.** Residential Work with the Elderly. *116 pp.*
● Social Work, Ageing and Society. *126 pp.*
● **Cheetham, Juliet.** Social Work with Immigrants. *240 pp. Crown 8vo.*
● **Cross, Crispin P.** (Ed.) Interviewing and Communication in Social Work. *Contributions by C. P. Cross, D. Laurenson, B. Strutt, S. Raven. 192 pp. Crown 8vo.*

● **Curnock, Kathleen** and **Hardiker, Pauline.** Towards Practice Theory. *Skills and Methods in Social Assessments. 208 pp.*

● **Davies, Bernard.** The Use of Groups in Social Work Practice. *158 pp.*

● **Davies, Martin.** Support Systems in Social Work. *144 pp.*

Ellis, June. (Ed.) West African Families in Britain. *A Meeting of Two Cultures. Contributions by Pat Stapleton, Vivien Biggs. 150 pp. 1 Map.*

● **Hart, John.** Social Work and Sexual Conduct. *230 pp.*

● **Hutten, Joan M.** Short-Term Contracts in Social Work. *Contributions by Stella M. Hall, Elsie Osborne, Mannie Sher, Eva Sternberg, Elizabeth Tuters. 134 pp.*

Jackson, Michael P. and **Valencia, B. Michael.** Financial Aid Through Social Work. *140 pp.*

● **Jones, Howard.** The Residential Community. *A Setting for Social Work. 150 pp.*

● (Ed.) Towards a New Social Work. *Contributions by Howard Jones, D. A. Fowler, J. R. Cypher, R. G. Walton, Geoffrey Mungham, Philip Priestley, Ian Shaw, M. Bartley, R. Deacon, Irwin Epstein, Geoffrey Pearson. 184 pp.*

Jones, Ray and **Pritchard, Colin.** (Eds) Social Work With Adolescents. *Contributions by Ray Jones, Colin Pritchard, Jack Dunham, Florence Rossetti, Andrew Kerslake, John Burns, William Gregory, Graham Templeman, Kenneth E. Reid, Audrey Taylor. About 170 pp.*

○ **Jordon, William.** The Social Worker in Family Situations. *160 pp. Crown 8vo.*

● **Laycock, A. L.** Adolescents and Social Work. *128 pp. Crown 8vo.*

● **Lees, Ray.** Politics and Social Work. *128 pp. Crown 8vo.*

● Research Strategies for Social Welfare. *112 pp. Tables.*

○ **McCullough, M. K.** and **Ely, Peter J.** Social Work with Groups. *127 pp. Crown 8vo.*

● **Moffett, Jonathan.** Concepts in Casework Treatment. *128 pp. Crown 8vo.*

Parsloe, Phyllida. Juvenile Justice in Britain and the United States. *The Balance of Needs and Rights. 336 pp.*

● **Plant, Raymond.** Social and Moral Theory in Casework. *112 pp. Crown 8vo.*

Priestley, Philip, Fears, Denise and **Fuller, Roger.** Justice for Juveniles. *The 1969 Children and Young Persons Act: A Case for Reform? 128 pp.*

● **Pritchard, Colin** and **Taylor, Richard.** Social Work: Reform or Revolution? *170 pp.*

○ **Pugh, Elisabeth.** Social Work in Child Care. *128 pp. Crown 8vo.*

● **Robinson, Margaret.** Schools and Social Work. *282 pp.*

○ **Ruddock, Ralph.** Roles and Relationships. *128 pp. Crown 8vo.*

● **Sainsbury, Eric.** Social Diagnosis in Casework. *118 pp. Crown 8vo.*

● Social Work with Families. *Perceptions of Social Casework among Clients of a Family Service. 188 pp.*

Seed, Philip. The Expansion of Social Work in Britain. *128 pp. Crown 8vo.*

● **Shaw, John.** The Self in Social Work. *124 pp.*

Smale, Gerald G. Prophecy, Behaviour and Change. *An Examination of Self-fulfilling Prophecies in Helping Relationships. 116 pp. Crown 8vo.*

Smith, Gilbert. Social Need. *Policy, Practice and Research. 155 pp.*

● Social Work and the Sociology of Organisations. *124 pp. Revised edition.*

● **Sutton, Carole.** Psychology for Social Workers and Counsellors. *An Introduction. 248 pp.*

● **Timms, Noel.** Language of Social Casework. *122 pp. Crown 8vo.*

● Recording in Social Work. *124 pp. Crown 8vo.*

● **Todd, F. Joan.** Social Work with the Mentally Subnormal. *96 pp. Crown 8vo.*

● **Walrond-Skinner, Sue.** Family Therapy. *The Treatment of Natural Systems. 172 pp.*

● **Warham, Joyce.** An Introduction to Administration for Social Workers. *Revised edition. 112 pp.*

● An Open Case. *The Organisational Context of Social Work. 172 pp.*

○ **Wittenberg, Isca Salzberger.** Psycho-Analytic Insight and Relationships. *A Kleinian Approach. 196 pp. Crown 8vo.*

Primary Socialization, Language and Education
General Editor Basil Bernstein

Adlam, Diana S., *with the assistance of Geoffrey Turner and Lesley Lineker.* Code in Context. *272 pp.*

Bernstein, Basil. Class, Codes and Control. *3 volumes.*

● 1. *Theoretical Studies Towards a Sociology of Language. 254 pp.*

2. *Applied Studies Towards a Sociology of Language. 377 pp.*

● 3. *Towards a Theory of Educational Transmission. 167 pp.*

Brandis, W. and **Bernstein, B.** Selection and Control. *176 pp.*

Brandis, Walter and **Henderson, Dorothy.** Social Class, Language and Communication. *288 pp.*

Cook-Gumperz, Jenny. Social Control and Socialization. *A Study of Class Differences in the Language of Maternal Control. 290 pp.*

● **Gahagan, D. M.** and **G. A.** Talk Reform. *Exploration in Language for Infant School Children. 160 pp.*

Hawkins, P. R. Social Class, the Nominal Group and Verbal Strategies. *About 220 pp.*

Robinson, W. P. and **Rackstraw, Susan D. A.** A Question of Answers. *2 volumes. 192 pp. and 180 pp.*

Turner, Geoffrey J. and **Mohan, Bernard A.** A Linguistic Description and Computer Programme for Children's Speech. *208 pp.*

Reports of the Institute of Community Studies

Baker, J. The Neighbourhood Advice Centre. A Community Project in Camden. *320 pp.*

● **Cartwright, Ann.** Patients and their Doctors. *A Study of General Practice. 304 pp.*

Dench, Geoff. Maltese in London. *A Case-study in the Erosion of Ethnic Consciousness. 302 pp.*

Jackson, Brian and **Marsden, Dennis.** Education and the Working Class: *Some General Themes Raised by a Study of 88 Working-class Children in a Northern Industrial City. 268 pp. 2 folders.*

Marris, Peter. The Experience of Higher Education. *232 pp. 27 tables.*

● Loss and Change. *192 pp.*

Marris, Peter and **Rein, Martin.** Dilemmas of Social Reform. *Poverty and Community Action in the United States. 256 pp.*

Marris, Peter and **Somerset, Anthony.** African Businessmen. *A Study of Entrepreneurship and Development in Kenya. 256 pp.*

Mills, Richard. Young Outsiders: *a Study in Alternative Communities. 216 pp.*

Runciman, W. G. Relative Deprivation and Social Justice. *A Study of Attitudes to Social Inequality in Twentieth-Century England. 352 pp.*

Willmott, Peter. Adolescent Boys in East London. *230 pp.*

Willmott, Peter and **Young, Michael.** Family and Class in a London Suburb. *202 pp. 47 tables.*

Young, Michael and **McGeeney, Patrick.** Learning Begins at Home. *A Study of a Junior School and its Parents. 128 pp.*

Young, Michael and **Willmott, Peter.** Family and Kinship in East London. *Foreword by Richard M. Titmuss. 252 pp. 39 tables.*

The Symmetrical Family. *410 pp.*

Reports of the Institute for Social Studies in Medical Care

Cartwright, Ann, Hockey, Lisbeth and Anderson, John J. Life Before Death. *310 pp.*
Dunnell, Karen and Cartwright, Ann. Medicine Takers, Prescribers and Hoarders. *190 pp.*
Farrell, C. My Mother Said. . . *A Study of the Way Young People Learned About Sex and Birth Control. 288 pp.*

Medicine, Illness and Society
General Editor   W. M. Williams

Hall, David J. Social Relations & Innovation. *Changing the State of Play in Hospitals. 232 pp.*
Hall, David J. and Stacey, M. (Eds) Beyond Separation. *234 pp.*
Robinson, David. The Process of Becoming Ill. *142 pp.*
Stacey, Margaret *et al.* Hospitals, Children and Their Families. *The Report of a Pilot Study. 202 pp.*
Stimson, G. V. and Webb, B. Going to See the Doctor. *The Consultation Process in General Practice. 155 pp.*

Monographs in Social Theory
General Editor   Arthur Brittan

● Barnes, B. Scientific Knowledge and Sociological Theory. *192 pp.*
Bauman, Zygmunt. Culture as Praxis. *204 pp.*
● Dixon, Keith. Sociological Theory. *Pretence and Possibility. 142 pp.*
The Sociology of Belief. *Fallacy and Foundation. About 160 pp.*
Goff, T. W. Marx and Mead. *Contributions to a Sociology of Knowledge. 176 pp.*
Meltzer, B. N., Petras, J. W. and Reynolds, L. T. Symbolic Interactionism. *Genesis, Varieties and Criticisms. 144 pp.*
● Smith, Anthony D. The Concept of Social Change. *A Critique of the Functionalist Theory of Social Change. 208 pp.*

Routledge Social Science Journals

The British Journal of Sociology. *Editor – Angus Stewart; Associate Editor – Leslie Sklair. Vol. 1, No. 1 – March 1950 and Quarterly. Roy. 8vo. All back issues available. An international journal publishing original papers in the field of sociology and related areas.*
Community Work. *Edited by David Jones and Marjorie Mayo. 1973. Published annually.*
Economy and Society. *Vol. 1, No. 1. February 1972 and Quarterly. Metric Roy. 8vo. A journal for all social scientists covering sociology, philosophy, anthropology, economics and history. All back numbers available.*

Ethnic and Racial Studies. *Editor – John Stone. Vol. 1 – 1978. Published quarterly.*

Religion. Journal of Religion and Religions. *Chairman of Editorial Board, Ninian Smart. Vol. 1, No. 1, Spring 1971. A journal with an inter-disciplinary approach to the study of the phenomena of religion. All back numbers available.*

Sociology of Health and Illness. *A Journal of Medical Sociology. Editor – Alan Davies; Associate Editor – Ray Jobling. Vol. 1, Spring 1979. Published 3 times per annum.*

Year Book of Social Policy in Britain. *Edited by Kathleen Jones. 1971. Published annually.*

Social and Psychological Aspects of Medical Practice
Editor   Trevor Silverstone

Lader, Malcolm. Psychophysiology of Mental Illness. *280 pp.*

● Silverstone, Trevor and Turner, Paul. Drug Treatment in Psychiatry. *Revised edition. 256 pp.*

Whiteley, J. S. and Gordon, J. Group Approaches in Psychiatry. *240 pp.*